THE OFFICIAL
F.A. Premier
League
Football Guide

This is a Carlton Book

Sky Sports™ & © 1998 British Sky Broadcasting Ltd

The Premier League™ & © 1998 The F.A. Premier League Ltd

Copyright © 1998 Carlton Books Limited

First published by Carlton Books Limited in 1998

ISBN   1 85868 595 8 (Hardback)
            1 85868 496 X (Paperback)

A CIP catalogue record for this book is available from the British Library

10 9 8 7 6 5 4 3 2 1

Project Editor: Chris Hawkes
Picture Research: Justin Downing
Project Art Direction: Diane Spender
Production: Garry Lewis

Author's Acknowledgements: I would like to thank the following for their help with this book: Debbie Millett; Martin Corteel and Chris Hawkes at Carlton; David Prole; Peter Neish; Steve Pearce; and John Kelly.

Picture: page 3
The Red Sea: Arsenal fans celebrate their FA Cup triumph.

The publishers would like to thank the following sources for their kind permission to reproduce the pictures in this book:
Allsport UK Ltd. 11tr, 21tl, 30, 44r, 66/Shaun Botterill 13tr, 17tl, 27tr, Clive Brunskill 56, 72t, 72b, 81, 86, David Cannon 68tc, Graham Chadwick 10, 19tr, Phil Cole 9tr, 21tr, 24tr, 37, 50, 65, 74r, 96l, 106, Michael Cooper 93, Stu Forster 11tl, 18, 25tl, 27tl, 29, 78, 88r, 88l, 89, Lawrence Griffiths 14, 34, 92r, Mike Hewitt 44l, Brian Kidd 15tl, Ross Kinnaird 17tr, 68c, Gary M Prior 13tl, 15tr, 38, 92l, 100, Ben Radford 3, 48c, Dave Rawcliffe 9tl, 58, 60, David Rogers 111, Tom Shaw 42, Dan Smith 74, 94, 104r, 108l, Mark Thompson 16, 54, 69: **Colorsport** 4, 25tr, 32l, 48l, 52, 53, 64l, 70, 82, 84, 90, 98, 101: **Empics/Neal Simpson** 57, 104l, Michael Steele 41, Leo Vogelzang 76l: **Popperfoto** 26/M.Fresco 24tl, D. Joiner 26, Kevin Lamarque/Reuters 20: **Sky Sports/Sam Teare** 6: **Sporting Pictures (UK) Ltd.** 8, 12, 19tl, 22, 24, 28, 32r, 36, 40, 46, 61, 62, 64r, 80, 85, 96r, 102, 108r, 109.

Every effort has been made to acknowledge correctly and contact the source and/copyright holder of each picture, and Carlton Books Limited apologises for any unintentional errors or omissions which will be corrected in future editions of this book.

SKY SPORTS

THE OFFICIAL F.A. Premier League Football Guide

GAVIN HAMILTON

CARLTON

Contents

Under Arsène Wenger, the Gunners have combined flair with their traditional grit and last season it won them the Double.

New boss John Gregory took over from Brian Little and guided the Midlands club to a spot in this season's UEFA Cup.

Rovers' final league position of sixth was their best finish since they won the title, and it also earned them a place in Europe.

Many think Charlton will go straight back down, but the Londoners are determined to stay in the Premiership.

Two cups last season for Gianluca Vialli's men, but they still seek their holy grail – the Premiership title.

Manager Gordon Strachan has turned the Sky Blues from perennial relegation dog-fighters to UEFA Cup contenders.

Foreword

The FA Carling Premier League is the most exciting League in the world, where the biggest stars of the world's greatest game can be seen – week in, week out.

In my 20 years as a player, with Dundee United, Glasgow Rangers, Aston Villa, Wolverhampton Wanderers, Everton and West Bromwich Albion, I thought I'd experienced enough excitement to last a lifetime. But the game has never been more exciting than it is today. The entertainment, the intrigue, the stars! They're out there every week for you to enjoy.

My playing days are well and truly over, but I'm doing the next best thing. On the opening day of the season yours truly will be in the Sky gantry for what promises to be another nine months of top-class football – there's no better place to be to catch all the action than with Sky Sports. Our exclusive live broadcasts and unrivalled reporting team give you the best possible coverage of the FA Carling Premier League. It means you can keep bang up to date with all the latest action, news and views.

The Official Premier League Football Guide is the perfect companion to Sky Sports' coverage. This superb book, crammed with colour photographs, is a real treasure trove of information. It gives you the lowdown on all the teams and their stars, and there are hundreds of player statistics and facts. You'll find it both informative and entertaining.

Last season was a real cracker. With two months to go, just about everybody thought the title would be staying put at Old Trafford yet again. Just about everybody, that is, bar a canny Frenchman in north London. Arsène Wenger's Arsenal finished the season in storming fashion, whisking the title from under Manchester United's nose, and then making off with the double when they beat Newcastle in the FA Cup.

But this season, the Gunners will face challengers wherever they look. United are out to regain their crown, while Liverpool will doubtless be inspired by football's new megastar – Michael Owen. There is also Chelsea, who are close to finding the level of consistency needed to sustain a serious challenge for the title.

All in all, the 1998–99 Premier League season promises to be a fascinating contest and we'll be with you all the way on Sky Sports.

Enjoy the book, and enjoy the season.

Andy Gray, Sky Sports Commentator,
London, July 1998

Review of the Season

August

Rovers return to the top

Manchester United started the new season in superb style, dispatching Chelsea in the Charity Shield. But Blackburn were the early leaders in the title race, reviving memories for their fans of 1994–95.

It was business as usual for Manchester United when the new season kicked off. The defending champions beat FA Cup-holders Chelsea on penalties in the Charity Shield at Wembley. United old boy Mark Hughes gave Chelsea the lead early in the second half, but the champions bounced back almost immediately and equalized through a headed corner from Norwegian defender Ronnie Johnsen. With the scores level after extra time, the match went to penalties. United's towering Danish goalkeeper Peter Schmeichel was the hero of the day, saving crucial penalties as Chelsea were beaten 4–2.

For United, the European Champions League was as important a target as the Premier League. They had spent the summer scouring Europe for big-name signings, but had so far been unsuccessful. Brazilian international defender Celio Silva and German national team centre-back Markus Babbel had both been targetted by United, but failed to make the move to Old Trafford. Instead, Norwegian international defender Henning Berg was signed for £5 million from Blackburn Rovers.

Blackburn, under new manager Roy Hodgson, sold England left-back Graeme Le Saux to Chelsea for a similar fee, but it didn't seem to affect the team. Blackburn soared to the top of the table, taking an early lead ahead of Manchester United and West Ham. When Blackburn won the Premier League title in 1995 they had Shearer and Sutton (the SAS) up front. Three years on, they had Gallacher and Sutton (the GAS) – and scoring goals was proving to be just that for Rovers. Sutton scored a hat-trick against Aston Villa, while Scottish international Gallacher hit five goals in his first five games of the season, including two against Sheffield Wednesday, who were demolished 7–2 at Ewood Park.

Slow out of the blocks

Liverpool, one of the pre-season favourites for the title after their signings of England's Paul Ince, Norway's midfielder Oyvind Leonhardsen and

Taking the Michael: Teenage star Michael Owen celebrates his spot kick against Wimbledon.

MANAGER OF THE MONTH

Roy Hodgson

The former Swiss national team coach made a huge impression at Blackburn Rovers following his arrival from Inter Milan.

PLAYER OF THE MONTH

Chris Sutton

His goals, including a hat-trick against Aston Villa, fired Blackburn to the top of the Premier League.

German striker Karlheinz Riedle, started slowly, drawing with Wimbledon and then losing at home to Leicester. An injury to Robbie Fowler gave teenage striker Michael Owen the chance to step under the spotlight. The youngster showed amazing maturity, winning and converting a penalty on the opening day of the season at Selhurst Park. He was definitely going to be one to watch.

The Anfield side were not the only team to get off to a poor start. Brian Little's Aston Villa lost their first three games and found themselves second from bottom at the end of August. And Wimbledon, without a win in their first four games, hit rock bottom. It was going to be a long, hard season.

The quest for European glory started early, with Newcastle United drawn against Croatia Zagreb in the qualifying rounds of the Champions League. After winning 2–1 at St James' Park, Kenny Dalglish's side took part in a thrilling second leg in Zagreb. The tie went to extra time, with new signing, the Georgian Temuri Ketsbaia, grabbing the winning goal with seconds remaining.

MILESTONES OF THE SEASON

AUGUST 3
Champions Manchester United beat cup winners Chelsea 4–2 on penalties after a 1–1 draw in the Charity Shield.

AUGUST 7
Arsenal sign striker Christopher Wreh from Monaco.

AUGUST 8
Bruce Grobbelaar, Hans Segars and John Fashanu are acquitted in the match-fixing trial.

AUGUST 9
The 1997–98 season kicks off with victories for West Ham, Blackburn, Coventry, Crystal Palace, Leicester, Newcastle and Bolton.

AUGUST 10
Manchester United start as they mean to carry on with a 2–0 win away at Tottenham.

AUGUST 12
Newcastle sign veteran midfielder John Barnes from Liverpool on a free transfer.

AUGUST 13
Blackburn, under new manager Roy Hodgson, thrash Aston Villa 4–0 at Villa Park. Newcastle beat Croatia Zagreb 2–1 in the first leg of the Champions League qualifying round.

AUGUST 15
Newcastle sign veteran striker Ian Rush from Leeds on a free transfer.

AUGUST 24
Chelsea run riot at Barnsley, hitting the newly-promoted side for six.

AUGUST 25
Roy Hodgson's Blackburn hit seven past Sheffield Wednesday to go top of the table.

AUGUST 27
Newcastle draw 2–2 in Zagreb to go through 4–3 on aggregate to the group stages of the UEFA Champions League.

PREMIER LEAGUE STANDINGS

August 30

		P	W	D	L	F	A	Pts
1	Blackburn Rovers	5	4	1	0	15	4	13
2	Manchester United	5	4	1	0	8	0	13
3	West Ham United	5	3	1	1	9	6	10
4	Chelsea	4	3	0	1	14	5	9
5	Arsenal	5	2	3	0	9	5	9
6	Leicester City	5	2	2	1	6	5	8
7	Tottenham Hotspur	5	2	1	2	5	6	7
8	Newcastle United	2	2	0	0	3	1	6
9	Crystal Palace	5	2	0	3	5	5	6
10	Barnsley	5	2	0	3	4	10	6
11	Liverpool	4	1	2	1	5	4	5
12	Coventry City	5	1	2	2	6	10	5
13	Bolton	3	1	1	1	4	4	4
14	Leeds United	5	1	1	3	4	7	4
15	Sheffield Wednesday	5	1	1	3	6	13	4
16	Derby County	3	1	0	2	1	2	3
17	Everton	3	1	0	2	3	5	3
18	Southampton	5	1	0	2	2	4	3
19	Aston Villa	5	1	0	4	3	9	3
20	Wimbledon	4	0	2	2	3	7	2

Arsenal at the top

Arsenal rose to the top of the Premiership thanks to some majestic goals from Dennis Bergkamp and the predatory instincts of Ian Wright, who broke Cliff Bastin's long-standing club record of 178 goals. Elsewhere, Manchester United started on their European Cup campaign with a 3–0 win over Kosice.

Blackburn Rovers may have been the early Premier League pacesetters, but it did not take Arsenal long to get into their stride. Manager Arsène Wenger had strengthened his side over the summer with the arrival of Dutch international Marc Overmars, a £5 million signing from Ajax, Frenchmen Emmanuel Petit and Gilles Grimandi from Monaco, teenage defender Matthew Upson and Liberian international striker Christopher Wreh. The Gunners had the look of title contenders and the early form of Dennis Bergkamp – he scored fabulous goals against Leicester, Chelsea and West Ham – suggested that the Dutchman was going to have a fantastic season. Ian Wright was also in terrific form in August and September and it was only a matter of weeks into the season before he was ready to overtake Cliff Bastin's record as Arsenal's all-time top scorer.

Wright finally beat Bastin's mark of 178 goals when he bagged a hat-trick at home to Bolton, Arsenal beat Bolton 4–1, Chelsea 3–2 (at Stamford Bridge thanks to a last-minute thunderbolt from Nigel Winterburn) and West Ham 4–0, and drew 3–3 at Leicester to go top of the table, ahead of Manchester United, who were getting into gear in the Premiership while also preparing their assault on the European Cup.

United opened up their European campaign with an emphatic 3–0 away win over Slovakian champions Kosice. Elsewhere on the European campaign trail, Liverpool and Celtic clashed in an all-British UEFA Cup tie. In the first leg in Glasgow, a wonderful goal from Liverpool's Steve McManaman in the dying seconds of the match squared the first leg at 2–2.

All roads lead to Rome

On the international front, England moved a step closer to the World Cup finals in France with a thumping 4–0 win over Moldova at Wembley, thanks to goals from Paul Scholes, Ian Wright (two) and Paul Gascoigne. And there was even better news that night from Tbilisi, where England's main rivals Italy had failed to beat Georgia. The result meant that Glenn Hoddle's side only needed to avoid defeat against Italy in Rome in their final group match in order to qualify for the World Cup.

September was a month full of surprises, and none more so than the return to football of Kevin Keegan – at Second Division

Suits you, sir: Chief of Operations Kevin Keegan in his new role at Fulham.

MANAGER OF THE MONTH

Arsène Wenger
Guided Arsenal to the top of the table with a mixture of English grit and Continental flair.

PLAYER OF THE MONTH

Ian Wright
Finally broke Cliff Bastin's long-standing Arsenal scoring record – and he celebrated in style.

Fulham. Keegan, who had walked out on Newcastle eight months earlier, was tempted back by Fulham owner Mohammed Al Fayed to guide the London club to promotion.

Comings and goings

At the bottom of the Premier League, it was already shaping up to be a battle against relegation. Struggling Southampton took an early plunge into the transfer market, signing Carlton Palmer from Leeds and Kevin Richardson from Coventry. Leeds offloaded the troublesome Tony Yeboah to German club Hamburg. West Ham sold Marc Rieper and Michael Hughes, to Celtic and Wimbledon respectively, to pay for the signing of QPR's Andrew Impey, and Bolton signed the South African international defender Mark Fish.

PREMIER LEAGUE STANDINGS

September 30

		P	W	D	L	F	A	Pts
1	Arsenal	9	5	4	0	22	10	19
2	Manchester United	9	5	3	1	12	4	18
3	Leicester City	9	5	3	1	13	6	18
4	Chelsea	8	5	1	2	22	10	16
5	Blackburn Rovers	9	4	4	1	19	9	16
6	Leeds United	9	4	1	4	11	11	13
7	West Ham United	9	4	1	4	12	14	13
8	Derby County	7	4	0	3	14	7	12
9	Liverpool	8	3	3	2	12	8	12
10	Newcastle United	6	4	0	2	6	5	12
11	Crystal Palace	9	3	2	4	9	11	11
12	Coventry City	9	2	5	2	8	11	11
13	Tottenham Hotspur	9	2	4	3	6	10	10
14	Aston Villa	9	3	1	5	10	15	10
15	Wimbledon	8	2	3	3	10	10	9
16	Everton	8	2	2	4	10	13	8
17	Bolton Wanderers	8	1	5	2	8	11	8
18	Sheffield Wednesday	9	1	3	5	11	22	6
19	Barnsley	9	2	0	7	7	23	6
20	Southampton	9	1	1	7	5	17	4

MILESTONES OF THE SEASON

SEPTEMBER 1
Calls are made for goal-line cameras after Bolton are denied a clear goal in a 0–0 draw with Everton.

SEPTEMBER 2
Liverpool's Steve McManaman and Robbie Fowler are left out of Glenn Hoddle's squad for the World Cup qualifier against Moldova.

SEPTEMBER 10
England move a step closer to France with a 4–0 defeat of Moldova at Wembley while Italy can only draw with Georgia.

SEPTEMBER 13
Arsenal demonstrate their championship credentials with a 4–1 defeat of Bolton in which Ian Wright scores a hat-trick and breaks Cliff Bastin's all-time Arsenal scoring record.

SEPTEMBER 16
Liverpool draw 2–2 with Celtic in Glasgow in the first round, first leg of the UEFA Cup. Arsenal go down 1–0 in Greece to PAOK Salonika. Aston Villa hold Bordeaux to a goalless draw in France. Leicester are beaten 2–1 by Atletico Madrid.

SEPTEMBER 17
Newcastle beat Barcelona 3–2 in a thrilling Champions League match at St James' Park. Faustino Asprilla scores a hat-trick. Manchester United open up their Champions League campaign with a 3–0 win in Slovakia over FC Kosice.

SEPTEMBER 18
Chelsea have a comfortable 2–0 victory over Slovakian side Slovan Bratislava in the first round, first leg of the European Cup-winners' Cup.

SEPTEMBER 21
Arsenal extend their unbeaten start to the season with a 3–2 win at Chelsea.

SEPTEMBER 24
Kevin Keegan returns to football as "Chief Operating Officer" of Second Division Fulham.

SEPTEMBER 30
Aston Villa beat Bordeaux 1–0 to reach the second round of the UEFA Cup. Liverpool go through on away goals after a goalless draw with Celtic. Leicester and Arsenal both go out.

Hoddle's heroes triumph in Rome

After the trauma of the last World Cup qualifying campaign when England failed to make it to USA '94, the expectation that preceded the make-or-break match in Rome against Italy was huge. But Glenn Hoddle's men performed heroics to earn a 0–0 draw and a place in France '98.

It was billed as the ultimate World Cup showdown. England versus Italy for the right to qualify automatically for France 98. England head coach Glenn Hoddle took his squad to the Olympic Stadium in Rome needing only a draw to reach France. Italy had beaten England earlier in the year at Wembley but had since stumbled on the qualifying trail, dropping points in a draw with Georgia in Tbilisi. England, in contrast, had won all of their qualifying matches since the defeat by Italy. They were in good shape and in a confident mood, especially after they had beaten Italy 2–0 in the summer's friendly Tournoi tournament in France.

The build-up to the showdown in Rome was intense – and was not helped by the over-exuberant treatment of England fans by the Italian police. Italy started with an attacking formation deploying three forwards, but England held firm and defended with guts and determination. Italy's Angelo Di Livio was sent off late in the first half – and England held out for a memorable result.

It could have all been so different. In the last minute of the match Ian Wright, one of England's heroes on the night, hit an Italian post. Within seconds, the ball was at the other end of the pitch and Christian Vieri headed just over David Seaman's crossbar. The match ended goalless – an invaluable result for Glenn Hoddle's men. They qualified automatically for the 1998 World Cup finals in France – and condemned Italy to a two-legged play-off against Russia.

English football achieved a notable double over the Italians in October. In addition to the national team's triumph, Manchester United took control of their Champions League group with a 3–2 victory over Juventus at Old Trafford. The scoreline flattered the Italians, who had taken a first-minute lead through Alessandro Del Piero. But three goals from United, including a stunning third from Ryan Giggs, gave the English champions a comprehensive victory, although Zinedine Zidane pulled a goal back for Juventus from a late free-kick. United's victory left many predicting that United were on course to win the European Cup for the first time since 1968.

Three Lions: David Beckham, Graeme Le Saux and Ian Wright show their pleasure at holding Italy to a 0–0 draw in Rome.

MANAGER OF THE MONTH

Alex Ferguson

Guided Manchester United back to the top of the table – in both the Premier League and Champions League.

PLAYER OF THE MONTH

Ryan Giggs

Gave a star performance as Manchester United stormed past Juventus in a crucial Champions League clash at Old Trafford.

Alex Ferguson's side were also getting into gear in the Premier League title race, despite the loss of captain Roy Keane. The Republic of Ireland international was ruled out for the rest of the season with damaged cruciate knee ligaments. Keane's injury didn't stop United – they thrashed newly promoted Barnsley 7–0 at Old Trafford to go top of the league. At the other end of the table, Everton and Sheffield Wednesday were struggling. David Pleat was looking over his shoulder at Wednesday, while Howard Kendall was finding it tough in his third spell in charge at Everton. Pleat reinforced his midfield with the signing of Norwegian international Petter Rudi, but was forced to sell striker David Hirst to Southampton to pay for it. One team who were doing surprisingly well were Derby. Jim Smith's side, with exciting foreign players such as Costa Rican Paolo Wanchope and Italian Francesco Baiano, forced their way into the top six.

PREMIER LEAGUE STANDINGS

October 31

		P	W	D	L	F	A	Pts
1	Manchester United	12	7	4	1	23	6	25
2	Arsenal	12	6	6	0	27	10	24
3	Blackburn Rovers	12	6	5	1	22	10	23
4	Leicester City	12	6	3	3	16	10	21
5	Chelsea	11	6	1	4	25	15	19
6	Liverpool	11	5	3	3	20	12	18
7	Derby County	11	5	2	4	19	15	17
8	Leeds United	12	5	2	5	15	13	17
9	Wimbledon	12	4	4	4	14	13	16
10	Newcastle United	9	5	1	3	9	10	16
11	West Ham United	11	5	1	5	15	17	16
12	Crystal Palace	12	4	3	5	12	14	15
13	Aston Villa	12	4	2	6	12	17	14
14	Tottenham Hotspur	12	3	4	5	11	16	13
15	Coventry City	12	2	7	3	8	13	13
16	Everton	11	3	3	5	13	16	12
17	Bolton Wanderers	11	2	5	4	9	15	11
18	Southampton	12	3	1	8	11	20	10
19	Sheffield Wednesday	12	2	3	7	17	29	9
20	Barnsley	12	3	0	9	9	35	9

MILESTONES OF THE SEASON

OCTOBER 1
Manchester United beat Juventus 3–2 in a thrilling Champions League match at Old Trafford. Newcastle snatch a draw against Dynamo Kiev in Ukraine.

OCTOBER 2
Manchester United captain Roy Keane is ruled out for the rest of the season after rupturing a cruciate ligament. Chelsea reach the second round of the Cup-winners' Cup after a 2–0 win in Slovakia.

OCTOBER 4
Arsenal thrash Barnsley 5–0.

OCTOBER 5
Patrik Berger scores a hat-trick as Liverpool beat Chelsea 4–2 at Anfield.

OCTOBER 11
England draw 0–0 with Italy to qualify for the World Cup finals.

OCTOBER 16
Chelsea's Uruguayan midfielder Gustavo Poyet is ruled out for the rest of the season with torn cruciate ligaments.

OCTOBER 18
Everton beat Liverpool 2–0 in the Merseyside derby.

OCTOBER 21
Aston Villa draw 0–0 with Athletic Bilbao in the second round, first leg of the UEFA Cup. Liverpool crash 3–0 to Strasbourg.

OCTOBER 22
Manchester United beat Feyenoord 2–1 in the third round of Champions League matches. Newcastle lose 1–0 to PSV Eindhoven in Holland.

OCTOBER 23
Chelsea lose 3–2 to Tromso in Arctic blizzard conditions in the first leg of the Cup-winners' Cup second round.

OCTOBER 25
Manchester United hit seven past Barnsley to go ahead of Arsenal at the top of the table.

OCTOBER 29
The Republic of Ireland draw 1–1 with Belgium in Dublin in the first leg of their World Cup qualifying play-off.

The Premiership's revolving door for managers was kept busy in November, but one boss staying put was Alex Ferguson who took Manchester United back to the top of the League despite a 3–2 loss to Arsenal.

Managers pay the price

Big Ron at Wednesday: Sheffield Wednesday fans welcome back Ron Atkinson for a second spell in charge at Hillsborough.

Sack race

The pressure on football managers is growing all the time – and Sheffield Wednesday's David Pleat and Tottenham's Gerry Francis paid the price for their clubs' failings in November.

Pleat had been close to the edge for some weeks, but a 6–1 thrashing by Manchester United at Old Trafford sealed his fate. He was sacked by Wednesday, who announced Ron Atkinson as his successor. Big Ron was a controversial choice because he had managed Wednesday before, guiding them to the League Cup in 1991, only to leave them in the lurch weeks later to join Aston Villa.

Pleat was immediately linked with a return to Tottenham, where Gerry Francis had resigned after a miserable start to the season. Spurs had been dogged by injuries, but Francis decided enough was enough, and quit the North London club. The man who Spurs chairman Alan Sugar picked as a successor to Francis was a surprise to everyone. Christian Gross had been a moderately successful coach with Swiss club Grasshopper, but he was seen as the man to bring continental class to Tottenham – just as Arsène Wenger had worked wonders for their North London rivals Arsenal.

Elsewhere in the League, George Graham's Leeds were doing

well and were earning a reputation as the comeback kids. They came from behind to beat Derby, West Ham and Barnsley in November.

Southampton, seen as relegation candidates at the start of the season, were doing well under manager Dave Jones. His new signings Kevin Davies, David Hirst and Carlton Palmer made an immediate impact and the Saints climbed away from the relegation zone.

While clubs like Tottenham and Wednesday rang the changes in a bid to revive their flagging season, Manchester United were busy running away with the League – and Alex Ferguson's men were not doing badly in Europe, either. United lost a thrilling League encounter at Highbury 3–2, with David Platt scoring the winner after Teddy Sheringham had scored twice to bring the scores level. But they followed up their setback against Arsenal with a 5–2 victory at Wimbledon and a 4–0 home win over title challengers Blackburn.

United did not seem to be missing Eric Cantona one bit. And while other teams looked to imported foreign stars to provide the inspiration, United's home-grown youngsters – Ryan Giggs, David Beckham, Paul Scholes and the Neville brothers, Gary and

Philip – seemed more than capable of allowing United to challenge for honours both at home and abroad. In the Champions League, United continued to impress. They beat Feyenoord and Kosice to ensure qualification for the quarter-finals in March. Alex Ferguson's young side looked unstoppable.

Elsewhere in Europe, Aston Villa qualified for the third round of the UEFA Cup after beating Athletic Bilbao, but Liverpool could not overcome French side Strasbourg. Chelsea continued their progress under Ruud Gullit and reached the quarter-finals of the European Cup-winners' Cup.

Glenn Hoddle's England started to look forward to France 98. Cameroon were the visitors for a friendly at Wembley and were seen off comfortably thanks to goals from Paul Scholes and Ian Wright. On the same day, the Republic of Ireland lost their World Cup play-off to Belgium, 3–2 on aggregate.

PREMIER LEAGUE STANDINGS

November 30

		P	W	D	L	F	A	Pts
1	Manchester United	15	9	4	2	36	12	31
2	Chelsea	16	10	1	5	35	17	31
3	Blackburn Rovers	15	8	6	1	27	13	30
4	Leeds United	16	9	2	5	26	19	29
5	Arsenal	15	7	6	2	30	17	27
6	Leicester City	16	7	5	4	21	14	26
7	Newcastle United	13	7	3	3	18	17	24
8	Derby County	15	7	2	6	28	24	23
9	Liverpool	14	6	4	4	25	14	22
10	Crystal Palace	15	5	4	6	15	17	19
11	Wimbledon	16	5	4	7	18	21	19
12	West Ham United	15	6	1	8	20	25	19
13	Aston Villa	16	5	3	8	16	23	18
14	Sheffield Wednesday	16	5	3	8	28	37	18
15	Coventry City	16	3	8	5	13	21	17
16	Southampton	16	5	1	10	20	26	16
17	Tottenham Hotspur	16	4	4	8	13	22	16
18	Bolton Wanderers	15	3	7	5	11	21	16
19	Barnsley	16	4	1	11	14	43	13
20	Everton	16	3	3	10	16	27	12

MILESTONES OF THE SEASON

NOVEMBER 1
Arsenal, without the suspended Dennis Bergkamp, go down 3–0 at Derby. Sheffield Wednesday are thrashed 6–1 by Manchester United at Old Trafford.

NOVEMBER 3
Sheffield Wednesday sack manager David Pleat.

NOVEMBER 4
Aston Villa beat Athletic Bilbao 2–1 at Villa Park to reach the third round of the UEFA Cup. Liverpool beat Strasbourg 2–0, but go out 3–2 on aggregate.

NOVEMBER 5
Manchester United beat Feyenoord 3–1 in the Champions League. Newcastle lose 2–0 at home to PSV Eindhoven.

NOVEMBER 6
Chelsea reach the quarter-finals of the Cup-winners' Cup in style, beating Tromso 7–1 at Stamford Bridge.

NOVEMBER 8
Manager-less Sheffield Wednesday beat Bolton 5–0. Liverpool defeat Tottenham 4–0.

NOVEMBER 9
Arsenal beat Manchester United 3–2 at Highbury.

NOVEMBER 13
Ron Atkinson returns to Sheffield Wednesday as manager.

NOVEMBER 15
England beat Cameroon 2–0 in a friendly at Wembley. The Republic of Ireland lose 2–1 to Belgium (3–2 on aggregate) in the World Cup play-offs.

NOVEMBER 19
Gerry Francis resigns as manager of Tottenham.

NOVEMBER 24
Christian Gross takes over as manager of Tottenham.

NOVEMBER 25
Aston Villa lose 2–1 to Steaua Bucharest in the first leg of the UEFA Cup third round.

NOVEMBER 26
Manchester United comfortably beat Kosice 3–0 in the Champions League. Newcastle go out of the competition after losing 1–0 to Barcelona in the Nou Camp.

NOVEMBER 30
Manchester United beat the early pace-setters Blackburn 4–0 at Old Trafford to stay top. A Steve McManaman goal gives Liverpool a 1–0 win at Arsenal.

Jürgen back at Tottenham

The old campaigner: Jurgen Klinsmann with Christian Gross.

Some Spurs fans viewed the return of Jürgen Klinsmann with scepticism, while Arsenal fans feared their season was in danger of disintegrating.

Tottenham's poor season looked up in December with the return of Jürgen Klinsmann to White Hart Lane. Klinsmann agreed to join Spurs on loan from Italian side Sampdoria until the end of the season as new manager Christian Gross tried to turn things around at Tottenham.

German international Klinsmann had not been having a good season in Italy. He could not win a first-team place at Sampdoria after a series of injuries and was worried about missing his chance with Germany's World Cup squad. He needed first-team football, which was exactly what Spurs could offer. In fact, Klinsmann reportedly had it written into his contract – he could not be dropped by Gross!

The German had starred for Spurs in the 1994–95 season and formed a lucrative partnership with Teddy Sheringham, but fell out with chairman Alan Sugar and went back to Germany, joining Bayern Munich. Three years on, there were doubts as to whether Klinsmann would be such a big hit second time around, especially as he had been troubled by injuries, but Spurs fans were glad to see him back at the Lane.

Spurs' North London rivals Arsenal, who had enjoyed such a great start to the season, started to falter in December, as injuries and suspensions took their toll. Without Dennis Bergkamp and Ian Wright, the general consensus was that the Gunners did not have the firepower to win the title. That view seemed to be proved right when Arsène Wenger's side went down 3–1 at home to fellow challengers Blackburn. After that defeat, questions were asked about the Arsenal defence. It was too old, people said, and Arsenal were not going to win the League with an ageing defence and foreign reserves who didn't seem up to the rigours of English football. Virtually the only person who didn't seem unduly worried was manager Arsène Wenger.

MANAGER OF THE MONTH

Alex Ferguson

The United manager kept his team on course for a Premier League and Champions League double.

PLAYER OF THE MONTH

Andy Cole

The Manchester United striker overcame the critics to score the goals which kept the champions on course.

Red Devils in heaven

While Arsenal's challenge stalled, Manchester United rolled on. They saw off the Premier League challenge from rivals Liverpool, winning 3–1 at Anfield in early December. There were further victories over Aston Villa and Newcastle, but United were given a nasty fright by Coventry, who beat the champions 3–2 at Highfield Road, with young striker Darren Huckerby scoring a sensational last-minute winner.

In Europe, United were drawn against French champions Monaco in the quarter-finals of the European Cup. Alex Ferguson's side had lost their final Champions League group match in Turin to Juventus, which allowed the Italian champions to squeeze into the quarter-finals as one of the best runners-up.

Jürgen Klinsmann was not the only foreign player to sign up for the Premier League. Romanian striker Viorel Moldovan joined Coventry in a record £3.25 million deal and Dutch midfielder George Boateng also moved to Highfield Road.

Everton took French striker Mickael Madar on a free transfer from Spanish side Deportivo La Coruna, and Liverpool finally got their man when American goalkeeper Brad Friedel signed from Major League Soccer. But two foreigners moved on to new challenges. Derby sold Croatian midfielder Aljosa Asanovic to Italian side Napoli and Manchester United offloaded Czech international Karel Poborsky to Portuguese side Benfica, now managed by former Liverpool manager Graeme Souness.

PREMIER LEAGUE STANDINGS

December 31

		P	W	D	L	F	A	Pts
1	Manchester United	21	14	4	3	49	16	46
2	Blackburn Rovers	21	11	8	2	38	21	41
3	Chelsea	21	12	3	6	46	21	39
4	Liverpool	20	11	4	5	36	19	37
5	Leeds United	21	10	5	6	30	23	35
6	Arsenal	20	9	7	4	35	23	34
7	Derby County	21	9	5	7	34	28	32
8	West Ham United	21	10	1	10	28	32	31
9	Leicester City	21	7	7	7	25	21	28
10	Aston Villa	21	7	5	9	25	27	26
11	Newcastle United	20	7	5	8	21	25	26
12	Wimbledon	20	6	6	8	21	24	24
13	Southampton	21	7	3	11	25	30	24
14	Coventry City	21	5	8	8	20	28	23
15	Crystal Palace	21	5	8	8	20	28	23
16	Sheffield Wednesday	21	6	5	10	32	44	23
17	Bolton Wanderers	21	4	9	8	19	33	21
18	Everton	21	5	5	11	20	31	20
19	Tottenham Hotspur	21	5	5	11	19	37	20
20	Barnsley	21	5	3	13	19	51	18

MILESTONES OF THE SEASON

DECEMBER 6
Manchester United beat Liverpool 3–1 at Anfield. Chelsea hit six past Tottenham at White Hart Lane.

DECEMBER 10
Manchester United lose to Juventus in the final round of Champions League group matches, but still finish top of the group.

DECEMBER 12
Manchester United are drawn against French side Monaco in the quarter-finals of the Champions League. Aston Villa will face Atletico Madrid in the quarter-finals of the UEFA Cup, while Chelsea will play Real Betis in the Cup-winners' Cup.

DECEMBER 13
Arsenal lose 3–1 at home to Blackburn.

DECEMBER 15
A Ryan Giggs goal gives Manchester United victory over Aston Villa.

DECEMBER 18
Coventry sign Dutch under-21 midfielder George Boateng from Feyenoord.

DECEMBER 21
Andy Cole gives Manchester United a 1–0 win over Newcastle at St James' Park.

DECEMBER 22
Tottenham bring Jürgen Klinsmann back to White Hart Lane for a second spell.

DECEMBER 28
Manchester United lose 3–2 at Coventry. Jürgen Klinsmann makes his first appearance back in Spurs colours, at home to Arsenal.

January

Man United get the jitters

Manchester United ran into soome rough water, but their closest rivals found the going equally tough. In the FA Cup, Newcastle United's players had to rough it with the minnows of Stevenage Town.

Alex Ferguson's side gave their best performance of the season in the FA Cup third round at Chelsea. They demolished Chelsea in a one-sided match which ended 5–3 after United had been 4–0 up at half-time. The result left everyone wondering what they had to do to beat United – they didn't have to wait long, as United slipped to unexpected defeats to mid-table sides Southampton and Leicester.

Arsenal, meanwhile, were busy putting together an unbeaten run which would continue right through to the last week of the season. They beat former manager George Graham's side, Leeds, 2–1, with a brace of goals from Dutch winger Marc Overmars, who was beginning to find his feet in English football – good news for Arsenal, bad news for all their rivals. Even so, by now Arsenal were way off the title pace in fifth place, but none of the teams above them – Chelsea, Liverpool and Blackburn – seemed capable of challenging Manchester United.

Liverpool failed to take advantage of United's dodgy spell, drawing with Leicester and Blackburn in the League and being knocked out of the FA Cup by Coventry, while Chelsea went down to Everton as doubts began to surface about Ruud Gullit's future as player-manager.

There were few upsets in the third round of the FA Cup. Non-league Stevenage were the big story. They knocked out First Division Swindon Town and were rewarded with a plum tie in the fourth round against Newcastle.

Shearer rides again

Kenny Dalglish's side were finding things tough in the Premier League after their exit from the Champions League – not least because they were without the injured Alan Shearer. The England captain returned to action in January after a six-month lay-off

The Italian Stallion from Stevenage: Giuliano Grazioli celebrates his equalizer against Newcastle in the FA Cup fourth round.

and helped the Magpies overcome an unexpectedly tough challenge from Stevenage in the FA Cup.

The non-league side refused to switch the tie to St James' Park, preferring instead to host the tie in their tiny ground. But Newcastle got their wish to play Stevenage on home soil after all. Shearer, starting in his first match since returning from injury, scored for Newcastle, but the part-timers equalized to force a replay at St James' Park, which Kenny Dalglish's side eventually won.

Newcastle were busy on the transfer front, despite the return of Shearer. Swedish striker Andreas Andersson was brought in from Milan to replace the outgoing Faustino Asprilla, who was sold back to Italian side Parma.

Elsewhere, Everton sold England left-back Andy Hinchcliffe for £2 million, a move which was forced on manager Howard Kendall, who was desperate for money to bring in reinforcements

to the troubled Merseyside club. In London, Tottenham bought former Italian international midfielder Nicola Berti from Inter Milan, while struggling Crystal Palace broke their transfer record to sign French under–21 defender Valerien Ismael, and West Ham signed England under–21 forward Trevor Sinclair from Queen's Park Rangers.

MILESTONES OF THE SEASON

JANUARY 3
Liverpool lose at home to Coventry in the FA Cup third round.

JANUARY 4
Manchester United demolish Chelsea 5–3 in the third round of the FA Cup at Stamford Bridge.

JANUARY 7
Middlesbrough, Arsenal, Liverpool and Chelsea all reach the semi-finals of the Coca-Cola Cup.

JANUARY 14
Sheffield Wednesday sell French defender Patrick Blondeau to Bordeaux for £1.2 million.

JANUARY 15
Struggling Crystal Palace sign French defender Valerien Ismael and decide to keep Swedish midfielder Tomas Brolin on until the end of the season.

JANUARY 19
Manchester United go down 1–0 at Southampton.

JANUARY 20
Aston Villa striker Savo Milosevic is transfer-listed after allegedly spitting at fans.

JANUARY 24
Arsenal beat Middlesbrough 2–1 in the FA Cup fourth round.

JANUARY 25
England captain Alan Shearer starts his first game for Newcastle since his return from serious injury, against Stevenage in the FA Cup fourth round.

JANUARY 27
Newcastle sign Swedish striker Andreas Andersson from Milan for £3 million. Liverpool beat Middlesbrough 2–1 in the first leg of the Coca-Cola Cup semi-final.

JANUARY 28
Arsenal beat Chelsea 2–1 at Highbury in the first leg of their Coca-Cola Cup semi-final.

JANUARY 31
Manchester United lose at home to Leicester.

PREMIER LEAGUE STANDINGS

January 31

		P	W	D	L	F	A	Pts
1	Manchester United	24	15	4	5	51	18	49
2	Chelsea	24	14	3	7	52	25	45
3	Blackburn Rovers	24	12	9	3	44	24	45
4	Liverpool	24	13	6	5	39	19	45
5	Arsenal	23	11	8	4	42	26	41
6	Derby County	24	11	6	7	39	30	39
7	Leeds United	24	11	5	8	34	27	38
8	West Ham United	24	11	2	11	36	35	35
9	Leicester City	24	8	9	7	27	22	33
10	Sheffield Wednesday	24	8	6	10	37	47	30
11	Newcastle United	23	8	5	10	24	29	29
12	Southampton	24	8	4	12	26	33	28
13	Coventry City	24	6	9	9	28	34	27
14	Everton	24	7	6	11	28	35	27
15	Aston Villa	23	7	6	10	26	34	27
16	Wimbledon	23	6	8	9	22	27	26
17	Crystal Palace	24	5	8	11	21	34	23
18	Tottenham Hotspur	24	6	5	13	21	41	23
19	Bolton Wanderers	24	4	10	10	21	40	22
20	Barnsley	24	6	3	15	20	59	21

Gullit sacking rocks Chelsea

Chelsea's glamorous player-manager Ruud Gullit exited the club amid a blaze of publicity. With Gianluca Vialli in charge, Chelsea bounced back with a win over Arsenal in the Coca-Cola Cup.

Close the door behind you: Ruud Gullit departs Chelsea in less than amicable circumstances following his sacking.

Chelsea pulled off one of the biggest surprises of the season in February when they sacked Ruud Gullit – and replaced him as player-manager with Italian striker Gianluca Vialli.

The news rocked football. Gullit, after all, was the man who had guided Chelsea to the FA Cup, their first trophy for more than a quarter of a century. He had also taken the London club to second place in the table behind Manchester United. But when Gullit presented Chelsea owner Ken Bates with his financial demands for a new contract, Bates backed off. He argued that nobody was worth the sort of money Gullit was asking for – £2 million a year – and especially not a manager whose side had

recently been beaten heavily by Manchester United in the FA Cup and by Arsenal in the League and the first leg of the semi-final of the League Cup. Gullit was devastated by Chelsea's decision. Vialli was surprised, but delighted to be given a new challenge. The Italian's first match in charge was the second leg of the League Cup semi-final against Arsenal. Chelsea needed to turn around a 2–1 deficit. They did so in style, beating Arsène Wenger's side 3–0 on the night and 4–2 on aggregate.

In the other semi-final, Bryan Robson's Middlesbrough overcame Liverpool to set up a repeat of the 1997 FA Cup final, which Chelsea had won 2–0.

MANAGER OF THE MONTH

Danny Wilson

Guided Barnsley past Manchester United – and into the sixth round of the FA Cup.

PLAYER OF THE MONTH

Michael Owen

The Liverpool teenager became the youngest England player this century after making his debut in the 2–0 defeat by Chile.

In the FA Cup fifth round, there were wins for Coventry, Leeds and Newcastle. Manchester United were held 1–1 at Old Trafford by Barnsley, who scored through John Hendrie after a rare blunder by Peter Schmeichel. In the replay at Oakwell, Barnsley, who had put out Tottenham after a replay in the fourth round, won 3–2 to set up a quarter-final clash with Newcastle, for whom the FA Cup was their only hope of silverware.

Manchester United continued at the top of the League in February, but Arsenal were catching up after wins over Crystal Palace and Chelsea.

On the international front, England coach Glenn Hoddle called up Liverpool teenager Michael Owen for the friendly against Chile. Owen was having a sensational season at Anfield and, if selected by Hoddle, would become the youngest England international this century. In the event, Owen started the match alongside another debutant, Coventry's Dion Dublin. Owen played well in a disappointing overall display by England which saw Chile striker Marcelo Salas score both goals in a 2–0 win for the South American visitors.

On the transfer front, Newcastle made further signings, bringing in Gary Speed from Everton, and Tottenham signed Algerian international Moussa Saib.

Another Premier League manager fell by the wayside in February. Brian Little paid the price for Aston Villa's poor results in the League. He resigned before he was pushed, and was replaced by former Villa player John Gregory.

MILESTONES OF THE SEASON

FEBRUARY 2
Liverpool teenager Michael Owen is called up to Glenn Hoddle's England squad.

FEBRUARY 4
In FA Cup fourth round replays, Barnsley beat Tottenham and Newcastle overcome non-league Stevenage.

FEBRUARY 6
Newcastle sign Everton captain Gary Speed for £5.5 million.

FEBRUARY 11
England are beaten 2–0 by Chile at Wembley. Michael Owen becomes the youngest England player this century.

FEBRUARY 12
Chelsea sack Ruud Gullit and appoint Gianluca Vialli as player-coach.

FEBRUARY 14
In the FA Cup fifth round, there are wins for Coventry, Leeds and Newcastle.

FEBRUARY 15
Manchester United are held to a 1–1 draw by Barnsley at Old Trafford in the FA Cup.

FEBRUARY 18
In Gianluca Vialli's first match in charge, Chelsea beat Arsenal 3–0 in the second leg of the Coca-Cola Cup semi-final to reach Wembley.

FEBRUARY 19
Tottenham sign Algerian international Moussa Saib from Valencia.

FEBRUARY 24
Brian Little resigns as manager of Aston Villa.

FEBRUARY 25
John Gregory succeeds Brian Little at Aston Villa. Barnsley beat Manchester United 3–2 in an FA Cup fifth round replay.

PREMIER LEAGUE STANDINGS

February 28

		P	W	D	L	F	A	Pts
1	Manchester United	28	18	5	5	57	19	59
2	Blackburn Rovers	27	13	9	5	49	33	48
3	Arsenal	25	13	8	4	45	25	47
4	Liverpool	28	13	8	7	46	28	47
5	Chelsea	27	14	3	10	52	30	45
6	Derby County	28	13	6	9	44	34	45
7	Leicester City	28	10	10	8	34	28	40
8	Leeds United	27	11	6	10	35	30	39
9	West Ham United	26	12	3	11	38	36	39
10	Coventry City	28	10	9	9	35	35	39
11	Southampton	28	11	4	13	34	37	37
12	Newcastle United	27	9	7	11	26	31	34
13	Sheffield Wednesday	28	9	7	12	41	54	34
14	Aston Villa	28	9	6	13	30	39	33
15	Wimbledon	26	8	8	10	28	30	32
16	Everton	28	7	9	12	32	40	30
17	Tottenham Hotspur	27	7	6	14	25	43	27
18	Barnsley	27	7	4	16	24	63	25
19	Bolton Wanderers	26	4	12	10	23	43	24
20	Crystal Palace	27	5	8	14	21	41	23

March

Arsenal blow the title race wide open

Manchester United experienced a miserable five days as they lost 1–0 at home to Arsenal, and were then bundled out of the European Cup by Monaco. Arsenal, meanwhile, had a steely look about them.

blew the title race wide open, although most pundits still tipped United for the title. They were six points clear of the London side even though Arsenal had three games in hand.

Within the space of a few days, United's season had turned upside down. Five days after the defeat by Arsenal, French champions Monaco were the visitors at Old Traffford in the second leg of the European Champions League quarter-final. Two weeks earlier, United had played out a goalless draw with Monaco in Monte Carlo. They needed to win at home in the second leg to reach the semi-finals and continue their quest for the elusive European Cup.

Shattered dreams

Monaco stunned Old Trafford early in the game when they took the lead through their teenage striker David Trezeguet. United equalized early in the second half, but the damage had already been done. Monaco held out for the draw and won the tie on away goals. United's European dreams were over for yet another season.

While United's hopes of silverware narrowed to the Premier League, Arsenal continued their challenge on two fronts. They followed up their crucial League win over United with victories over Sheffield Wednesday and Bolton, and beat West Ham on penalties in the FA Cup quarter-final. The double was beginning to look like a distinct possibility rather than a distant dream. The Gunners were drawn against Wolves in the FA Cup semi-final. In the other tie, Newcastle, who had defeated Barnsley in their quarter-final had to face Sheffield United, amid a welter of outrage and shock on Tyneside following a Sunday newspaper article that portrayed club directors Freddie Sheppard and Douglas Hall in a less than flattering light. The allegations were so serious that the pair resigned a week later. Meanwhile, Chelsea were learning to live without Ruud Gullit. They overcame Real Betis of Spain to reach the semi-finals of the Cup-winners' Cup and then went one better at home, beating Middlesbrough 2–0 in the Coca-Cola Cup final at Wembley. Middlesbrough had new signing Paul Gascoigne on the bench, but even Gazza could not prevent Chelsea win-

Gazz-attack: The introduction of Paul Gascoigne failed to spark Middlesbrough in the Coca-Cola final.

Manchester United were still the favourites to win the Premier League title when Arsenal visited Old Trafford in March. Arsène Wenger's side travelled to Manchester on the back on an unbeaten League run which stretched back to mid-December. They were in no mood to give in to United – and they beat the champions in their own back yard.

Marc Overmars scored the only goal of the game late in the second half to give the Gunners a priceless victory. The result

ning the match in extra time. Gianluca Vialli had only been in the job a matter of weeks and he had already delivered his first trophy.

On the international front, England drew 1–1 in Switzerland, a disappointing result, but Michael Owen again impressed – and there was an encouraging return to international action for Middlesbrough's Paul Merson.

Transfer activity in the run-up to deadline day was surpris-

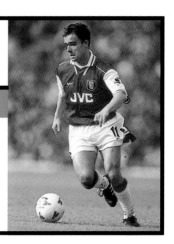
ingly limited, with the relegation strugglers making a last desperate bid to stay in the Premier League. Crystal Palace bought Yugoslav midfielder Sasa Curcic from Aston Villa, while Newcastle brought in Greek international defender Nicoa Dabizas from Olympiakos. And an era came to an end at Wimbledon when Vinnie Jones, the original Crazy Gang member, was sold to QPR.

PREMIER LEAGUE STANDINGS
March 31

		P	W	D	L	F	A	Pts
1	**Manchester United**	32	19	6	7	60	23	63
2	**Arsenal**	29	16	9	4	48	26	57
3	**Liverpool**	31	15	9	7	54	34	54
4	**Chelsea**	30	15	3	12	59	35	48
5	**Leeds United**	31	14	6	11	45	33	48
6	**Blackburn Rovers**	29	13	9	7	49	38	48
7	**West Ham United**	30	14	5	11	44	38	47
8	**Derby County**	30	13	6	11	44	40	45
9	**Coventry City**	30	11	10	9	36	35	43
10	**Southampton**	31	13	4	14	41	43	43
11	**Aston Villa**	32	12	6	14	38	42	42
11	**Leicester City**	30	10	10	10	35	32	40
12	**Sheffield Wednesday**	31	10	7	14	45	58	37
13	**Wimbledon**	29	9	8	12	30	34	35
14	**Newcastle United**	30	9	8	13	28	35	35
15	**Tottenham Hotspur**	31	9	7	15	32	48	34
16	**Everton**	31	8	9	14	35	46	33
17	**Barnsley**	30	9	4	17	31	69	31
18	**Bolton Wanderers**	30	6	12	12	29	47	30
19	**Crystal Palace**	31	6	8	17	27	54	26

MILESTONES OF THE SEASON

MARCH 3
Aston Villa go down 1–0 to Atletico Madrid in the first leg of their UEFA Cup quarter-final.

MARCH 4
Manchester United hold Monaco to a goalless draw in Monte Carlo in the first leg of their Champions League quarter-final.

MARCH 5
Chelsea win 2–1 at Real Betis in the first leg of their Cup-winners' Cup quarter-final.

MARCH 6
Jürgen Klinsmann says he will leave Tottenham at the end of the season.

MARCH 7
Wolves beat Leeds 1–0 in the FA Cup quarter-finals.

MARCH 8
Newcastle beat Barnsley 2–1 to reach the semi-finals of the FA Cup.

MARCH 13
Relegation-threatened Crystal Palace appoint Attilio Lombardo as player-coach until the end of the season.

MARCH 14
Arsenal win 1–0 at Old Trafford.

MARCH 15
Newcastle fans are shocked and angered by newspaper allegations about United directors Freddie Sheppard and Douglas Hall.

MARCH 16
Paul Gascoigne is left out of England's squad to play Switzerland.

MARCH 17
Aston Villa beat Atletico Madrid 2–1 at Villa Park in the UEFA Cup but go out on the away goals rule. In the FA Cup quarter-final replays, there are wins for Arsenal and Sheffield United on penalties.

MARCH 18
Manchester United draw 1–1 with Monaco at Old Trafford and go out of the Champions League on the away goals rule.

MARCH 19
Chelsea beat Betis 3–1 at Stamford Bridge to win their Cup-winners' Cup quarter-final 5–2 on aggregate.

MARCH 24
First Division Middlesbrough sign Paul Gascoigne from Rangers for £3 million. Crystal Palace sign Yugoslav midfielder Sasa Curcic from Aston Villa for £1 million. Freddie Sheppard and Douglas Hall quit Newcastle over sleaze allegations.

MARCH 25
England draw 1–1 with Switzerland in a friendly.

MARCH 29
Chelsea beat Middlesbrough 2–0 at Wembley to win the Coca-Cola Cup.

MARCH 30
Leeds United players have a lucky escape when their plane crash-lands at Stanstead airport.

April

Arsenal take control

Alex Ferguson indulged in his usual mind games as the season approached its climax, but if Manchester United fans were hoping for a repeat of Newcastle's spectacular collapse in 1996, they were to be disappointed as Arsenal went from strength to strength – in the League as well as the FA Cup.

After their crucial win over Manchester United at Old Trafford, Arsenal took control of the race for the Premier League title – and the Gunners also reached the FA Cup final.

After overcoming Wolves at Villa Park in the FA Cup semi-final, Arsenal hammered home their advantage over Manchester United. The champions beat Blackburn 3–1 at Ewood Park, but could only draw with Liverpool – a match which saw teenager Michael Owen sent off after he had given Liverpool the lead – and Newcastle at Old Trafford. Arsenal, in contrast, were going from strength to strength. They comfortably beat Newcastle in a dress rehearsal for the FA Cup final and then emphasized their championship credentials with a stunning 4–1 win over Blackburn at Ewood Park.

Ray Parlour, who was emerging as a key man in Arsenal's season, scored twice as the Gunners went 3–0 up within 14 minutes. In their next match, they hit five past Wimbledon at Highbury. Further wins followed away at Barnsley and Derby. The championship looked to be heading to Highbury.

Ian who?, who?, who?

Arsenal had put together a sensational run of form in the League despite the absence through injury of striker Ian Wright. Under George Graham and Bruce Rioch, it was said that Arsenal were only an Ian Wright-injury away from being a very average team. Under Arsène Wenger, the criticism of Arsenal was that

Ginger nut: Manchester United's Paul Scholes heads one of his side's three goals in the 3–0 win against Crystal Palace.

MANAGER OF THE MONTH

Arsène Wenger

Arsenal's French guru took his team to the brink of a League and Cup Double.

PLAYER OF THE MONTH

Emmanuel Petit

Arsenal's French international midfielder established a partnership with Patrick Vieira which formed the basis for the Gunners' League and Cup success.

the reserve strikers brought in by the manager – Christopher Wreh and Nicolas Anelka – were not up to the rigours of English football.

In April, Wenger's side proved the critics wrong. Wreh stepped into Ian Wright's shoes in style for the FA Cup semi-final against Wolves, scoring the only goal of the game. Anelka, replacing the injured Dennis Bergkamp, scored twice in the League win over Newcastle and again against Blackburn.

While Arsenal consolidated their domestic supremacy, Gianluca Vialli was busy guiding Chelsea to European success. In the European Cup-winners' Cup semi-final, Chelsea went down 1–0 in the first leg in Vicenza. They went further behind early in the second leg at Stamford Bridge before a dramatic fightback, culminating in a stunning Mark Hughes goal, secured an outstanding 3–1 aggre-

gate victory and a place in the final against German Cup-holders VFB Stuttgart.

At the wrong end of the Premier League table, things looked grim for the three sides who had been promoted from the First Division a year earlier. Crystal Palace's relegation was confirmed after a comprehensive 3–0 home defeat by Manchester United, while Bolton and Barnsley teetered on the brink.

MILESTONES OF THE SEASON

APRIL 2
Chelsea go down 1–0 in Vicenza in the first leg of the Cup-winners' Cup semi-final.

APRIL 5
Dennis Bergkamp is voted the Players' Player of the Year. Arsenal beat Wolves and Newcastle overcome Sheffield United in the FA Cup semi-finals.

APRIL 10
Michael Owen is sent off as Liverpool draw 1–1 with Manchester United at Old Trafford.

APRIL 11
Arsenal beat Newcastle 3–1 at Highbury.

APRIL 13
Arsenal win 4–1 at Blackburn to close in on the title.

APRIL 16
Chelsea beat Vicenza 3–1 at Stamford Bridge to win their Cup-winners' Cup semi-final 3–2 on aggregate.

APRIL 18
Arsenal thrash Wimbledon 5–0 at Highbury. Manchester United can only draw with Newcastle, while Crystal Palace beat Derby 3–1 at Selhurst Park, their first home win in the Premier League all season.

APRIL 22
England beat Portugal 3–0 in a friendly international at Wembley.

APRIL 25
Arsenal win 2–0 away at Barnsley to move a step closer to the League title.

APRIL 27
Manchester United beat Crystal Palace 3–0 to send Palace down.

PREMIER LEAGUE STANDINGS

April 30

		P	W	D	L	F	A	Pts
1	Arsenal	34	21	9	4	63	28	72
2	Manchester United	36	21	8	7	68	26	71
3	Chelsea	35	19	3	13	68	39	60
4	Liverpool	35	16	11	8	59	41	59
5	Leeds United	36	17	7	12	56	42	58
6	Blackburn Rovers	35	14	10	11	55	50	52
7	West Ham United	35	15	7	13	49	46	52
8	Aston Villa	36	15	6	15	45	47	51
9	Leicester City	35	12	13	10	47	37	49
10	Derby County	35	14	7	14	49	48	49
11	Coventry City	35	11	14	10	43	43	47
12	Southampton	36	14	5	17	49	52	47
13	Sheffield Wednesday	36	12	8	16	51	63	44
14	Wimbledon	35	10	12	13	31	39	42
15	Newcastle United	35	10	10	15	29	42	40
16	Tottenham Hotspur	36	10	10	16	37	53	40
17	Everton	36	9	12	15	40	51	39
18	Bolton Wanderers	36	8	13	15	36	57	37
19	Barnsley	36	10	5	21	37	79	35
20	Crystal Palace	35	7	8	20	31	63	29

Arsenal clinch the double

Arsène Wenger's Arsenal side emulated the achievements of their 1971 predecessors by winning the League and Cup Double. The Gunners secured the title with a 4–0 thrashing of Everton and then broke the hearts of the Toon army with a cruising 2–0 win at a sun-drenched Wembley.

Arsenal confirmed what Manchester United fans had been fearing ever since the title decider at Old Trafford in March – the Gunners won the Premier League title with two matches of the season remaining.

Arsène Wenger's side had double vision as they prepared to play Everton at Highbury. Victory over the Merseyside team and Arsenal would claim the title and still leave them two weeks to prepare for their FA Cup final showdown with Newcastle.

The match against Everton was Arsenal's last home game of the season. If they didn't beat Everton, the Gunners would have to get a result away at Aston Villa or Liverpool to seal the title. They needn't have worried. A Slaven Bilic own goal from a corner gave Arsenal an early lead, and they cruised to the title from there on in.

Marc Overmars, Arsenal's biggest threat during the unbeaten run, scored twice, either side of half-time. And captain Tony Adams, who rarely ventured out of his own penalty area under George Graham, scored a memorable fourth, appearing from nowhere in the Everton penalty box to confirm just how much has changed under Arsène Wenger at Highbury.

Arsenal lost their last two League matches of the season, away at Liverpool and Aston Villa, but by now their thoughts were focused on the FA Cup final. Dennis Bergkamp was fighting a losing battle with a hamstring injury, and with Ian Wright also injured, the Gunners started the final with second-choice strikers Nicolas Anelka and Christopher Wreh. Just as was the case earlier in the season, it didn't matter. Marc Overmars gave Arsenal the lead in the first-half after he outpaced Newcastle's Italian defender Alessandro Pistone to fire past keeper Shay Given. And Nicolas Anelka sealed the victory in the second half. It was a devastating blow for the thousands of members of the Toon Army who had travelled down from Newcastle, but Arsenal deserved their victory. It was the Highbury club's second Double and only the sixth by any club this century, and the success owed an enormous debt to their French coach Wenger.

Super Sub: Chelsea's Gianfranco Zola scores the winning goal against Stuttgart in the final of the Cup-winners' Cup.

MANAGER OF THE MONTH

Arsène Wenger

The Frenchman masterminded an historic second double for Arsenal.

PLAYER OF THE MONTH

Dennis Bergkamp

Arsenal Dutch maestro missed the FA Cup final but was voted Footballer of the Year by players and journalists.

Subhead needed here

London teams swept the board. Chelsea, with the League Cup already in the trophy cabinet, went one better in Stockholm when they won the Cup-winners' Cup final. Gianfranco Zola was the hero on the night as Gianluca Vialli's side beat German side Stuttgart. The little Italian battled to be fit for the final, but could only claim a place on the bench. After a goalless 70 minutes, Chelsea coach Graham Rix took the decision to replace Tore Andre Flo with Zola. The Italian was on the pitch for less than a minute when Dennis Wise played him through a square German defence to score the only goal of the game.

There was another lucky escape for Everton on the last day of the season. They stayed up only because Chelsea beat Bolton, who joined Barnsley and Palace back in the First Division.

The final match of the English season turned out to be the most exciting. In the First Division play-off at Wembley Charlton were promoted after beating Sunderland in a dramatic penalty shoot-out. The match had finished 4–4 after extra time.

MILESTONES OF THE SEASON

MAY 2
Barnsley are relegated after losing 1–0 at Leicester.
MAY 3
Arsenal beat Everton 4–0 at Highbury to clinch the title.
MAY 6
Internazionale beat Lazio 3–0 in Paris to win the UEFA Cup.
MAY 10
Everton escape the drop on the last day of the season after drawing 1–1 with Coventry, but Bolton go down after losing at Chelsea.
MAY 13
Chelsea beat Stuttgart 1–0 in Stockholm to win the European Cup-winners' Cup.
MAY 15
Dennis Bergkamp is named as Footballer of the Year by the Football Writers' Association.
MAY 17
Arsenal do the "double" after beating Newcastle 2–0 in the FA Cup final.
MAY 20
Real Madrid beat Juventus 1–0 in Amsterdam to win the Champions League final.
MAY 23
England draw 0–0 with Saudi Arabia at Wembley in the final World Cup warm-up game on home turf.
MAY 25
Charlton beat Sunderland on penalties after a thrilling First Division play-off final ends 4–4 after extra time at Wembley.
MAY 27
A Michael Owen goal gives England victory over Morocco in a World Cup warm-up game in Casablanca.
MAY 29
England draw 0–0 with Belgium and lose on penalties in the King Hassan II Cup in Morocco.

PREMIER LEAGUE STANDINGS

May 31

		P	W	D	L	F	A	Pts
1	Arsenal	15	9	4	2	29	13	31
2	Newcastle United	15	9	2	4	26	17	29
3	Liverpool	14	8	4	2	24	13	28
4	Wimbledon	15	8	4	3	26	16	28
5	Manchester United	15	7	5	3	29	22	26
6	Aston Villa	15	7	3	5	19	15	24
7	Chelsea	14	6	6	2	23	19	24
8	Everton	15	6	5	4	23	18	23
9	Derby County	15	5	6	4	17	17	21
10	Sheffield Wednesday	15	5	6	4	16	18	21
11	Tottenham Hotspur	14	6	2	6	15	14	20
12	Sunderland	15	4	5	6	13	18	17
13	West Ham United	15	4	5	6	13	18	17
14	Leicester City	15	5	2	8	14	21	17
15	Leeds United	14	5	1	8	13	20	16
16	Middlesbrough	15	3	5	7	20	26	14
17	Southampton	15	3	4	8	23	28	13
18	Blackburn Rovers	15	2	6	7	15	20	12
19	Coventry City	15	1	7	7	9	21	10
20	Nottingham Forest	15	1	6	8	12	25	9

Teams of the premier league

The FA Premier League is fast becoming the most exciting, star-laden championship in the world. No other league boasts as many big-name clubs and few have more World Cup stars on display week in, week out. From champions Arsenal and runners-up Manchester United to Liverpool and Chelsea, through to Newcastle, Tottenham and Everton, English football has great strength in depth – and world-class players to boot.

Last season, Arsenal did everybody a great favour. By preventing Manchester United from winning their third successive Premier League title, the Gunners have shown that Alex Ferguson's side are not invincible. The Premiership is there for the taking – for the team that is prepared to fight for it.

While Manchester United and Arsenal are again among the favourites this season, they will be pushed all the way by some heavyweight contenders. Liverpool are desperate to take the title back to Anfield, after a gap of nearly ten years, while Chelsea's continental connections continue to grow. They will hoping that the arrival at Stamford Bridge of the likes of Brian Laudrup, Pierluigi Casiraghi and Marcel Desailly can help them make the switch from Cup kings to league champions.

The Premier League is full of teams with great traditions – Aston Villa, Sheffield Wednesday, Blackburn Rovers, Leeds United – whose fans demand success, while others such as Everton, Newcastle and Tottenham, will be hoping to put last season's miserable campaigns behind them. Then there are those smaller clubs who are looking to greater things after avoiding last season's battle against relegation: Derby, West Ham, Coventry, Southampton, Leicester and Wimbledon.

The newcomers this season – Nottingham Forest, Middlesbrough and Charlton Athletic – have a simple objective over the next nine months: to stay up and avoid the fate of last season's newly promoted sides, instant relegation. The Premier League is the place to be for any aspiring club. The rewards for clubs and players alike are too great to miss out on.

Manchester United's Andy Cole is the centre of a celebration sandwich with Teddy Sheringham and David Beckham against Chelsea, while (opposite page) Alan Shearer tussles with a bottle-blond Charvet of Chelsea.

Arsenal
The Gunners

At Highbury, they are celebrating the French revolution, the Arsène Wenger revolution to be precise. Last season, Arsenal's French manager delivered a sensational League and Cup Double to Highbury. Wenger now plans to take the Gunners to the top in Europe.

Wenger arrived at Highbury from Japan in September 1996 after one of the most difficult times in the club's history. The Frenchman was the fourth manager in a matter of weeks, following Bruce Rioch, Stewart Houston and Pat Rice. Club captain Tony Adams had confessed to being an alcoholic just as former manager George Graham (banned from football for allegedly receiving a transfer "bung") took charge at Leeds.

Under George Graham, Arsenal fans had got used to success (two League titles, the FA Cup, Cup-winners' Cup and two League Cups) but at the expense of attractive football. The arrival of Bruce Rioch as manager in the summer of 1995 promised changes, especially with the signing of Dutch striker Dennis Bergkamp. But Bergkamp took time to settle in and Rioch also had problems. The former Bolton Wanderers boss steered Arsenal away from Graham's more direct style and into the UEFA Cup, but had run-ins with key players, notably Ian Wright, and Highbury bosses decided to move for Frenchman Wenger.

Everybody thought the new manager would steady a very shaky ship and then hope for the best. Highbury was in for a difficult season, with little chance of any success. In fact, Arsenal finished the season in third place and in better shape than they'd been for many years, with European success in the UEFA Cup a real possibility.

Last season Arsenal astounded everyone by beating Manchester United to the Premier League title, and then strolling past Kenny Dalglish's Newcastle in the FA Cup final to complete an historic Double. "No one thought us capable of it," said Wenger. "This is the best moment in my sporting life. My players have shown quality. It is your dream always when you work together to achieve something like this. You believe in the players and I would say they did well – but they surprised me as well."

Wenger had been quick to ring the changes at Highbury. He surprised many by retaining Arsenal's ageing defence of Tony Adams, Steve Bould, Lee Dixon and Nigel Winterburn, but had a clear-out of the reserves. That paved the way for a new continental class. In came Frenchmen Patrick Vieira, Remi Garde and Nicolas Anelka, and they were joined at the start of last season by major new arrivals.

Wenger splashed out £7 million on Dutch winger Marc Overmars. The French connection was maintained by the signing of Emmanuel Petit and Gilles Grimandi from Wenger's old club, Monaco. Wenger is also bringing in young English players – he paid £1million for Luton's teenage defender Matthew Upson. In an attempt to balance the books a little, Wenger and the Highbury board made the shock sale of fans' favourite Paul

Ray of sunshine: Ray Parlour was the most improved member of the Arsenal squad last season

ARSENAL

Formed: 1886.
Nickname: The Gunners.
Stadium: Highbury.
Capacity: 38,500.
Address: Arsenal Stadium,
Highbury: London N5 1BU.
Telephone: 0171 704 4000.
Clubcall: 0891 202021.
Fax: 0171 704 4001.
Website: www.fa-carling.com/club/a.fc
Manager: Arsène Wenger.

COLOURS

RECORDS

Record Premier League victory:
5–0 (v Barnsley, Oct 4, 1997; v
Wimbledon, April 18, 1998).
Record Premier League defeat:
4–0 (v Liverpool, May 6 1998).
Record transfer fee received:
£4.5 million from Middlesbrough for Paul
Merson, July 1997.
Record transfer fee paid:
£7.5 million to Inter for Dennis Bergkamp,
June 1995.
Record attendance:
73,295, v Sunderland, Division 1, 9.3.35.

HONOURS

League (11):
1930–31, 1932–33, 1933–34, 1934–35,
1937–38, 1947–48, 1952–53, 1970–71,
1988–89, 1990–91, 1997–98.
FA Cup (7): 1930, 1936, 1950, 1971,
1979, 1993, 1998.
League Cup (2): 1987, 1993.
European Cup-winners' Cup (1):
1994.
European Fairs Cup (1): 1970.

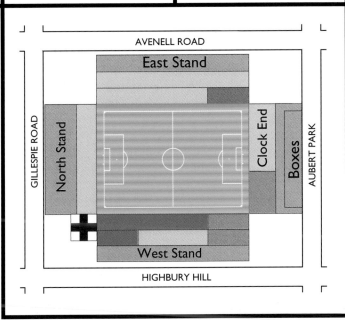

FIXTURES 1998–99

15 AUG	NOTTINGHAM FOREST	H	____ : ____
22 AUG	LIVERPOOL	A	____ : ____
29 AUG	CHARLTON ATHLETIC	H	____ : ____
9 SEPT	CHELSEA	A	____ : ____
12 SEPT	LEICESTER CITY	A	____ : ____
19 SEPT	MANCHESTER UNITED	H	____ : ____
26 SEPT	SHEFFIELD WEDNESDAY	A	____ : ____
3 OCT	NEWCASTLE UNITED	H	____ : ____
17 OCT	SOUTHAMPTON	H	____ : ____
24 OCT	BLACKBURN ROVERS	A	____ : ____
31 OCT	COVENTRY CITY	A	____ : ____
7 NOV	EVERTON	H	____ : ____
14 NOV	TOTTENHAM HOTSPUR	H	____ : ____
21 NOV	WIMBLEDON	A	____ : ____
28 NOV	MIDDLESBROUGH	H	____ : ____
5 DEC	DERBY COUNTY	A	____ : ____
12 DEC	ASTON VILLA	A	____ : ____
19 DEC	LEEDS UNITED	H	____ : ____
26 DEC	WEST HAM UNITED	H	____ : ____
28 DEC	CHARLTON ATHLETIC	A	____ : ____
9 JAN	LIVERPOOL	H	____ : ____
16 JAN	NOTTINGHAM FOREST	A	____ : ____
30 JAN	CHELSEA	H	____ : ____
6 FEB	WEST HAM UNITED	A	____ : ____
13 FEB	MANCHESTER UNITED	A	____ : ____
20 FEB	LEICESTER CITY	H	____ : ____
27 FEB	NEWCASTLE UNITED	A	____ : ____
6 MAR	SHEFFIELD WEDNESDAY	H	____ : ____
13 MAR	EVERTON	A	____ : ____
20 MAR	COVENTRY CITY	H	____ : ____
3 APR	SOUTHAMPTON	A	____ : ____
5 APR	BLACKBURN ROVERS	H	____ : ____
10 APR	TOTTENHAM HOTSPUR	A	____ : ____
17 APR	WIMBLEDON	H	____ : ____
24 APR	MIDDLESBROUGH	A	____ : ____
1 MAY	DERBY COUNTY	H	____ : ____
8 MAY	LEEDS UNITED	A	____ : ____
16 MAY	ASTON VILLA	H	____ : ____

Merson to newly-relegated Middlesbrough, towards the end of the summer.

The fresh arrivals quickly settled down and Arsenal played some delightful football, with Dennis Bergkamp in breathtaking form. Striker Ian Wright even broke Cliff Bastin's long-standing record to become the Gunners' all-time top-scorer. Boring, boring Arsenal have become scoring, scoring Arsenal under Wenger. The manager is committed to playing attacking football. "I think every manager can only be successful if he gets his team to play the way that he holds deeply within himself," he said.

"When I came to the club I didn't pay too much attention to the previous style, although I was aware of the tradition. But for me, we played the kind of football we did because it was the way we could be successful. I would not change my philosophy."

The Wenger revolution at Arsenal has not just taken place on the pitch. Players now follow strict diets and Wenger has masterminded the construction of a new training complex which will incorporate a youth development centre.

The future looks bright for the Gunners. Further big-name signings were planned over the summer as Arsène Wenger's men prepared to take on the cream of Europe in the Champions League. The sceptics who questioned Wenger's appointment at Highbury have been well and truly silenced.

PREMIER LEAGUE TABLES

SEASON	POS.	P	W	D	L	F	A	PTS	TOP SCORER	AV. GATE
1993–94	4th	42	18	17	7	53	28	71	Wright 23	30,563
1994–95	12th	42	13	12	17	52	49	51	Wright 18	35,330
1995–96	5th	38	17	12	9	49	36	63	Wright 15	37,568
1996–97	3rd	38	19	11	8	62	32	68	Wright 23	37,822
1997–98	1st	38	23	9	6	68	33	78	Bergkamp 16	38,053

Bergkamp started his career in his native Holland with Ajax, the Amsterdam club famous around the world for its youth policy. He made his debut for Ajax as a teenager just as another Ajax legend, Marco Van Basten, was leaving. Bergkamp took over Van Basten's goalscoring role for Ajax and the Dutch national team and eventually followed his hero to Italy.

However, Dennis's time in Italy, with Milan club Internazionale, was not a happy one, but he did win the UEFA Cup. Arsenal broke the bank to bring him to England in the summer of 1995.

He took time to score his first goal for the Gunners – Highbury waited what seemed like ages, but it was a memorable strike when it did arrive, against Southampton on September 23, 1995.

Until the appointment of Arsène Wenger, many Arsenal fans thought their team were too reliant on Ian Wright for goals. Now Dennis Bergkamp's stunning contributions have taken taken the Gunners to new heights.

Tony Adams

After his much-publicized problems off the pitch, Arsenal captain Tony Adams has found a new lease of life at Highbury under manager Arsène Wenger.

The England defender – whose trademark was, and still is, the arm held aloft, appealing for offside – can often be seen in unfamiliar places these days. Adams, a one-club man with nearly 450 appearances for Arsenal since his debut 15 years ago, has been encouraged by Wenger to get forward into attacking positions more often. His goal against Everton at Highbury last season, which helped to clinch the Premier League title, was typical

Dutch master: Bergkamp was the player of the 1997–98 season.

Dennis Bergkamp

It took time for Dennis Bergkamp to settle in at Highbury, but last season Arsenal fans saw the sensational best from the player known simply as "The Iceman". The Dutchman's goals helped Arsenal to an historic League and FA Cup Double, and he was voted Footballer of the Year by both players and journalists alike.

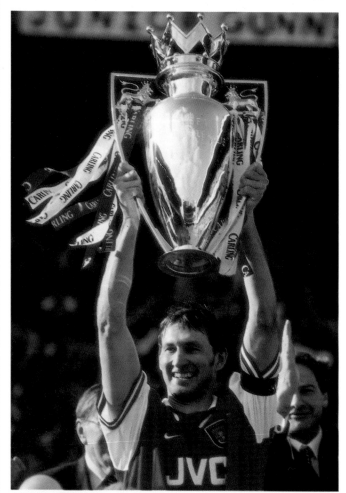

King Tony: The Arsenal captain lifts the Premiership crown.

Player Records

	BORN	NATIONALITY	HEIGHT	WEIGHT	APPS	GOALS	PREVIOUS TEAMS
GOALKEEPERS							
Alex Manninger	11.6.77 Salzburg	Austrian	6-2	12-2	7	0	Salzburg, Grazer AK (Aut)
David Seaman	19.9.63 Rotherham	English	6-4	14-10	587	0	Leeds U, Peterborough U, Birmingham C, QPR.
DEFENDERS							
Tony Adams	10.10.66 London	English	6-3	13-11	421	30	none.
Steve Bould	16.11.62 Stoke	English	6-4	14-2	459	11	Stoke C, Torquay U.
Lee Dixon	17.3.64 Manchester	English	5-8	11-8	530	31	Burnley, Chester C, Bury, Stoke C.
Remi Garde	3.4.66 L'Arbresle	French	5-8	11-4	21	0	L'Arbresle, Lyon, Strasbourg (Fra),
Gilles Grimandi	11.1.70 Gap	French	5-11	11-11	22	1	Monaco (Fra).
Martin Keown	24.7.66 Oxford	English	6-1	12-4	418	6	Arsenal, Brighton & HA, Aston Villa, Everton.
Scott Marshall	1.5.73 Edinburgh	Scottish	6-1	12-5	51	2	Rotherham U, Oxford U, Sheffield U, Luton T.
Matthew Upson	18.4.79 Hartismere	English	6-1	11-5	6	0	
Nigel Winterburn	11.12.63 Coventry	English	5-8	11-4	547	16	Birmingham C, Oxford U, Wimbledon.
MIDFIELDERS							
Jason Crowe	30.9.78 Sidcup	English	5-9	10-9	0	0	none.
Stephen Hughes	18.9.76 Wokingham	English	6-0	12-8	32	3	none.
Alberto Mendez	24.10.74 Nuremburg	German	5-9	11-8	3	0	Feucht (Ger).
Marc Overmars	29.3.73 Emst	Dutch	5-7	10-8	0	0	Go Ahead Eagles, Willem II, Ajax (Hol).
Emmanuel Petit	22.9.70 Dieppe	French	6-1	12-6	30	2	Monaco (Fra).
Ray Parlour	7.3.73 Romford	English	5-10	11-12	169	11	none.
Patrick Vieira	26.6.76 Dakar	French	6-3	12-10	64	4	Cannes (Fra), Milan (Ita).
FORWARDS							
Nicolas Anelka	14.3.79 Versailles	French	6-0	12-2	30	6	Paris St Germain (Fra).
Dennis Bergkamp	18.5.69 Amsterdam	Dutch	6-0	12-5	90	39	Ajax (Hol), Internazionale (Ita).
Luis Boa Morte	4.8.77 Lisbon	Portuguese	5-9	11-2	15	0	Sporting Lisbon (Por).
Isaiah Rankin	22.5.78 London	English	5-10	11-0	1	0	none.
Christopher Wreh	14.5.75 Monrovia	Liberian	5-9	11-5	16	3	Monaco (Fra).

of the Arsenal captain's new attacking ambitions.

George Graham probably isn't very impressed with Adams's new-found forward thinking, but Arsenal now have the tactical flexibility they lacked under their old manager. And Adams is a player reborn.

Patrick Vieira

Few, if any, knew much about Frenchman Patrick Vieira when he arrived at Highbury from Milan two years ago, but it didn't take long for Arsenal fans to realize the club had unearthed a real find.

"He comes from Senegal, he plays for Arsenal," was one of the favourite chants on Highbury's North Bank last season, proof that the Senegalese-born Vieira has won the hearts, minds and voices of the Arsenal faithful.

The 22-year-old midfielder now provides the link between defence and attack that had been lacking at Highbury in recent years. His intelligent passing, combined with tough tackling, provided the perfect base for forwards Ian Wright and Dennis Bergkamp. "We discovered we needed players to bridge the gap between defence and attack," says Bergkamp. "Now Vieira forms the link we were missing."

Vieira's form for Arsenal earned him a full international debut for France – as well as a place in their World Cup squad – and manager Arsène Wenger, who first spotted Vieira playing for French side Cannes in July 1994, was quick to praise him. "Patrick is remarkable for such a young player, and potentially he could become a very big force," said the Highbury boss.

The central midfield partnership which Vieira established with Emmanuel Petit last season was crucial to Arsenal's Double success. In Petit, a fellow French international midfielder, Vieira has found a player who complements his own instinctive attacking skills perfectly. Whereas Vieira relishes the opportunity to launch counter-attacks at the opposition using his long-striding pace to great effect, Petit is a more defensive player whose reputation for tackling has given many a Premiership striker a sleepless night prior to a trip to Highbury.

In the eyes of many of the Arsenal fans, Vieira was the club's most consistent player last season. Having worked hard to control his volatile temper, Vieira is fast becoming the finished article. Tall, fast, strong and blessed with a unique footballing talent, it's hard to believe he's still in his early twenties.

Aston Villa
The Villans

Aston Villa are one of England's great football clubs. Their proud tradition and history demand success. It also means that Villa set their standards high – any manager who fails to meet those standards can expect to lose his job.

Last season Brian Little, a former Villa favourite as a player, was the latest in a long line of Villa managers to lose his job – the 11th in 30 years, in fact. Little was replaced by John Gregory, another former player, who successfully steered Villa from the edge of the relegation zone to finish in seventh place, a result which was good enough to qualify Villa for the UEFA Cup.

Gregory knows that his initial success will count for nothing if he cannot deliver this season. It is now almost 20 years since Ron Saunders steered Villa to the League title, the club's first since 1910. A year later, Saunders's successor Tony Barton guided the club to their finest hour yet, the European Cup. Striker Peter Withe was the hero in Rotterdam as Villa beat German champions Bayern Munich 1–0 in the final. Villa have never been able to match the achievements of the early 1980s. The club suffered the ignominy of relegation to the old Second Division in 1987, but bounced back at the first attempt under Graham Taylor, who took Villa to a second-place finish in the League before departing to take charge of England. Villa then brought in Czech manager Dr Josef Venglos, who was not a great success, before employing the flamboyant Atkinson in 1992.

Big Ron quickly built an impressive outfit, with striker Dean Saunders a major signing from Liverpool. Saunders finished the 1992–93 season as the club's top scorer as Villa finished in second place. The following season saw Villa's League position slip to 10th, but consolation came in the form of a League Cup final victory over Manchester United.

A dramatic win on penalties over Italian side Internazionale in the UEFA Cup promised great things during the 1994–95 season, but by November Big Ron was gone and the call went out to Brian Little.

Former Villa hero Little did a great job in rescuing an ageing and demoralized side from relegation (Villa finished the season in 18th place), and set about building a new era at Villa Park. That summer, Little brought in Gareth Southgate, Savo Milosevic and Mark Draper to join

Sharpshooter: For the third successive season, Dwight Yorke was top-scorer for Villa.

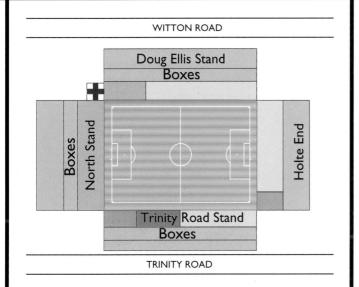

existing stars Mark Bosnich, Steve Staunton, Andy Townsend and Dwight Yorke. Patiently and without a great deal of fuss, the Little revolution took effect at Villa Park. Dwight Yorke has emerged as a talented goalscorer and it was his goals which took Villa to the 1996 League Cup final, where Villa outclassed Leeds United, winning 3–0. Gareth Southgate, a midfielder at his previous club, Crystal Palace, has been converted to a central defender of international standing.

In the 1996–97 season, Villa, like many other Premier League clubs, added a few more Continental touches with the purchases of Serbian midfielder Sasa Curcic and Portuguese defender Fernando Nelson. There was disappointment in the UEFA Cup (defeat by Swedish part-timers Helsingborgs), but compensation in the form of a top-five placing – and another UEFA Cup campaign.

Last season, Villa had a disastrous start – and Little paid the price. In came Gregory, who took the club on a successful run in which they only narrowly lost to Atletico Madrid in the quarter-finals of the UEFA Cup, and qualified for this season's competition by virtue of Chelsea's European Cup-winners' Cup triumph.

Gregory was busy in the transfer market over the summer, selling Savo Milosevic to Real Zaragoza, signing Bolton midfielder Alan Thompson and promising to get the best out of maverick striker Stan Collymore. He knows that he if cannot get his players to perform, he too will go the same way as Brian Little.

Gareth Southgate

He's the man who missed that penalty and unfortunately some people will never let him forget it! But it is a great tribute to the character of Gareth Southgate that his career has survived that terrible night at Wembley, when the hopes of a whole nation fell on his shoulders. He remains a crucial part of John Gregory's plans at Aston Villa and was a key member of Glenn Hoddle's squad at the World Cup finals in France.

Watford-born Gareth was first called up for England duty by Terry Venables, who recognized his great versatility – he started as a full-back for Crystal Palace, making his League debut against Liverpool at Anfield in April 1991, before moving into midfield. It was as a midfielder that Southgate was first spotted by Brian Little, who was looking for players for a new-look three-man central defence at Villa Park. When Palace were relegated in 1995, Villa moved in, signing Southgate for £2 million. Southgate has committed himself to Aston Villa for the foreseeable future, making it likely that he will play the best years of his career at Villa Park. Intelligent and eloquent both on and off the pitch, few would be surprised if Southgate went into football management when he retires.

Ugo Ehiogu

At the age of 25, defender Ugo Ehiogu is fast becoming a Villa Park veteran. Last season, Ehiogu started all but one of Villa's Premier League matches and was again impressive in central defence.

London-born Ehiogu started his career not with Arsenal, Spurs or West Ham, but in the Midlands with West Bromwich Albion. He made only two appearances in the 1990–91 season for Albion before Villa's Ron Atkinson stepped in with a £200,000 bid and took the tall centre-back down the road to Villa Park.

Ehiogu took his time settling in under Atkinson, making eight appearances in the 1991–92 season and four the next. His career really took off with the arrival of Brian Little. The new boss had plans for a new-look three-man defence – and Ehiogu was to play a full role alongside Paul McGrath and Gareth Southgate.

Ehiogu is now firmly established at the heart of Villa's defence and has even received international recognition. He was called up by former England manager Terry Venables just prior to Euro 96 and was desperately unlucky to be left out of the tournament squad.

Mark Draper

Midfielder Mark Draper has the potential to be one of English football's leading midfielders. Although he has yet to win his first international cap, Draper has long been tipped to play for England.

Brian Little signed Draper from his old club Leicester in the summer of 1995. The 26-year-old had spent one season at Filbert Street and despite Leicester's poor run of results (they were relegated), Draper stood out as their star performer. Villa paid £3.25 million for Draper, which gave Leicester a £2 million profit on the £1.25 million they paid Draper's first club Notts County. A lot of money, but for Villa it has been money well spent.

Here we Ugo: Defender Ehiogu has become a mainstay in the Aston Villa defence.

Player Records

	BORN	NATIONALITY	HEIGHT	WEIGHT	APPS	GOALS	PREVIOUS TEAMS
GOALKEEPERS							
Mark Bosnich	13.1.72 Fairfield	Australian	6-1	13-7	167	1	Sydney Croatia, (Aus), Manchester U.
Michael Oakes	30.10.73 Northwich	English	6-1	12-7	29	0	Scarborough, Tranmere R.
Adam Rachel	10.12.76 Birmingham	English	5-11	12-8	0	0	none.
DEFENDERS							
Gary Charles	13.4.70 London	English	5-9	11-8	194	6	Nottingham F, Leicester C, Derby Co.
Ugo Ehiogu	3.11.72 London	English	6-2	13-3	181	9	West Brom.
Riccardo Scimeca	13.6.75 Leamington Spa	English	6-1	12-9	55	0	none.
Gareth Southgate	3.9.70 Watford	English	6-0	12-8	243	17	Crystal Palace.
Alan Wright	28.9.71 Ashton under Lyne	English	5-4	9-5	293	4	Blackpool, Blackburn R.
Alan Thompson	22.12.73 Newcastle	English	6-0	12-8	173	34	Newcastle United, Bolton W.
MIDFIELDERS							
Darren Byfield	29.9.76 Birmingham	English	5-11	11-11	6	0	none.
Mark Draper	11.11.70 Long Eaton	English	5-10	12-4	357	50	Notts Co, Leicester C.
Simon Grayson	16.12.69	English	5-11	12-10	208	13	Leeds U, Leicester C
Fernando Nelson	5.11.71 Oporto	Portuguese	5-10	11-2	58	0	FC Porto (Por), Sporting Lisbon (Por).
Ian Taylor	4.6.68 Birmingham	English	6-1	12-0	210	41	Port Vale, Sheffield W.
Richard Walker	8.11.77 Birmingham	English	6-0	12-0	1	0	none.
FORWARDS							
Stan Collymore	22.1.71 Stone	English	6-3	14-10	201	89	Crystal Palace, Southend U, Nottingham F, Liverpool.
Lee Hendrie	18.5.77 Birmingham	English	5-8	10-3	17	3	none.
Julian Joachim	20.9.74 Peterborough	English	5-6	12-11	151	37	Leicester C.
Dwight Yorke	3.11.71 Canaan, Tobago	Trinidad & Tobago	5-10	11-13	231	73	Signal Hill (Tob).

Stan Collymore

Controversy has marked Stan Collymore's career more closely than even the most accomplished defenders. Last season, his first in Aston Villa's colours, was no exception.

Collymore arrived at Villa Park amid a blaze of publicity following his £7 million transfer from Liverpool. He was now playing for the team he supported as a boy. It should have been the dream move, but Collymore left his shooting boots on Merseyside – he scored just six goals in 25 Premier League appearances. That's £1.166 million per League goal. Stan is the first to admit that he did not perform up to expectations last season. He says: "I know that I haven't done myself justice, but I know that I can do the business for the club and I will be going flat out to do so this season. I am the first to admit that these 12 months have not been the best for me either on or off the pitch.

"But I have learned a lot from what has happened, and that will stand me in good stead in the future. I will be looking to score goals in the kind of numbers that I did not manage last season."

Villa fans will be hoping to see a repeat of the sort of form that saw Liverpool pay Nottingham Forest £8.5 million for Stan's services. Collymore scored 41 League goals in two seasons for Forest following a season with Southend. Collymore started his professional career with Crystal Palace, after signing from Stafford Rangers in 1991, but a series of personality clashes and his inability to displace first-choice striker Ian Wright did not make his time at Palace a happy one.

Stan the Bad Man: Collymore is running out of chances at Villa.

Blackburn Rovers

Blackburn Rovers are back where they believe they belong – among the elite of English football. Under manager Roy Hodgson, the 1995 Premier League champions have re-established themselves among the top teams in the Premiership – last season they finished sixth and qualified to play in the UEFA Cup.

Hodgson arrived at Blackburn in the summer of 1997 with a big reputation, bags of exeperience and a simple plan. He was one of Europe's most experienced and respected coaches, after spells in Sweden, Switzerland (where he took the national team to the World Cup finals) and Italy, where he occupied one of the hottest seats in Serie A – as coach of Internazionale. His objective at Blackburn was simple enough – to stabilize a shaky ship. "My job is to make sure we don't challenge for the title one year and then fight against relegation the next."

Hodgson took charge of Rovers when there was a danger that they could slip away into obscurity. The 1996–97 season had been a series of embarrassments for Rovers, with the club struggling to overcome the loss of Kenny Dalglish. The Scot had quit as director of football early in the season after his stint as manager had overseen the most successful period in the club's recent history – earning promotion to the Premier League in 1992 and then, within three years, winning the Premier League.

Dalglish may have built a successful championship-winning team around striker Alan Shearer, but the man who made it all possible was Jack Walker. Blackburn's multi-millionaire backer has provided the cash for all recent player purchases (almost £40 million) and has financed the rebuilding of Ewood Park to the tune of £25 million.

Shearer scored 34 goals in the 1994–95 season as Dalglish's men pipped Manchester United to the title, and he was bound to be missed following the move to his home-town club Newcastle in the summer of 1996. In his four seasons at Ewood, Shearer notched up 112 goals in 138 Premier League games – an amazing goal-to-game ratio and it was no surprize that Rovers struggled without his goals.

In 1996–97, Rovers went 11 League matches without a win before beating Liverpool 3–0 in November. By then manager Ray Harford had resigned – the pressure had got too much following a home defeat by Second Division Stockport County in the League Cup. Harford's assistant Tony Parkes took charge of first-team affairs while the club looked for a replacement.

Great Scot!: Kevin Gallacher was one of several Blackburn players to take part in the 1998 World Cup finals.

BLACKBURN ROVERS

Formed: 1875.
Nickname: Rovers.
Stadium: Ewood Park.
Capacity: 31,367.
Address: Ewood Park, Blackburn;
BB2 4JF.
Telephone: 01254 698888.
Clubcall: 0898 121179.
Fax: 01254 671042.
Website: www.fa-carling.com/club/br.fc
Manager: Roy Hodgson.

COLOURS

RECORDS

Record Premier League victory:
7–0 (v Nottingham F, Nov 18, 1995).
Record Premier League defeat:
5–0 (v Coventry C, Dec 9, 1995).
Record transfer fee received:
£15 million from Newcastle U for Alan
Shearer, July 1996.
Record transfer fee paid:
£7.5 million to Southampton for Kevin
Davies, May 1998.
Record attendance:
61,783, v Bolton W, FA Cup sixth round,
Mar 2, 1929.

HONOURS

League (3):
1911–12, 1913–14, 1994–95.
FA Cup (6):
1884, 1885, 1886, 1890, 1891, 1928.

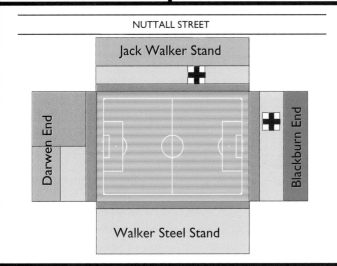

NUTTALL STREET

Jack Walker Stand

Darwen End

Blackburn End

Walker Steel Stand

FIXTURES 1998–99

15 AUG	DERBY COUNTY	A	____ : ____
22 AUG	LEEDS UNITED	A	____ : ____
29 AUG	LEICESTER CITY	H	____ : ____
9 SEPT	TOTTENHAM HOTSPUR	A	____ : ____
12 SEPT	SHEFFIELD WEDNESDAY	A	____ : ____
19 SEPT	CHELSEA	H	____ : ____
26 SEPT	EVERTON	A	____ : ____
3 OCT	WEST HAM	H	____ : ____
17 OCT	MIDDLESBROUGH	A	____ : ____
24 OCT	ARSENAL	H	____ : ____
31 OCT	WIMBLEDON	A	____ : ____
7 NOV	COVENTRY CITY	H	____ : ____
14 NOV	MANCHESTER UNITED	A	____ : ____
21 NOV	SOUTHAMPTON	H	____ : ____
28 NOV	LIVERPOOL	A	____ : ____
5 DEC	CHARLTON ATHLETIC	H	____ : ____
12 DEC	NEWCASTLE UNITED	H	____ : ____
19 DEC	NOTTINGHAM FOREST	A	____ : ____
26 DEC	ASTON VILLA	H	____ : ____
28 DEC	LEICESTER CITY	A	____ : ____
9 JAN	LEEDS UNITED	H	____ : ____
16 JAN	DERBY COUNTY	A	____ : ____
30 JAN	TOTTENHAM HOTSPUR	H	____ : ____
6 FEB	ASTON VILLA	A	____ : ____
13 FEB	CHELSEA	A	____ : ____
20 FEB	SHEFFIELD WEDNESDAY	H	____ : ____
27 FEB	WEST HAM	A	____ : ____
6 MAR	EVERTON	H	____ : ____
13 MAR	COVENTRY CITY	A	____ : ____
20 MAR	WIMBLEDON	A	____ : ____
3 APR	MIDDLESBROUGH	H	____ : ____
5 APR	ARSENAL	A	____ : ____
10 APR	MANCHESTER UNITED	H	____ : ____
17 APR	SOUTHAMPTON	A	____ : ____
24 APR	LIVERPOOL	H	____ : ____
1 MAY	CHARLTON ATHLETIC	A	____ : ____
8 MAY	NOTTINGHAM FOREST	H	____ : ____
16 MAY	NEWCASTLE UNITED	A	____ : ____

Hodgson had been Blackburn's first-choice as choice, but after he initially turned them down, Rovers tried to hire Swedish coach Sven Goran Eriksson. When Eriksson turned them down, they went back to Hodgson – and finaly got their man.

Although Hodgson had money to spend on new players, he didn't need it. In fact, Rovers sold Henning Berg (to Manchester United) and Graeme Le Saux (to Chelsea) at the start of last season and still managed to climb to the top of the table. They stayed up with the title challengers almost all season, only faltering towards the end, eventually finishing sixth. Hodgson was a happy man. He said, "Although I am delighted, it's not just delight for me personally – I am particularly pleased for Jack Walker who cares so deeply for this club. He was so happy in the first half of the season when our form was excellent, but he was knocked for six during our late bad run.

"By qualifying for Europe we have not only achieved our pre-season goal but we have made him very happy. I would have been shattered if we had missed out after all the work we've put in. People have worked incredibly hard and this is the icing on the cake."

The record signing of Kevin Davies from Southampton kicked off a summer of spending at Ewood Park and the manager has set a place in next season's Champions League as the target for Rovers. "That is something we will be working towards," says Hodgson, "and we can already look back with a lot of satisfaction on what we have achieved."

PREMIER LEAGUE TABLES

SEASON	POS.	P	W	D	L	F	A	PTS	TOP SCORER	AV. GATE
1993–94	2nd	42	25	9	8	63	36	84	Shearer 31	17,721
1994–95	1st	42	27	8	7	80	39	89	Shearer 34	25,272
1995–96	7th	38	18	7	13	61	47	61	Shearer 31	27,716
1996–97	13th	38	9	15	14	42	43	42	Sutton 11	24,947
1997–98	6th	38	16	10	12	57	52	58	Sutton 18	25,253

Kevin Davies

Blackburn Rovers' record signing Kevin Davies still can't believe how much his life has changed in the past 18 months. He finished the 1996–97 season as a Second Division player with Chesterfield. He starts the 1998–99 season as a £7.5 million hitman with Blackburn on a weekly wage of £20,000.

Davies joined Rovers in the summer from Southampton, who had signed the youngster for just £700,000 from Chesterfield in the summer of 1997. Last season Davies scored 12 goals for Southampton and was shortlisted for the PFA Young Player of the Year award.

Davies, who holds the record for the youngest player to appear in the Coca-Cola Cup when he came on against West Ham in September 1993 aged 16 years and 180 days, has been tipped for future England honours by his former manager at Chesterfield, John Duncan. "I've not been surprized by what he has done so far," says Duncan. "We always knew he had talent. For someone so young he had this incredible physical presence, but with his power he also had a good brain. He was always willing to learn and he picked up things very quickly. "When the ball is close to him any defender would have trouble getting near him. No matter what the quality of the defence, he will always be hard to handle."

Tim Flowers

Since his transfer from Southampton for a British record (for a goalkeeper) of £2.4 million in November 1993, Tim Flowers has established himself as one of the most charismatic goalkeepers in the Premier League.

Flowers is a regular in Glenn Hoddle's England squad after making his international debut in a 1–1 draw with Brazil in June 1993. He is now well into double figures after establishing himself as England's number two behind David Seaman.

Flowers is used to being an understudy. He moved to Southampton from Wolves for £70,000 in 1986 to be Peter Shilton's number two and stayed there for eight seasons before the move to Ewood Park.

Chris Sutton

Chris Sutton spent the summer of 1998 wondering what might have been. He finished the Premier League season as joint top scorer and could have reasonably expected to have been included in England's World Cup plans. He reckoned without Glenn Hoddle. Sutton made his England debut against Cameroon last November but then refused to play for England B against Russia B in February. Hoddle took exception to what he saw as an arrogant and selfish act and ruled the Rovers' striker out of contention for the World Cup.

Sutton became Britain's most expensive player when Blackburn signed him from Norwich for £5 million in the summer of 1994. That figure has since been eclipsed a number of times, notably by Sutton's former striking partner Alan Shearer.

It was with Shearer that Sutton formed the lethal SAS (Shearer and Sutton) partnership. Between them, the pair scored 49 League goals as Rovers won the 1994–95 title. Sutton signalled his intentions early on in that campaign with a hat-trick against Coventry. But the following season was not a happy one for Nottingham-born Sutton – he failed to score in the League and was even used in his original role at Norwich in the centre of defence.

The achievements of Blackburn under Roy Hodgson last season owe a great deal to Sutton's goalscoring exploits. This season he will be aiming to finish as Rovers' top scorer for the third successive year – and to get a change of heart from Glenn Hoddle.

Kevin Gallacher

After being plagued by injuries for four years, Scottish striker Kevin Gallacher is finally repaying the £1.5 million Blackburn paid Coventry for his services in March 1993.

Gallacher broke a leg and played just one League game for Rovers in their 1994–95 title-winning season. He was injured almost immediately on his comeback and only re-established himself in the Rovers' first team in the 1996–97 season. He had already done enough to win a place in Scotland's Euro 96 squad, though, and he came on as a substitute against Holland at Villa

Say it with Flowers: The Blackburn goalie is England's deputy.

Player Records

	BORN	NATIONALITY	HEIGHT	WEIGHT	APPS	GOALS	PREVIOUS TEAMS
GOALKEEPERS							
Alan Fettis	1.2.71 Belfast	Northern Irish	6-1	11-8	146	0	Nottingham Forest, Hull C, West Brom.
John Filan	8.2.70 Sydney	Australian	5-11	12-10	22	0	Coventry C., Cambridge Utd.
Tim Flowers	3.2.67 Kenilworth	English	6-3	14-4	428	0	Wolves, Southampton, Swindon T.
DEFENDERS							
Marlon Broomes	28.11.77 Birmingham	English	6-0	12-11	16	0	Swindon T.
Gary Croft	17.2.74 Stafford	English	5-9	11-8	177	4	Grimsby T.
Callum Davidson	25.6.76 Stirling	Scottish	5-10	11-0	1	0	St Johnstone.
Stephane Henchoz	7.9.74 Switzerland	Swiss	6-2	12-8	36	0	Neuchatel Xamax (Swi), Hamburg (Ger).
Colin Hendry	7.1.65 Keith	Scottish	6-1	12-7	440	41	Dundee, Blackburn R, Manchester C.
Jeff Kenna	28.8.70 Dublin	Irish	5-11	12-3	229	5	Southampton.
Darren Peacock	3.2.68 Bristol	English	6-1	12-12	346	12	Newport Co, Hereford U, QPR.
Tore Pedersen	29.8.69 Ferdirkstad	Norwegian	6-1	12-4	5	0	St Pauli (Ger).
Adam Reed	18.2.75 Bishop Auckland	English	6-0	11-0	52	1	Darlington.
Patrick Valery	3.7.69 Brignoles	France	5-11	11-9	15	0	Monaco (Fra), Bastia (Fra).
MIDFIELDERS							
Anders Andersson	15.3.74 Tomellia	Sweden	5-9	11-9	4	0	Malmo.
Garry Flitcroft	6.11.72 Bolton	English	6-0	12-9	191	16	Manchester C, Bury.
Billy McKinlay	22.4.69 Glasgow	Scottish	5-8	11-4	296	27	Dundee U.
Tim Sherwood	2.2.69 St Albans	English	6-1	12-9	300	34	Watford, Norwich C.
Jason Wilcox	15.7.71 Bolton	English	6-0	11-0	218	28	none.
FORWARDS							
James Beattie	27.2.78 Lancaster	English	6-1	12-0	3	0	Stockport County.
Martin Dahlin	16.4.68 Sweden	Swedish	6-0	12-8	20	4	Malmo, Borussia MG (Ger), Roma (Ita).
Kevin Davies	26.3.77 Sheffield	English	6-0	13-5	134	38	Chesterfield, Southampton.
Damien Duff	2.3.79 Ballyboden	Irish	5-10	9-7	27	4	Lourdes Celtic.
Kevin Gallacher	23.11.66 Clydebank	Scottish	5-8	11-3	354	96	Dundee U, Coventry C.
Chris Sutton	10.3.73 Nottingham	English	6-3	13-7	215	79	Norwich.

Park as the Scots came mighty close to reaching the quarter-finals.

Clydebank-born Gallacher spent six-and-a-half seasons with Dundee United before moving south of the border to Coventry for a £900,000 fee. He was also a key man in Scotland's World Cup 98 campaign in France after finishing as top scorer in the qualifiers.

Blackballed: Despite his 18 League goals, Chris Sutton made himself unpopular with England by refusing to play for the B team.

Charlton Athletic
The Addicks

Top-flight football is back at the Valley – after a gap of 13 years. Charlton won promotion in the most dramatic fashion with the last kick of the last game of last season.

Charlton were last in the top division in 1990, but were forced to play all their matches at Selhurst Park, home of local rivals Crystal Palace. They had been forced to leave the Valley, their home since 1924, and the stadium fell into disrepair. Then, after a long campaign by fans, which included forming their own political party for the local elections, Charlton finally made a triumphant return to a rebuilt Valley in 1992.

The new-look stadium was very different to the old one. Once upon a time, the Valley regularly saw crowds of 50,000 and 60,000. In February 1938, more than 75,000 crammed on to the terraces for an FA Cup tie against Newcastle. That was during a golden era for the club. They stayed in the top division from 1936 to 1957, winning the FA Cup in 1947 after finishing as losing side at Wembley a year earlier.

Charlton stayed out of the top flight until 1986, and even spent a spell in the old Third Division in the early 1970s. It was under the managership of Lennie Lawrence that the Addicks made the return to the top division. They won promotion in 1986 with former West Ham and Birmingham midfielder Alan Curbishley in the ranks. Curbishley had joined Charlton for £38,000 from Aston Villa in December 1984, making 69 appearances

and scoring six goals, before Lawrence sold him to Brighton and Hove Albion in 1987 for £30,000. He returned for a second spell with Charlton in June 1990, this time as a player and reserve-team coach. He became first-team coach in October 1990, and when Lawrence left to manage Middlesbrough, Curbishley stepped into the manager's hotseat, along with Steve Gritt.

By now, Charlton were back in the old Second Division and playing their home games at Upton Park, home of West Ham United. It was hardly an ideal arrangement, but Curbishley and Gritt steered the team close to the First Division promotion play-offs as the club struggled to find the money to move back to the Valley. The move finally took place in December 1992, but Curbishley and Gritt were forced to sell winger Robert Lee to Newcastle to help pay for the refurbishment of the stadium. Charlton finished the 1992–93 season way off the promotion pace in mid-table. Two more average seasons followed until Curbishley was put in sole charge of teams affairs in the summer of 1995.

Under Curbishley, Charlton made it to the promotion play-offs in 1996, but lost to local rivals Crystal Palace in the semi-finals over two legs. Curbishley had been forced to sell some of his best young players – Lee Bowyer and Scott Minto – but in the summer of 1997, Charlton paid a club record £700,000 for Grimby's Clive Mendonca. The striker played a key role in keeping Charlton in contention for promotion all season – but nobody could predict that it would finish in such dramatic fashion. Charlton pushed Nottingham Forest, Sunderland and Middlesbrough hard for the automatic promotion spots, but had to be content with a

CHARLTON ATHLETIC

Formed: 1905.
Nickname: The Addicks.
Stadium: The Valley.
Capacity: 16,000.
Address: The Valley, Floyd Rd,
London SE7 8BL
Telephone: 0181 333 4000
Fax: 0181 333 4001
Manager: Alan Curbishley.

COLOURS

RECORDS

Record Premier League victory:
None
Record Premier League defeat:
None
Record transfer fee received:
£2.8 million from Leeds United for Lee
Bowyer, July 1996.
Record transfer fee paid:
£700,000 to Grimsby for Clive Mendonca,
May 1997.
Record attendance:
75,301 v Newcastle United, FA Cup fifth
round, 12 February, 1938.

HONOURS

League:
Runners-up Division One 1936–37.
FA Cup (1): 1947.

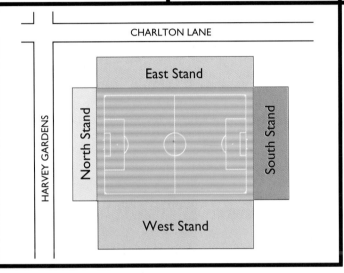

CHARLTON LANE

East Stand

North Stand

South Stand

HARVEY GARDENS

West Stand

FIXTURES 1998–99

Date	Opponent	H/A	Score
15 AUG	NEWCASTLE UNITED	A	____ : ____
22 AUG	SOUTHAMPTON	H	____ : ____
29 AUG	ARSENAL	A	____ : ____
8 SEPT	MANCHESTER UNITED	H	____ : ____
12 SEPT	DERBY COUNTY	H	____ : ____
19 SEPT	LIVERPOOL	A	____ : ____
26 SEPT	COVENTRY CITY	H	____ : ____
3 OCT	NOTTINGHAM FOREST	A	____ : ____
17 OCT	CHELSEA	A	____ : ____
24 OCT	WEST HAM UNITED	H	____ : ____
31 OCT	TOTTENHAM HOTSPUR	A	____ : ____
7 NOV	LEICESTER CITY	H	____ : ____
14 NOV	MIDDLESBROUGH	H	____ : ____
21 NOV	LEEDS UNITED	A	____ : ____
28 NOV	EVERTON	H	____ : ____
5 DEC	BLACKBURN ROVERS	A	____ : ____
12 DEC	SHEFFIELD WEDNESDAY	A	____ : ____
19 DEC	ASTON VILLA	H	____ : ____
26 DEC	WIMBLEDON	A	____ : ____
28 DEC	ARSENAL	H	____ : ____
9 JAN	SOUTHAMPTON	A	____ : ____
16 JAN	NEWCASTLE UNITED	H	____ : ____
30 JAN	MANCHESTER UNITED	A	____ : ____
6 FEB	WIMBLEDON	H	____ : ____
13 FEB	LIVERPOOL	H	____ : ____
20 FEB	DERBY COUNTY	A	____ : ____
27 FEB	NOTTINGHAM FOREST	H	____ : ____
6 MAR	COVENTRY CITY	A	____ : ____
13 MAR	LEICESTER CITY	A	____ : ____
20 MAR	TOTTENHAM HOTSPUR	H	____ : ____
3 APR	CHELSEA	H	____ : ____
10 APR	MIDDLESBROUGH	A	____ : ____
17 APR	LEEDS UNITED	H	____ : ____
24 APR	EVERTON	A	____ : ____
1 MAY	BLACKBURN ROVERS	H	____ : ____
8 MAY	ASTON VILLA	A	____ : ____
16 MAY	SHEFFIELD WEDNESDAY	H	____ : ____

place in the play-offs. In the semi-final, Charlton met an Ipswich side similar to themselves – young and talented. The South Londoners came out on top to earn a trip to Wembley and a meeting with Sunderland.

The north-east side, under the inspired leadership of Peter Reid, had just missed out on automatic promotion in their first season back in the First Division, finishing third behind Middlesbrough and Forest. They were considered the favourites at Wembley, but lost out in the most dramatic play-off final yet.

Charlton took an early lead through Clive Mendonca, but Sunderland bounced through Kevin Phillips and Niall Quinn. Mendonca equalized for the Addicks, but when Quinn added a third for Sunderland, it looked to be all over for Charlton. Then, with minutes remaining of normal time, Richard Rufus, who had never scored a goal in his professional career, rose above everyone else at a corner to head home an equalizer for Charlton and take the match into extra time.

Mendonca completed his hat-trick but Sunderland equalized as the match finished 4–4. Promotion to the Premier League was decided by a penalty shoot-out. Charlton goalkeeper Sasa Ilic was the hero of the day, saving Michael Gray's spot-kick with the shoot-out in sudden death. Charlton were back in the top flight after an absence of eight years and in the Premier League for the first time.

Last summer, work continued to add extra capacity to the Valley as Charlton prepared for the Premier League big boys. Happy days are back at the Valley.

Clive Mendonca

Striker Clive Mendonca is hoping to have the same effect on the Premier League as he had on last season's play-off final at Wembley. Mendonca became the first player to score a hat-trick in a play-off final when he hit three past Sunderland in the 4–4 draw.

After the Wembley win, Mendonca said: "I think if I can get the chances I can score goals. This was the second hat-trick I've scored for Charlton and the sixth of my career. I always feel positive and I felt this morning it was going to be a great day."

The goals helped repay some of the £700,000 which Charlton had splashed out on Mendonca in May 1997 to make him the club's record signing. He joined Charlton from Grimsby after spells with Sheffield United, Rotherham and Doncaster Rovers.

Mendoca was born in London, but brought up on Wearside, although he never got the chance to play for Sunderland. Now, at the age of 30, he has a chance to prove himself in the top flight. "Charlton are a good team," he says, "and I know that we can be a danger in the Premiership and it will give me the opportunity to show I have got the ability to put chances away if they come along." After his hat-trick at Wembley, and more than 20 goals for Charlton last season, we probably haven't heard the last of Mendonca.

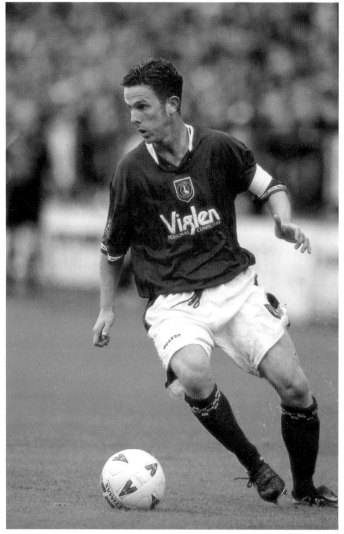

The Boss: Kinsella will need to lead by example this season.

Mark Kinsella

Mark Kinsella was an unlikely hero when he captained Charlton to their dramatic play-off success last May against Sunderland at Wembley.

The young Irish midfielder was Charlton's discovery of the season last year after arriving at the Valley from Colchester in September 1996 for a modest £200,000. However, he quickly repaid that fee with accomplished displays in midfield and some spectacular goals from long range, including an effort at St James' Park in the FA Cup third round against Newcastle which earned Charlton a lucrative replay at the Valley.

The Dubliner's performances for Charlton earned him a debut for the Republic of Ireland B team against Northern Ireland in February 1998, the month when he took over the captincy of the Addicks.

Shaun Newton

Charlton have never been able to pay huge amounts of money in the transfer market. They have always had to rely on "growing their own" talent. Winger Shaun Newton is an example of the Charlton youth system at its best. The youngster is 23, but has already had six seasons of League action after making his League debut at the end of the 1992–93 season.

Last season was Newton's best yet as

Defying gravity: Charlton will be hoping for more acrobatics from Newton.

he scored crucial goals for the Addicks, inlcuding one against Ipswich in the play-off semi-final. Newton's form for Charlton has earned him recognition at England under-21 level, and he scored for a Football League side a 1–1 draw with an Italian Serie B selection in February 1997.

John Robinson

Welsh international John Robinson was the man Charlton signed in September 1992 to replace the Newcastle-bound Robert Lee. Zimbabwe-born Robinson started his playing career on the south coast with Brighton, where he played more than 60 games in just over three seasons before the move to London. He took his time to find his feet at the Valley but has since become a firm favourite with Addicks fans and was voted player of the 1995–96 season.

Player Records

	BORN	NATIONALITY	HEIGHT	WEIGHT	APPS	GOALS	PREVIOUS TEAMS
GOALKEEPERS							
Andy Petterson	26.9.69 Freemantle, Australia	Australian	6-2	14-12	100	0	Luton, Ipswich (loan), Swindon (loan), Charlton, Bradford (loan), Plymouth (loan)
Mike Salmon	14.7.64 Leyland	English	6-2	12-12	411	0	Wrexham, Bolton, Stockport, Chester.
Sasa Ilic	18.7.72	Yugoslavian	6-3	13-4	17	0	St. Leonards.
DEFENDERS							
Stuart Balmer	20.6.9 Falkirk	Scottish	6-1	12-4	264	9	Celtic.
Anthony Barness	25.3.73 Lewisham	English	5-10	12-1	124	4	Southend, Middlesbrough (both loan) Chelsea, Charlton.
Mark Bowen	7.12.63 Neath	Welsh	5-8	11-6	404	27	Shimizu S-Pulse (Jap), West Ham, Norwich City, Tottenham Hotspur.
Steve Brown	6.12.73 Brighton	English	6-1	13-10	168	6	none.
Paul Konchesky	15.5.81 London	English	5-9	12-5	4	0	none.
Gary Poole	11.9.67 Stratford	English	6-0	11-0	254	1	Birmingham City, Southend United, Plymouth Argyle, Barnet, Cambridge United, Tottenham Hotspur.
Richard Rufus	12.1.75 Lewisham	English	6-1	10-5	165	1	none.
Eddie Youds	3.5.70 Liverpool	English	6-1	13-3	137	10	Everton, Cardiff, Wrexham (both loan), Ipswich T, Bradford.
MIDFIELDERS							
Matt Holmes	1.8.69 Luton	English	5-7	11-0	218	14	Blackburn, West Ham, Cardiff, Bournemouth.
Keith Jones	14.10.65 Dulwich	English	5-9	11-0	443	37	Southend, Brentford, Chelsea.
Mark Kinsella	12.8.72 Dublin	Irish	5-9	11-5	272	40	Colchester, Home Farm.
Paul Mortimer	8.5.68 Kensington	English	5-11	11-3	245	35	Crystal Palace, Aston Villa, Charlton.
Shaun Newton	20.8.75 Camberwell	English	5-8	11-0	203	19	none.
Kevin Nicholls	2.1.79 Newham	English	N/A	N/A	16	1	none.
John Robinson	29.8.71 Zimbabwe	Welsh	5-10	11-2	280	35	Brighton.
FORWARDS							
Bradley Allen	13.9.71 Romford	English	5-7	10-7	128	38	QPR.
Mark Bright	6.6.62 Stoke	English	6-0	11-0	464	166	FC Sion (Swi), Sheffield W, Millwall (loan), Crystal Palace, Leicester, Port Vale, Leek T.
Steve Jones	17.3.70 Cambridge	English	5-11	12-3	128	37	West Ham, Bournemouth.
Kevin Lisbie	17.10.78 Hackney	English	5-9	11-4	47	2	none.
Clive Mendonca	9.9.68 Islington	English	5-10	12-9	322	119	Grimsby, Sheffield U, Rotherham, Doncaster (loan).

Robinson loves to attack on the right-hand flank, but his overall ability and work-rate mean he can also play at right-back and in a central midfield position. For the Welsh national side, where Robinson is now a regular, he plays as a right wing-back.

Richard Rufus

Central defender Richard Rufus has long been a target for other Premier League clubs, but he has displayed rare loyalty by sticking with Charlton and was rewarded with promotion last season after five seasons at the Valley.

Rufus made an impressive full debut for the Addicks – against Sunderland in a 1–1 draw in November 1994 – after working his way through the youth system at the Valley. His performances for Charlton earned him recognition at England under-21 level and he went on to captain the under-21 side during the 1996–97 season.

Though he has made more than 150 appearances for Charlton, Rufus had failed to score – that is until last season's play-off final against Sunderland – when his header took the Wembley decider into extra time. And the rest, as they say, is history.

Chelsea
The Blues

The Continental changes are sweeping through Stamford Bridge. Last season, the Coca-Cola Cup and the European Cup-winners' Cup were added to the Chelsea trophy cabinet, alongside the FA Cup which the Blues won in 1997 under Ruud Gullit, who was so sensationally sacked by chairman Ken Bates halfway through last season.

Gianluca Vialli is carrying on where Gullit left off. The foreign stars keep on arriving – Brian Laudrup, Pierluigi Casiraghi and Marcel Desailly were three big names who signed up in the summer – and the manager now has the Premier League title in his sights. After Chelsea triumphed in the Cup-winners' Cup final last May, Vialli said: "We don't want to stop here. We want to keep on improving and next season start thinking about winning the Premier League. That is now our target."

It is a far cry from the early 1980s when Chelsea struggled in the old Second Division having been on the brink of major success after winning the 1970 FA Cup. The club had a reputation for unruly fans and controversial chairman Ken Bates even threatened to install electric fences at Stamford Bridge to control them.

Glenn Hoddle got the ball rolling at Stamford Bridge in 1993 before leaving to manage England three years later. It was Hoddle who signed Gullit on a free transfer from Italian Serie A side Sampdoria in the summer of 1995. Hoddle changed Chelsea's playing style to a more continental approach, which brought immediate success – the Blues reached the 1994 FA Cup final and the semi-final two years later, losing to Manchester United on both occasions.

Gullit was the overwhelming choice of Chelsea fans to succeed Hoddle – and he did not disappoint them. As a player, Gullit experienced phenomenal success, winning the Italian League, European Cup and World Club Cup with Milan and the 1988 European Championship with Holland. As one of the world's most famous footballers, Gullit was always going to be in a strong position to attract other world-class players. And he did just that.

Italian striker Gianluca Vialli, who had just won the European Cup with Juventus and was looking for a new challenge, not to mention a final pay day, was one of Gullit's first major signings as Chelsea boss. Vialli was joined by fellow-Italian and midfielder Roberto Di Matteo and French defender Frank Leboeuf.

Gullit changed Chelsea's training methods, employing a full-time fitness coach, former international sprinter Ade Mafe, and encouraged the players to change their diets. Chips were out, salads were in.

Gullit's first season in charge ended in Wembley glory for the Blues. His multi-national stars beat Middlesbrough 2–0 in the FA Cup final to claim the club's first trophy for 26 years. Vialli was already a hero at Stamford Bridge, but another Italian was to make a bigger impact. Gianfranco Zola, who Gullit had tried to buy during the summer of 1996, fell out

Reach for the Sky: Under Vialli, Chelsea have their sights on the title.

CHELSEA

Formed: 1905.
Nickname: The Blues.
Stadium: Stamford Bridge.
Capacity: 31,791.
Address: Stamford Bridge, London SW6 1HS.
Telephone: 0171 385 5545.
Clubcall: 0891 121159.
Fax: 0171 381 4831.
Website: www.fa-carling.com/club/c.fc
Manager: Gianluca Vialli.

COLOURS

RECORDS

Record Premier League victory:
6–0 (v Barnsley, Aug 24, 1997).
Record Premier League defeat:
5–1 (v Liverpool, Sept 21, 1996).
Record transfer fee received:
£2.2 million from Tottenham H for Gordon Durie, July 1991.
Record transfer paid:
£5.4 million to Lazio for Pierluigi Casiraghi, May 1998.
Record attendance:
82,905, v Arsenal, Division 1, Oct 12, 1935.

HONOURS

League (1): 1954–55.
FA Cup (2): 1970, 1997.
League Cup (2): 1965, 1998.
European Cup-winners' Cup (2): 1971, 1998.

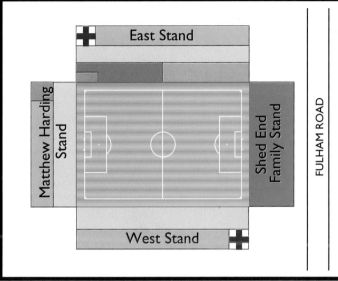

FIXTURES 1998–99

15 AUG	COVENTRY CITY	A	____	:	____
22 AUG	NEWCASTLE UNITED	H	____	:	____
9 SEPT	ARSENAL	H	____	:	____
12 SEPT	NOTTINGHAM FOREST	H	____	:	____
19 SEPT	BLACKBURN ROVERS	A	____	:	____
23 SEPT	MANCHESTER UNITED	A	____	:	____
26 SEPT	MIDDLESBROUGH	H	____	:	____
3 OCT	LIVERPOOL	A	____	:	____
17 OCT	CHARLTON ATHLETIC	H	____	:	____
24 OCT	LEEDS UNITED	A	____	:	____
31 OCT	ASTON VILLA	H	____	:	____
7 NOV	WEST HAM	A	____	:	____
14 NOV	WIMBLEDON	H	____	:	____
21 NOV	LEICESTER CITY	A	____	:	____
28 NOV	SHEFFIELD WEDNESDAY	H	____	:	____
5 DEC	EVERTON	A	____	:	____
12 DEC	DERBY COUNTY	A	____	:	____
19 DEC	TOTTENHAM HOTSPUR	H	____	:	____
26 DEC	SOUTHAMPTON	A	____	:	____
28 DEC	MANCHESTER UNITED	H	____	:	____
9 JAN	NEWCASTLE UNITED	A	____	:	____
16 JAN	COVENTRY CITY	H	____	:	____
30 JAN	ARSENAL	A	____	:	____
6 FEB	SOUTHAMPTON	H	____	:	____
13 FEB	BLACKBURN ROVERS	H	____	:	____
20 FEB	NOTTINGHAM FOREST	A	____	:	____
27 FEB	LIVERPOOL	H	____	:	____
6 MAR	MIDDLESBROUGH	A	____	:	____
13 MAR	WEST HAM	H	____	:	____
20 MAR	ASTON VILLA	A	____	:	____
3 APRIL	CHARLTON ATHLETIC	A	____	:	____
5 APR	LEEDS UNITED	H	____	:	____
10 APR	WIMBLEDON	A	____	:	____
17 APR	LEICESTER CITY	H	____	:	____
24 APR	SHEFFIELD WEDNESDAY	A	____	:	____
1 MAY	EVERTON	H	____	:	____
8 MAY	TOTTENHAM HOTSPUR	A	____	:	____
16 MAY	DERBY COUNTY	H	____	:	____

with his Serie A club Parma and agreed to move to Stamford Bridge in November 1996. The little Sardinian made a huge impact, striking up a partnership with Welshman Mark Hughes which, despite keeping Vialli out of the side, took Chelsea to the FA Cup final and sixth place in the League, their highest placing for more than a quarter of a century.

Further progress was expected last season after more foreign reinforcements arrived in the form of Norwegian striker Tore Andre Flo, Dutch goalkeeper Ed De Goey, Uruguayan midfielder Gustavo Poyet and Nigerian teenager Celestine Babayaro. They were joined by England international Graeme Le Saux. Chelsea were going places, but in February a bombshell exploded under Stamford Bridge. Gullit was sacked as manager because, as chairman Ken Bates said, he wanted too much money. Vialli took over as player-manager and guided Chelsea to two cup finals. In the Coca-Cola Cup, they comfortably beat Middlesbrough 2–0 in a repeat of the 1997 FA Cup final. And then Gianfranco Zola was the hero in Stockholm when he scored the only goal of the game against Stuttgart in the Cup-winners' Cup final.

Chelsea are once again a fashionable club to support, just as they were in the late 1960s and early 1970s when the nearby King's Road was the centre of the fashion universe. However, this time round, under the player-management of Ruud Gullit and now Gianluca Vialli, it might well be a little longer before Chelsea go out of fashion.

PREMIER LEAGUE TABLES

SEASON	POS.	P	W	D	L	F	A	PTS	TOP SCORER	AV. GATE
1993–94	14th	42	13	12	17	49	53	51	Stein 13	19,416
1994–95	11th	42	13	15	14	50	55	54	Spencer 11	21,057
1995–96	11th	38	12	14	12	46	44	50	Spencer 13	25,466
1996–97	6th	38	16	11	11	58	55	59	Vialli 9	27,617
1997–98	4th	38	20	3	15	71	43	63	Vialli/Flo 11	33,387

Casiraghi was a hero in Italy after he scored the goal in the play-off against Russia which secured qualification for France 98. But he was desperately unlucky to miss out on Cesare Maldini's final squad of 22 that travelled to France for the finals.

Brian Laudrup

Danish international Brian Laudrup's free transfer from Glasgow Rangers to Chelsea was clouded in controversy. His move was at the centre of allegations made by departing manager Ruud Gullit when he was replaced by Gianluca Vialli last season – and Rangers made a desperate bid to stop the Dane transferring to London, despite the fact that the player's contract with the Scottish club had expired.

Chelsea is the latest stop on a career that has taken Laudrup across Europe. Brian, whose elder brother Michael is also a leading international, left Denmark to play in Germany, for Bayer Uerdingen and Bayern Munich, before moving to Italy, for Fiorentina and then Milan. His move to Rangers in 1994, resulted in the most successful period in his career. He won three League championships and collected the Footballer of the Year award – the first foreign player to do so – in his first season.

Brian has also been Player of the Year in Denmark a record three years – 1989, 1992 and 1995 – and he was one of the stars of Denmark's sensational victory at the 1992 European Championships. Laudrup can play as a winger or as a forward playing behind a main target. Either way, he's a world-class talent.

New recruit: Casiraghi is the latest Italian at Chelsea.

Pierluigi Casiraghi

Italian international striker Pierluigi Casiraghi is the latest star to join the contienental crusade at Stamford Bridge. He joined fellow Italians Gianluca Vialli, Gianfranco Zola and Roberto Di Matteo in London after a £5.4 million transfer from Lazio. The 29-year-old forward signed a four-year deal and promised to give everything in Chelsea's bid to win the Premier League. He says: "It will be our aim to put in a strong title challenge. I had been at Lazio for the last five years and with the changes that were going on it was time to move."

Casirasghi was a transfer target for Roy Hodgson's Blackburn Rovers, but the presence of Vialli as player-manager persuaded the former Juventus man to sign for Chelsea. "It was important that Vialli was here. That was one of the reasons I decided to come. I played with Vialli for one year in Juventus and it was a great forward line," he says. "I know him as a player and not a manager, but he is a great player, he has had some great results in his first season as a manager and I think in time he will become a great one."

Frank Leboeuf

Few people knew much about Frank Leboeuf when he joined Chelsea in the summer of 1996. He had been a member of the French squad, but did not play in England during Euro 96.

Any doubts about Leboeuf, though, quickly went out of the window after his opening games in a Chelsea shirt.

Ball control: Gianfranco Zola has developed a knack of scoring goals at crucial times for Chelsea.

Player Records

	BORN	NATIONALITY	HEIGHT	WEIGHT	APPS	GOALS	PREVIOUS TEAMS
GOALKEEPERS							
Ed de Goey	20.12.66 Gouda	Dutch	6-4	14-2	28	0	Feyenoord (Hol).
Kevin Hitchcock	5.10.62 Custom House	English	6-1	13-4	292	0	Nottingham F, Mansfield T, Northampton T, West Ham U.
Dmitri Kharine	16.8.68 Moscow	Russian	6-2	13-9	117	0	Torpedo Moscow (Rus), Dynamo Moscow (Rus), CSKA Moscow (Rus).
DEFENDERS							
Celestine Babayaro	29.8.78 Nigeria	Nigerian	5-7	10-5	8	0	Plateau U (Nig), Anderlecht (Bel).
Steve Clarke	29.8.63 Saltgate	Scottish	5-10	12-5	440	13	St Mirren.
Marcel Desailly	7.9.68 Accra, Ghana	French	6-2	13-3	0	0	Nantes, Marseille (Fra), Milan (Ita).
Michael Duberry	14.10.75 Enfield	English	6-1	13-6	68	1	Bournemouth.
Danny Granville	19.1.75 Islington	English	5-11	12-5	103	12	Cambridge U.
Bernard Lambourde	11.5.71 Guadeloupe	French	6-2	13-9	7	0	Bordeaux (Fra).
Frank Leboeuf	22.1.68 Marseille	French	6-0	11-4	64	11	Hyeres, Laval, Strasbourg (Fra).
Graeme Le Saux	17.10.68 Jersey	English	5-10	12-2	245	16	Chelsea, Blackburn R.
Dan Petrescu	22.12.67 Bucharest	Romanian	5-8	9-5	117	13	Steaua Bucharest (Rom), Foggia (Ita), Genoa (Ita), Sheffield W.
Frank Sinclair	3.12.71 Lambeth	Jamaican	5-9	12-9	175	8	West Brom.
MIDFIELDERS							
Roberto Di Matteo	29.5.70 Schaffhausen	Italian	5-10	11-9	64	11	Schaffhausen (Swi), Zurich (Swi), Lazio (Ita).
Paul Hughes	19.4.76 Hammersmith	English	6-0	11-7	21	2	none.
David Lee	26.11.69 Kingswood	English	6-3	15-1	170	17	Reading, Plymouth A, Portsmouth.
Jody Morris	22.12.78 London	English	5-5	9-0	25	1	none.
Andy Myers	3.11.73 Hounslow	English	5-10	12-11	73	2	none.
Eddie Newton	13.12.71 Hammersmith	English	6-0	12-8	173	12	Cardiff C.
Mark Nicholls	30.5.77 Hillingdon	English	5-9	9-10	25	3	none.
Gustavo Poyet	15.11.67 Montevideo	Uruguayan	6-1	13-0	12	4	River Plate (Uru), Grenoble (Fra), Real Zaragoza (Spa).
Dennis Wise	16.12.66 Kensington	English	5-6	10-0	379	73	Southampton, Wimbledon.
FORWARDS							
Pierluigi Casiraghi	4.3.69 Monza	Italian	6-1	12-2	0	0	Monza, Juventus, Lazio (Ita).
Tor Andre Flo	15.6.73 Norway	Norwegian	6-2	13-2	38	11	Tromse IL (Nor), SK Brann (Nor).
Brian Laudrup	22.9.69 Denmark	Danish	5-11	12-3	0	0	Brondby (Den), Bayer Uerdingen, Bayern Munich (Ger), Fiorentina, Milan (Ita), Rangers (Sco).
Gianluca Vialli	9.7.64 Cremona	Italian	5-11	12-1	49	22	Cremonese (Ita), Sampdoria (Ita), Juventus (Ita).
Gianfranco Zola	5.7.66 Oliena	Italian	5-5	10-3	50	16	Nuorese (Ita), Torres (Ita), Napoli(Ita), Parma (Ita).

He is that rare commodity in English football – a tough-tackling centre-back who is also comfortable on the ball. He has a range of passing which few, if any, English defenders can match, although if he does have a weakness, it is in the air.

Gianfranco Zola

He may have missed much of last season through injury and a loss of form, but Gianfranco Zola was again one of the stars of Chelsea's season. The little Italian, who dented England's World Cup hopes when he scored the only goal of the game for Italy against England at Wembley in February 1997, has a habit of scoring crucial goals.

The 1997 Footballer of the Year came off the bench to score the winner against Stuttgart in the European Cup-winners' Cup final. He had been on the pitch less than a minute when he struck the vital blow. "It was quite incredible for me," Zola said after the final. "I couldn't contain myself." It was touch and go right up until the day of the final whether Zola would be fit to play. In the end he was cleared to play, but was only named as a substitute only. "I want to thank the masseur who treated me. He did a fantastic job …you must imagine my situation. Eighteen days ago, my dream turned into nothing. Then after treatment, suddenly I'm the man of the match. I came on, scored, and won the Cup!" It could have come from the pages of *Boys' Own*.

Coventry City
The Sky Blues

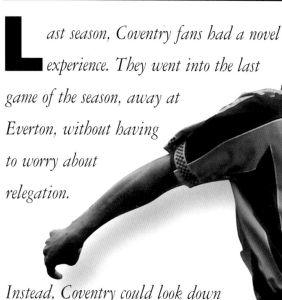

Last season, Coventry fans had a novel experience. They went into the last game of the season, away at Everton, without having to worry about relegation.

Instead, Coventry could look down on the basement scrappers safe in the knowledge that manager Gordon Strachan has built a side which has its sights set on Europe, not the First Division.

Coventry players seem to have an annual fight against relegation written into their contracts – they have been involved in the fight against the drop in nine of the past 11 seasons. Miraculously, they have survived on every occasion while other wealthier, more glamorous clubs have fallen by the wayside.

City have never been a very fashionable club, but ever since the days of Jimmy Hill, the TV pundit who as manager took them from the Fourth to the First Division in six years, they have been part of the elite of English football. Coventry have now been in the top division since 1967 – only Liverpool, Arsenal and Everton have been around for longer.

The Sky Blues have never experienced much success in the top division – their best placing was sixth in 1969–70 – but they have achieved success in the FA Cup, winning it in 1987. Under joint managers John Sillett and George Curtis, City reached the FA Cup final for the first time in their history. In an exciting match at Wembley they beat Tottenham 3–2.

Despite the Cup win, City fared no better in the League, and only survived in 1992 when Luton lost on the last day of the season. In the early 1990s, Coventry gained a reputation for starting the League campaign well, only to fade fast after Christmas. With a view to stopping that worrying trend, manager Phil Neal left the club in February 1995 and was replaced by Ron Atkinson, recently sacked by Aston Villa.

Big Ron spent almost £20 million in less than two years – bringing in the likes of Gary McAllister, Dion Dublin, Noel Whelan and Paul Telfer – but with limited success. Despite the extensive changes to the defence, City continued to leak goals. Not even the switch of striker Dion Dublin to centre-back improved matters and by November 1997 the Sky Blues were struggling at the wrong end of the table.

Gordon Strachan had been brought in as Atkinson's assistant with a view to succeeding Big Ron in the long term. But with City's Premier League status in doubt, the change

**Dublin's fair city:
Dion has helped give
Coventry more firepower.**

COVENTRY CITY

Formed: 1883.
Nickname: Sky Blues.
Stadium: Highfield Road.
Capacity: 23,500.
Address: King Richard Street,
Coventry CV2 4FW.
Telephone: 01203 234000.
Clubcall: 0891 121166.
Fax: 01203 234099.
Website: www.fa.carling.com/club/cv.fc
Manager: Gordon Strachan.

COLOURS

RECORDS

Record Premier League victory:
5–0 (v Blackburn R, Dec 9, 1995).
Record Premier League defeat:
5–0 (v Manchester U, Dec 28, 1992).
Record transfer fee received:
£3.6 million from Liverpool for Phil Babb,
Sept 1994.
Record transfer fee received:
£3.5 million to Grasshopper Zurich for
Viorel Moldova, December 1997.
Record attendance:
51,455, v Wolves, Division 2, April 29,
1967.

HONOURS

League:
Best finish sixth, Division One, 1969–70.
FA Cup (1):
1987.
League Cup:
semi-finalists 1981, 1990.

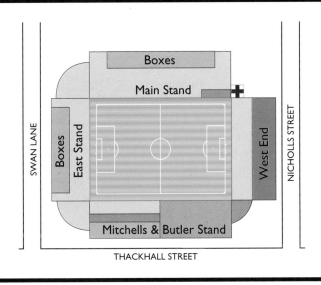

FIXTURES 1998–99

15 AUG	CHELSEA	H	____ : ____
22 AUG	NOTTINGHAM FOREST	A	____ : ____
29 AUG	WEST HAM UNITED	H	____ : ____
9 SEPT	LIVERPOOL	A	____ : ____
12 SEPT	MANCHESTER UNITED	A	____ : ____
19 SEPT	NEWCASTLE UNITED	H	____ : ____
26 SEPT	CHARLTON ATHLETIC	A	____ : ____
3 OCT	ASTON VILLA	H	____ : ____
17 OCT	SHEFFIELD WEDNESDAY	H	____ : ____
24 OCT	SOUTHAMPTON	A	____ : ____
31 OCT	ARSENAL	H	____ : ____
7 NOV	BLACKBURN ROVERS	A	____ : ____
14 NOV	EVERTON	H	____ : ____
21 NOV	MIDDLESBROUGH	A	____ : ____
28 NOV	LEICESTER CITY	H	____ : ____
5 DEC	WIMBLEDON	A	____ : ____
12 DEC	LEEDS UNITED	A	____ : ____
19 DEC	DERBY COUNTY	H	____ : ____
26 DEC	TOTTENHAM HOTSPUR	H	____ : ____
28 DEC	WEST HAM UNITED	A	____ : ____
9 JAN	NOTTINGHAM FOREST	H	____ : ____
16 JAN	CHELSEA	A	____ : ____
30 JAN	LIVERPOOL	H	____ : ____
6 FEB	TOTTENHAM HOTSPUR	A	____ : ____
13 FEB	NEWCASTLE UNITED	A	____ : ____
20 FEB	MANCHESTER UNITED	H	____ : ____
27 FEB	ASTON VILLA	A	____ : ____
6 MAR	CHARLTON ATHLETIC	H	____ : ____
13 MAR	BLACKBURN ROVERS	H	____ : ____
20 MAR	ARSENAL	A	____ : ____
3 APR	SHEFFIELD WEDNESDAY	A	____ : ____
5 APR	SOUTHAMPTON	H	____ : ____
10 APR	EVERTON	A	____ : ____
17 APR	MIDDLESBROUGH	H	____ : ____
24 APR	LEICESTER CITY	A	____ : ____
1 MAY	WIMBLEDON	H	____ : ____
8 MAY	DERBY COUNTY	A	____ : ____
16 MAY	LEEDS UNITED	H	____ : ____

over happened earlier than expected, with Atkinson moving upstairs to the newly-created position of "director of football". Strachan, the former Aberdeen, Manchester United and Leeds midfielder, was still playing despite turning 40, thanks largely to an unlikely diet of bananas and seaweed pills. He faced a tough task in keeping Coventry in the top flight, but somehow pulled it off.

The Sky Blues travelled to Tottenham on the last day of the season on a wing and a prayer. They needed to beat Spurs at White Hart Lane and then hope that other results went in their favour. The 2–1 victory over Tottenham, and Middlesbrough's failure to beat Leeds and Sunderland's defeat by Wimbledon ensured Coventry's 31st consecutive season of top-flight football.

The Scot was busy in the transfer market last season, shopping during the pre-season in Scandinavia for Norwegian international Trond Egil Soltvedt, Dane Martin Johansen and the Swedish pair Magnus Hedman and Roland Nilsson. During the season, Romanian international striker Viorel Moldovan arrived for a club record £3.25 million and Dutch under-21 midfielder George Boateng signed from Feyenoord in a deal which turned out to be one of the bargains of the season.

The new players gelled together quickly as the Sky Blues cruised through the season in mid-table. Under Gordan Strachan, Coventry City, the Premier League's great survivors, seem more capable than ever of preserving the top-flight status which they have held since 1967.

PREMIER LEAGUE TABLES

SEASON	POS.	P	W	D	L	F	A	PTS	TOP SCORER	AV. GATE
1993–94	11th	42	14	14	14	43	45	56	Ndlovu 11	13,352
1994–95	16th	42	12	14	16	44	62	50	Dublin 13	15,980
1995–96	16th	38	8	14	16	42	60	38	Dublin 14	18,507
1996–97	17th	38	9	14	15	38	54	41	Dublin 14	19,608
1997–98	11th	38	12	16	10	46	44	52	Dublin 18	19,722

Dion Dublin

Dion Dublin has to be one of the unluckiest men in English football. He was tipped by almost all the pundits to be included in England's final 22-man squad for the World Cup in France after impressing in pre-World Cup friendlies – in defence as well as attack. But Spurs striker Les Ferdinand got the nod ahead of Dublin, leaving the Coventry captain to wonder what might have been.

Hoddle said: "Choosing between Les Ferdinand and Dion Dublin was the real tough decision. Dion was so close to getting into the 22. What decided it for me was that I felt that I needed some more pace up front. Michael Owen has great pace, but if anything happened to him then we might have been short."

However, Hoddle has not ruled out an international recall for Dublin. The England coach said: "It was a tough call, but Dion has done himself a load of favours with me as England coach with the way he has performed and conducted himself. It certainly would not surprise me, if he has a good season, to find that he will be back in the frame with England."

Dublin is the sort of player every manager likes to call upon. He adds pace, power and aerial punch to any attack, provides leadership on the pitch and is versatile enough to play in defence if required.

Leicester-born Dublin has come a long way since the days when he turned out for non-League Oakham United, after being released as a teenager by Norwich City. He was spotted by Fourth Division Cambridge City and spent the 1988–89 season in their reserves before making his League debut at Wrexham on December 13. On January 3, in only his second League appearance, he smashed a hat-trick past Peterborough. Dion Dublin had arrived.

Dublin's goals helped Cambridge into the FA Cup sixth round and promotion before Manchester United stepped in with a £1 million bid in July 1992. He scored the winner on his full debut at Southampton, but broke a leg against Crystal Palace and spent the rest of the season on the sidelines. He made only a handful of appearances before moving to Coventry for £2 million in September 1994.

He has become a popular figure at Highfield Road, not just for his goals, but also for his willingness to drop back into defence when required.

George Boateng

Dutch midfielder George Boateng proved to be one of the transfer bargains of last season. He moved to Coventry last December from Feyenoord for £250,000. He had received offers from Spain and Italy in addition to the Sky Blues, but had made up his mind in the summer of 1996 during the European Championships that he wanted to play in England. He says: "I went to Wembley for the England–Holland game with a Feyenoord team-mate and was one of the few Dutch supporters not wearing orange!

"That was a great night for England [who won 4–1] and I said to my team-mate the next time I come back here it will be to play – and that's what has happened."

George has adapted to life in England very well. "I love the Premiership. In Holland there are basically only three teams – Ajax, Feyenoord and PSV Eindhoven – in with a shout for the title. They basically decide the championship in the matches among themselves every year, whereas in England every team can be beaten – top can lose to bottom."

It hasn't all been plain sailing though. He says: "I did wonder after the first game at Liverpool what I had let myself in for. It was so cold that at half-time I held a cup of tea in both hands so I could feel my fingers again! And I have struggled to get used to the roundabouts! At first I didn't know what I was doing. In the end I would wait at the junction, wave the person behind me past and then follow them until I got to the turn I wanted. It was a nightmare but I've got better."

Viorel Moldovan

Big things were expected of Romanian international striker Viorel Moldovan when he became Coventry's record signing last season. He joined the Sky Blues in a £3.25 million deal after he shot to the top of the European goalscorers' charts during his time with Swiss club Grasshopper Zurich. He had made his name in Romania with Gloria Bistrita and Dinamo Bucharest.

But it was in Switzerland that Moldovan, one of the stars of Romania's successful France 98 qualification campaign, made his name as a goalscorer. He hit 19 goals for Neuchatel Xamax in the 1995–96 season, 29 in 1996–97 for Grasshopper, and 16 last season before the move to Coventry.

Floating Boateng: Dutchman George has made a good impression since arriving at Highfield Road.

Player Records

	BORN	NATIONALITY	HEIGHT	WEIGHT	APPS	GOALS	PREVIOUS TEAMS
GOALKEEPERS							
Steve Ogrizovic	12.9.57 Mansfield	English	6-5	15-0	606	0	Chesterfield, Liverpool, Shrewsbury T.
Magnus Hedman	19.3.73 Sweden	Swedish	6-4	14-8	14	0	AIK Solna (Swe).
DEFENDERS							
Gary Breen	12.12.73 London	Irish	6-1	11-12	196	3	Maidstone U, Gillingham, Peterborough U, Birmingham C.
David Burrows	25.10.68 Dudley	English	5-10	11-8	314	5	West Brom, Liverpool, West Ham U, Everton.
Liam Daish	23.9.68 Portsmouth	Irish	6-2	13-5	244	9	Portsmouth, Cambridge U, Birmingham C.
Marcus Hall	24.3.76 Coventry	English	6-1	12-2	68	0	none.
Roland Nilsson	27.11.63 Sweden	Swedish	5-10	12-0	32	0	Helsingborgs (Swe), IFK Gothenburg (Swe), Sheff W., Helsingborgs (Swe).
Richard Shaw	11.9.68 Brentford	English	5-9	12-8	300	3	Crystal Palace, Hull C.
Paul Williams	26.3.71 Burton	English	6-0	12-10	247	30	Derby Co, Lincoln C.
MIDFIELDERS							
George Boateng	5.8.75 Accra, Ghana	Dutch	6-0	12-0	14	1	Feyenoord (Hol)
Willie Boland	6.8.75 Ennis	Irish	5-9	11-2	63	0	none.
Gary McAllister	25.12.64 Motherwell	Scottish	6-0	12-7	543	90	Motherwell, Leicester C, Leeds U.
Michael O'Neill	5.7.69 Portadown	NorthernIrish	5-11	10-10	214	45	Newcastle, Hibernian.
John Salako	11.2.69 Nigeria	English	5-9	12-3	300	29	Crystal Palace, Swansea C.
Sam Shilton	21.7.78 Nottingham	English	5-10	10-0	2	0	Plymouth A.
Trond Egil Soltvedt	15.2.67 Norway	Norwegian	6-1	12-11	30	1	Rosenborg (Nor).
Gavin Strachan	23.12.78 Aberdeen	Scottish	5-10	10-7	12	0	none.
Paul Telfer	21.10.71 Edinburgh	Scottish	5-9	11-6	242	23	Luton T.
Noel Whelan	30.12.74 Leeds	English	6-2	12-3	125	27	Leeds U.
FORWARDS							
Dion Dublin	22.4.69 Leicester	English	6-2	12-4	303	151	Norwich C, Cambridge U, Man. U.
Andrew Ducros	16.9.77 Evesham	English	5-4	9-8	8	0	none.
Simon Haworth	30.3.77 Cardiff	Welsh	6-3	13-8	10	0	Cardiff C.
Darren Huckerby	23.4.76 Nottingham	English	5-10	11-11	88	24	Lincoln C, Newcastle U.
Martin Johansen	22.7.72 Denmark	Danish	5-6	10-5	2	0	FC Copenhagen (Den).
Viorel Moldovan	8.8.72 Romania	Romanian	5-11	11-8	10	1	Grasshopper (Swi), Dinamo Bucharest (Rom), Gloria Bistrita (Rom).

However, Moldovan had problems settling in and he was quoted in a Romanian newspaper as criticising Gordan Strachan's training methods and branding the Sky Blues a "very, very poor side" who played "kick-and-rush football". Strachan accepted Moldovan's claims that he was misquoted. "Viorel says he didn't even give the interview, let alone have his words twisted. He faxed me saying he was very embarrassed when he heard the stories and insisted that he is very happy here with us."

Record-breaker: Viorel Moldovan.

Darren Huckerby

Striker Darren Huckerby has come a long way in a very short space of time. Huckerby only played a handful for games for his first club Lincoln when he was signed by Newcastle boss Kevin Keegan from Lincoln for £500,000. 21-year-old Huckerby soon found life tough at St James' Park, especially with the arrival of £15-million-man Alan Shearer. Keegan had disbanded the reserve team (they messed up the pitch at St James' Park, he claimed) and first-team football was hard to come by.

Nottingham-born Huckerby went on loan to Coventry during the 1996–97 season, and soon found his temporary stay converted to a permanent £1-million deal after striking a rich vein of goalscoring form. His goals for the Sky Blues even earned him a call-up to the England B team. Last season, he proved he was no one-season wonder by weighing in with 14 League goals for the Sky Blues.

DERBY COUNTY

Derby County
The Rams

Derby County continue to make slow progress up the Premier League – and they would not have it any other way.

Last season, the Rams finished the League campaign in ninth place, an impressive result when you consider that they were promoted only two seasons ago and are still finding their Premiership feet – as well as settling in at their new, high-tech stadium, Pride Park.

That Derby are competing in the top flight at all owes a great deal to the commitment, and cash, of club chairman Lionel Pickering. His backing helped Derby to clinch promotion to the Premier League two seasons ago after two previous play-off failures.

The other person County have to thank for their recent success is manager Jim Smith. He has put together an impressive side, spending less money than most of his rivals, while having more success than most with foreign imports.

However, Smith will have to go a long way before he matches the achievements of the most successful manager in Derby's history, Brian Clough. Under Clough, County won the League in 1972 and became established in the top division, winning the title again in 1975 under Dave Mackay.

The club entered one of the darkest periods in their history during the 1980s. They were relegated to the old Second Division in 1980 and slumped even further in 1984, when they slipped into the Third Division. Under manager Arthur Cox, County clawed their way back up and by 1990 were back in the big time, albeit for just one season. After relegation back to the old Second division, they faced a long haul back. Derby experienced double disappointment, first in the semi-finals of the 1992 play-offs and then defeat at the hands of Leicester at Wembley in 1994. Cox stayed on at the Baseball Ground until 1993 while chairman Pickering dug deep to buy success, but it eluded County.

Derby finally made the step up to the Premier League under Jim Smith, the "Bald Eagle", who arrived in

Basket case: Paolo Wanchope has made a stunning switch from basketball player to football sharpshooter.

DERBY COUNTY

Formed: 1884.
Nickname: The Rams.
Stadium: Pride Park Stadium.
Capacity: 30,000.
Address: Pride Park Stadium,
Pride Park, Derby DE24 8XL.
Telephone: 01332 340105.
Clubcall: 0891 121187.
Fax: 01332 360988.
Website: www.fa-carling.com/club/dc.fc
Manager: Jim Smith.

COLOURS

RECORDS

Record Premier League victory:
4-0 (v Bolton W, April 14, 1998; v Southampton Sep 27, 1997).
Record Premier League defeat:
5-0 (v Leeds U, March 14, 1998).
Record transfer fee received:
£2.9 million from Liverpool for Dean Saunders, July 1991.
Record transfer fee paid:
£2.7 million to Rosario Central for Horacio Carbonari, June 1998.
Record attendance:
41,826, v Tottenham H, Division One, 20 Sept, 1969.

HONOURS

League (2): 1971–72, 1974–75.
FA Cup (1): 1946.
League Cup: Semi-finalists 1968.

Stadium diagram: Boxes / Toyota Stand / Boxes / Colombo Street / Boxes / Osmaston Stand / Normanton Stand / Vulcan Street / Main Stand

FIXTURES 1998–99

15 AUG	BLACKBURN ROVERS	A	____ : ____
22 AUG	WIMBLEDON	H	____ : ____
29 AUG	MIDDLESBROUGH	A	____ : ____
9 SEPT	SHEFFIELD WEDNESDAY	H	____ : ____
12 SEPT	CHARLTON ATHLETIC	A	____ : ____
19 SEPT	LEICESTER CITY	H	____ : ____
26 SEPT	ASTON VILLA	A	____ : ____
3 OCT	TOTTENHAM HOTSPUR	H	____ : ____
17 OCT	NEWCASTLE UNITED	A	____ : ____
24 OCT	MANCHESTER UNITED	H	____ : ____
31 OCT	LEEDS UNITED	H	____ : ____
7 NOV	LIVERPOOL	A	____ : ____
14 NOV	NOTTINGHAM FOREST	A	____ : ____
21 NOV	WEST HAM UNITED	A	____ : ____
28 NOV	SOUTHAMPTON	A	____ : ____
5 DEC	ARSENAL	H	____ : ____
12 DEC	CHELSEA	H	____ : ____
19 DEC	COVENTRY CITY	A	____ : ____
26 DEC	EVERTON	A	____ : ____
28 DEC	MIDDLESBROUGH	H	____ : ____
9 JAN	WIMBLEDON	A	____ : ____
16 JAN	BLACKBURN ROVERS	H	____ : ____
30 JAN	SHEFFIELD WEDNESDAY	A	____ : ____
6 FEB	EVERTON	H	____ : ____
13 FEB	LEICESTER CITY	A	____ : ____
20 FEB	CHARLTON ATHLETIC	H	____ : ____
27 FEB	TOTTENHAM HOTSPUR	A	____ : ____
6 MAR	ASTON VILLA	H	____ : ____
13 MAR	LIVERPOOL	H	____ : ____
20 MAR	LEEDS UNITED	A	____ : ____
3 APR	NEWCASTLE UNITED	H	____ : ____
5 APR	MANCHESTER UNITED	A	____ : ____
10 APR	NOTTINGHAM FOREST	H	____ : ____
17 APR	WEST HAM UNITED	A	____ : ____
24 APR	SOUTHAMPTON	H	____ : ____
1 MAY	ARSENAL	A	____ : ____
8 MAY	COVENTRY CITY	H	____ : ____
16 MAY	CHELSEA	A	____ : ____

June 1995 and steered County to promotion in his first season. After being one of the biggest fish in the First Division, County were now one of the smallest clubs in the Premiership. However, in manager Smith, Derby had one of the shrewdest operators in the transfer market.

For Derby's first season back in the top flight, Smith brought in Croatian midfielder Aljosa Asanovic, Danish defender Jacob Laursen and Scottish midfielder Christian Dailly – all at knockdown prices. With other new arrivals, such as Costa Rican forward Paolo Wanchope, and local talents, such as striker Dean Sturridge, they combined to keep County comfortably in midtable all season, eventually finishing in 12th place.

Last season, further reinforcements arrived from the Continent, as Derby settled into their new home after 102 years at the Baseball Ground. Former Italian international Stefano Eranio moved to the Midlands on a free transfer from Milan and was joined by fellow Italian Francesco Baiano, a £650,000 signing from Fiorentina. County proved to be one of the season's surprise packages, staying in the top six for most of the campaign and eventually finishing in ninth place.

Manager Jim Smith was happy with season's achievements. "We've made progress," he said. "We're nine points and three places up on last year. I call that progress, and if we show a similar improvement over the next 12 months, we'll be getting there."

PREMIER LEAGUE TABLES

SEASON	POS.	P	W	D	L	F	A	PTS	TOP SCORER	AV. GATE
1996–97	12th	38	11	13	14	45	58	46	Sturridge 11	17,889
1997–98	9th	38	16	7	15	52	49	55	Wanchope 13	29,105

Horacio Carbonari

Derby manager Jim Smith continues to delve into the foreign transfer market for new players. The latest player to arrive at Pride Park from abroad is Argentinian defender Horacio Carbonari. The 24-year-old became Derby's record signing in the summer when his £2.7 million transfer from Buenos Aires side Rosario Central eclipsed the £2.5 million Derby paid Notts County for Craig Short in 1992.

Carbonari was first spotted by club scout Archie Gemmill. Manager Jim Smith followed up Gemmill's recommendation and saw Carbonari in the flesh before going ahead with the deal. "We didn't think we would get him," Smith admitted. "But I am very excited by this signing. Horacio can play as a sweeper or central defender, he can play left or right and he scores a lot of goals. He is the sort of player I was looking for – it should make it very exciting next season."

Carbonari had an impressive goalscoring record in the Argentinian League – he notched up 36 goals in 137 appearances for Rosario.

Paolo Wanchope

Costa Rican striker Paolo Wanchope burst onto the Premier League scene in the 1996–97 season when he scored a sensational goal for Derby County against Manchester United at Old Trafford. That should have served as a warning to defenders that the Central American hitman meant business. But last season, Wanchope continued on the goalscoring trail – including more valuable goals against Manchester United.

All in all, Wanchope scored 17 goals in 36 starts for Derby last season and finshed as County's top scorer in the League with 13 goals. His performances for Derby have been all the more impressive as he has only been playing football for a relatively short period of time. In fact, Wanchope, who stands 6ft 4ins tall,

started out as a basketball player and only switched to football a few years ago.

Most players would find it hard to surpass Wanchope's feats last season. But the Costa Rican insists that he can do better this season. He says: "I'm someone who has a lot of belief in myself and my ability. If I stay fit and stay in the side, I can score more than 20."

Deon Burton

When striker Deon Burton joined Derby during the summer of 1996 in a £1 million move from First Division Portsmouth, he had little idea that, 12 months later, he would be playing in the World Cup finals. But a holiday to Jamaica turned into an invitation to join the Jamaican campaign to qualify for France 98.

Deon was born in Berkshire, but he qualifies to play for the Caribbean country through his Jamaican-born father. The decision to play for Jamaica was a controversial move, but it quickly paid off for the 21-year-old, who was joined in the Jamaican side by Wimbledon's Robbie Earle and his former Portsmouth team-mates Paul Hall and Fiztroy Simpson.

"The local Jamaican players were a bit uneasy to start with," says Burton. "But scoring vital goals helps you fit in. Now I'm definitely one of the Reggae Boyz." Burton made a sensational start to his international career with Jamaica. He scored vital goals in four successive World Cup qualifiers for the Reggae Boyz, being voted Jamaican Sportsman of the Year, and earning the young striker the nickname "One-love", because of the Bob Marley song – and the wins his goals gave Jamaica on the road to France 98.

One of the Boyz: Jamaican Deon Burton experienced World Cup fever in France.

Player Records

	BORN	NATIONALITY	HEIGHT	WEIGHT	APPS	GOALS	PREVIOUS TEAMS
GOALKEEPERS							
Russell Hoult	22.11.72 Leicester	English	6-4	14-5	121	0	Leicester C, Lincoln C, Blackpool, Bolton W, Lincoln C.
Mart Poom	3.2.72 Tallinn	Estonian	6-4	13-7	44	0	FC Wil (Est), Flora Tallinn (Est), Portsmouth, Flora Tallinn (Est).
DEFENDERS							
Horacio Carbonari	2.5.74 Argentina	Argentinian	6-3	??	0	0	Rosario Central (Arg).
Lee Carsley	28.2.74 Birmingham	English	5-9	12-7	112	4	none.
Steve Elliott	29.10.78 Derby	English	6-2	13-11	4	0	none.
Robbie Kozluk	5.8.77 Mansfield	English	5-8	11-9	9	0	none.
Jacob Laursen	6.10.71 Veijle	Danish	5-10	12-6	64	2	Veijle (Den), Silkeborg (Den).
Chris Powell	8.9.69 Lambeth	English	5-10	11-7	354	4	Crystal Palace, Aldershot, Southend U.
Gary Rowett	6.3.74 Bromsgrove	English	6-1	12-6	191	12	Cambridge U, Everton, Blackpool.
Igor Stimac	6.9.67 Metkovic	Croatian	6-2	13-2	70	3	Hajduk Split (Cro), Cibalia Vinkovci (Cro), Cadiz (Spa), Hajduk Split (Cro).
Dean Yates	26.10.67 Leicester	English	6-2	12-6	382	36	Notts Co.
MIDFIELDERS							
Lars Bohinen	8.9.66 Vadso, Norway	Norwegian	6-0	12-2	129	15	Blackburn R, Nottingham F, Young Boys (Swi), Viking (Nor), Valerengen (Nor).
Christian Dailly	23.10.73 Dundee	Scottish	6-0	12-10	210	1	Dundee U.
Rory Delap	6.7.76 Sutton Coldfield	English	6-0	12-3	69	0	Carlisle U.
Stefano Eranio	29.12.66 Genoa	Italian	5-11	11-9	23	5	Genoa (Ita), Milan (Ita).
Jonathan Hunt	2.11.71 London	English	5-10	11-0	156	23	Barnet, Southend.
Darryl Powell	15.1.71 Lambeth	English	6-1	11-2	223	22	Portsmouth.
Mauricio Solis	13.12.72 Costa Rica	Costa Rican	5-8	11-10	9	0	Heridiano (CR).
Robin Van Der Laan	5.9.68 Schiedam	Dutch	5-11	13-8	241	32	Port Vale.
FORWARDS							
Francesco Baiano	1.9.68 Italy	Italian	5-10	11-11	31	12	Fiorentina.
Deon Burton	25.10.76 Ashford	Jamaican	5-8	10-9	96	15	Portsmouth, Cardiff City.
Dean Sturridge	27.7.73 Birmingham	English	5-7	11-13	132	45	Torquay U.
Ron Willems	20.9.66 Epe	Dutch	6-0	12-11	59	13	PEC Zwolle (Hol), Twente (Hol), Grasshopper (Swi).
Paulo Wanchope	31.1.76 Costa Rica	Costa Rican	6-4	12-5	37	14	Herediano.

Stefano Eranio

County manager Jim Smith is good at spotting a bargain, and that's exactly what he got when he signed Italian international midfielder Stefano Eranio on a free transfer from Milan in the summer of 1996.

Milan had been hoping to persuade Eranio to sign a new contract and stay in Italy. But the player had other ideas, and after seeing Derby's stunning new stadium, Eranio signed a three-year deal. Under the Bosman ruling, Derby paid Milan no transfer fee and the Rams' couldn't believe their good fortune.

Eranio spent eight seasons with his home-town club Genoa before making the move to Milan in the summer of 1992. In five seasons with the Italian giants, Eranio collected three Italian League winners' medals, a European Cup and a Supercup, as well as being a regular in the Italian national side.

The Italian experienced some problems with injuries in his first season with Derby, but he still weighed in with five goals in 23 League matches – an impressive performance from right wing-back.

Bargain Buy: Derby's piggy bank was left untouched when Eranio arrived from Milan.

Everton
The Toffees

Nordic Invasion: Thomas Myhre joined Everton from Norway's Viking Stavanger.

Everton survived in the Premier League by the skin of their teeth last season. Only Bolton's defeat at Chelsea maintained the top-flight status which Everton have enjoyed since 1955.

The miraculous last-day escape was no cause for celebration, though. Veteran captain Dave Watson said: "We got away with murder throughout the season and for it to go down to last game and for us to just scrape through is not a matter for celebrating. It is a matter of making sure it does not happen again."

"Never again" is the message that will be repeated time and time again this season as Everton bid to reclaim their place as one of the "Big Five" clubs of English football. Plans are still being laid to relocate Everton away from Goodison Park to a new purpose-built, 60,000-capacity stadium in Kirkby.

Goodison Park is still an impressive stadium and one of a handful of Premier League grounds which can hold more than 40,000 supporters. But Liverpool's Anfield, less than a mile away across Stanley Park, was chosen ahead of Goodison Park as a venue for Euro 96. And there's the rub. Everton have been playing second fiddle to Liverpool for too long, and chairman Peter Johnson feels a new stadium is the best way to put the club back on the map.

The rivalry goes back more than a century, to when the two clubs were one and the same. Everton, founder members of the Football League in 1888, played at Anfield Road. A row broke out in 1892 over the team using a pub as the club HQ. This led to Everton moving down the road to Goodison. The pub's landlord stayed at Anfield and formed a new team – Liverpool.

Everton may have lived in Liverpool's shadow in recent years, but they have a pretty impressive history, enjoying three golden eras: the 1930s, the 1960s and the 1980s. They won their first title in 1891 and were runners-up six times before doing it again in 1915, by which time they had also bagged their first FA Cup, in 1906. In the 1928–29 season, striker William "Dixie" Dean set an as-yet-unbroken record of 60 League goals as Everton were crowned champions again.

The 1930s saw two more Championships (1932 and 1939) and an FA Cup win in 1933. However, Everton could not sustain their success after the Second World War and were relegated in 1951. They spent four seasons out of the top division before, under manager Harry Catterick, they were at last able to renew the successes of the 1930s, winning the League twice (1962–63 and 1969–70) and the FA Cup once (1966). They were not to taste such success again until the arrival of former Everton player, Howard Kendall, as manager in 1981. Thereafter the club challenged for honours on a regular basis, winning the League (1984–85 and 1986–87), FA Cup (1984) and European Cup-

EVERTON

Formed: 1878.
Nickname: The Toffees.
Stadium: Goodison Park.
Capacity: 40,200.
Address: Goodison Park, Liverpool
L4 4EL.
Telephone: 0151 330 2200.
Clubcall: 0891 121199.
Fax: 0151 286 9112.
Website: www.fa-carling/club.e.fc
Manager: Walter Smith.

COLOURS

RECORDS

Record Premier League victory:
7–1 (v Southampton, Nov 16, 1996).
Record Premier League defeat:
5–1 (v Norwich C, Sept 25, 1993;
v Sheffield W, April 2, 1994).
Record transfer fee received:
£7 million from Fiorentina for Andrei
Kanchelskis, Mar 1997.
Record transfer fee paid:
£5.75 million to Middlesbrough for Nick
Barmby, Oct 1996.
Record attendance: 78,299,
v Liverpool, Division One, 18 Sept, 1948.

HONOURS

League (9):
1890–91, 1914–15, 1927–28, 1931–32,
1938–39, 1962–63, 1969–70, 1984–85,
1986–87.
FA Cup (5):
1906, 1933, 1966, 1984, 1995.
League Cup:
runners-up 1977, 1988.
European Cup-winners' Cup (1):
1985.

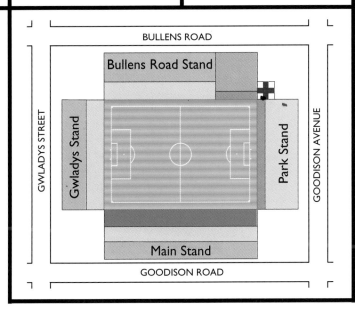

FIXTURES 1998–99

15 AUG	ASTON VILLA	H	____ : ____
22 AUG	LEICESTER CITY	A	____ : ____
29 AUG	TOTTENHAM HOTSPUR	H	____ : ____
9 SEPT	NOTTINGHAM FOREST	A	____ : ____
12 SEPT	LEEDS UNITED	H	____ : ____
19 SEPT	MIDDLESBROUGH	A	____ : ____
26 SEPT	BLACKBURN ROVERS	H	____ : ____
3 OCT	WIMBLEDON	A	____ : ____
17 OCT	LIVERPOOL	H	____ : ____
24 OCT	SHEFFIELD WEDNESDAY	A	____ : ____
31 OCT	MANCHESTER UNITED	H	____ : ____
7 NOV	ARSENAL	A	____ : ____
14 NOV	COVENTRY CITY	A	____ : ____
21 NOV	NEWCASTLE UNITED	H	____ : ____
28 NOV	CHARLTON ATHLETIC	A	____ : ____
5 DEC	CHELSEA	H	____ : ____
12 DEC	SOUTHAMPTON	H	____ : ____
19 DEC	WEST HAM UNITED	A	____ : ____
26 DEC	DERBY COUNTY	H	____ : ____
28 DEC	TOTTENHAM HOTSPUR	A	____ : ____
9 JAN	LEICESTER CITY	H	____ : ____
16 JAN	ASTON VILLA	A	____ : ____
30 JAN	NOTTINGHAM FOREST	H	____ : ____
6 FEB	DERBY COUNTY	A	____ : ____
13 FEB	MIDDLESBROUGH	H	____ : ____
20 FEB	LEEDS UNITED	A	____ : ____
27 FEB	WIMBLEDON	H	____ : ____
6 MAR	BLACKBURN ROVERS	A	____ : ____
13 MAR	ARSENAL	H	____ : ____
20 MAR	MANCHESTER UNITED	A	____ : ____
3 APR	LIVERPOOL	A	____ : ____
5 APR	SHEFFIELD WEDNESDAY	H	____ : ____
10 APR	COVENTRY CITY	H	____ : ____
17 APR	NEWCASTLE UNITED	A	____ : ____
24 APR	CHARLTON ATHLETIC	H	____ : ____
1 MAY	CHELSEA	A	____ : ____
8 MAY	WEST HAM UNITED	H	____ : ____
16 MAY	SOUTHAMPTON	A	____ : ____

winners' Cup (1985). They were losing FA Cup finalists a further three times (twice to Liverpool) and, despite 30 goals from Gary Lineker, finished second in the League behind Liverpool in 1986. The post-Heysel ruling barring English clubs from European competition denied Everton a chance at the European Cup the year after their League triumphs of 1985 and 1987, but it was still an impressive record.

Kendall left to coach Spanish side Athletic Bilbao and was replaced by his assistant Colin Harvey, who could not keep up the winning ways. Kendall returned in 1990, but to no avail. After a brief period under the stewardship of Mike Walker, during which Everton flirted with relegation, the club turned to an old hero, Joe Royle.

Royle had had great success keeping Oldham Athletic in the top division, and quickly took Everton away from the relegation zone and into the 1995 FA Cup final. A Paul Rideout goal was enough to beat Manchester United at Wembley. The League proved a tougher nut to crack, and Royle parted company with the club at the end of the 1996–97 season.

Howard Kendall's return for a third stint as manager was not a happy one last season. He struggled to find the money to buy new players and was forced to place a lot of responsibility on youngsters such as Danny Cadermateri, Michael Ball and Gareth Farelly in the fight against relegation.

PREMIER LEAGUE TABLES

SEASON	POS.	P	W	D	L	F	A	PTS	TOP SCORER	AV. GATE
1993–94	17th	42	12	8	22	42	63	44	Cottee 16	22,876
1994–95	15th	42	11	17	14	44	51	50	Rideout 14	31,291
1995–96	6th	38	17	10	11	64	44	61	Kanchelskis 16	35,435
1996–97	15th	38	10	12	16	44	57	42	Ferguson 10	36,204
1997–98	17th	38	9	13	16	41	56	40	Ferguson 11	35,355

Squad Info
KEY PLAYERS TO WATCH

Nick Barmby

Everton fans have yet to see the best of Nick Barmby, but there is no doubt the young forward is one of the most talented players of his generation.

As a kid, Hull-born Barmby's talent was spotted early on and he was one of the first to graduate from the FA School of Excellence at Lilleshall. Tottenham beat off a host of clubs to sign Barmby in February 1991 and he made his League debut against Sheffield Wednesday in September 1992. The former Tottenham Hotspur manager, Terry Venables, gave Barmby an international debut in March 1995. His career may have been progressing well, but the homesick forward never made any secret of his desire to move back north.

Middlesbrough manager Bryan Robson came to Barmby's rescue, signing him in August 1995 for £5.25 million, and he scored on his debut against Arsenal. However, the arrival of Juninho and Ravanelli restricted Barmby's development at 'Boro and he made the move to Everton in October 1996 for £5.75 million.

Duncan Ferguson

Everton's top scorer last season has been dogged by disciplinary problems during his short career, but is determined to be recognized for what he does best – scoring goals.

The big striker, who stands 6ft 4ins tall, scored 11 times and was troubled by injuries in what was another disappointing League campaign for Everton. It was only his second full season since his conviction and imprisonment for headbutting Raith Rovers defender John McStay while playing for Rangers in a Scottish Premier League match in April 1994. He spent 44 days in Glasgow's tough Barlinnie jail during the 1995–96 season as a result.

Stirling-born Ferguson has never been far from the headlines. He was still at Dundee United, his first club, when he made his full international debut for Scotland, against the United States in 1992. He already had a reputation as a player who was difficult to handle, but Rangers beat off a host of other clubs to sign him in the summer of 1993, for a then record British transfer fee of £4 million.

The big man was plagued by a serious knee injury during his time in Glasgow and made just 14 League appearances in two seasons. But Everton manager Joe Royle offered Ferguson a chance to resurrect his career over the border in England and, after an initial loan period, Everton signed the big Scot for a then club record £4 million.

Despite his off-the-pitch problems Ferguson has given Everton's attack a focus which few teams can match, and his height and heading ability cause problems for the Premier League's finest defenders. The danger for Everton is that they may have become too dependent on their Scottish striker for goals.

Thomas Myhre

It was never going to be easy replacing a Goodison Park legend, but Norwegian goalkeeper Thomas Myhre has quickly made the Everton number one jersey his own – ending Neville Southall's 18-year association with the club.

The giant 24-year-old keeper arrived at Goodison Park last November, a virtual unknown from Norwegian club Viking Stavanger for just £800,000. The transfer proved to be an inspired piece of business by Everton manager Howard Kendall. Myhre was one of the stars of a disappointing season for the Toffees and was rewarded when he was given an international debut by Norway manager Egil Olsen.

Myhre appeared as second-half substitute for Tottenham goalkeeper Frode Grodas in Norway's 2–0 defeat of Denmark. "I was just delighted to have at last got the call," says Myhre. "My aim had been to keep my place at Everton and do well in the Premier League and hope that would get me some recognition." He ended up earning a place in Norway's World Cup squad which, given his position (a completely unknown figure just six months previously), was quite an achievement.

Michael Ball

There weren't many good points about Everton last season, but teenager Michael Ball was one of the them. The youngster performed so well at left-back that manager Howard Kendall felt confident enough about selling England international Andy Hinchcliffe to Sheffield Wednesday.

Kendall said: "The fact that Ball was emerging was a key factor in the decision to sell Andy because his breakthrough meant we could spend the money to strengthen other areas."

Hinchcliffe is a big Ball fan and understood why Everton sold him: "I saw that Ball was going to be a good player and I could see Howard's point of view over the financial side of the deal.

"I think Michael has got to be given time to develop, but he has got everything you could possibly need. He can play in several positions – wing-back, left-back and centre-half as well as in midfield – and that is great for a manager.

"I could see on a football level the reasons why I was going to move on. Ball was a very good prospect who would mature in the team and go on and do wonders. As long as he develops and gains more and more experience against the better players, everything will follow."

On the Ball: Youngster Michael has a bright future ahead of him.

Player Records

	BORN	NATIONALITY	HEIGHT	WEIGHT	APPS	GOALS	PREVIOUS TEAMS
GOALKEEPERS							
Paul Gerrard	22.1.73 Heywood	English	6-2	13-1	126	1	Oldham Ath.
Thomas Myhre	16.10.73 Sarpsborg	Norwegian	6-4	14-2	22	0	Viking Stavanger (Nor).
DEFENDERS							
Michael Ball	2.10.79 Liverpool	English	5-10	11-2	30	1	none.
Slaven Bilic	11.9.68 Croatia	Croatian	6-2	13-6	72	0	Hajduk Split (Cro), Karlsruhe (Ger), West Ham U.
Richard Dunne	21.9.79 Dublin	Irish	6-2	15-0	10	0	none.
John O'Kane	15.11.74 Nottingham	English	5-10	12-2	27	0	Manchester U, Bury.
Terry Phelan	16.3.67 Manchester	Irish	5-7	9-0	357	2	Leeds U, Swansea C, Wimbledon.
Craig Short	25.6.68 Bridlington	English	6-3	13-8	386	26	Scarborough, Notts Co, Derby Co.
Tony Thomas	12.7.71 Liverpool	English	5-11	12-5	265	12	Tranmere Rovers.
Carl Tiler	11.2.70 Sheffield	English	6-4	13-0	179	5	Sheffield U, Aston Villa, Swindon T, Nottingham F, Barnsley.
Dave Watson	20.1.61 Liverpool	English	6-0	13-7	607	34	Liverpool, Norwich C., Manchester C, Chelsea.
Danny Williamson	5.12.73 West Ham	English	5-10	11-6	79	6	Doncaster Rovers, West Ham United.
MIDFIELDERS							
Graham Allen	8.4.77 Bolton	English	6-1	11-12	6	0	none.
Gareth Farrelly	28.8.75 Dublin	Irish	6-1	12-7	34	1	Aston Villa, Rotherham.
Tony Grant	14.11.74 Liverpool	English	5-9	10-0	45	2	Swindon T.
Don Hutchison	9.7.71 Gateshead	English	6-2	11-8	146	23	Sheffield U, West Ham, Liverpool, Hartlepool.
Joe Parkinson	11.6.71 Eccles	English	6-1	13-0	239	10	Wigan Ath, Bournemouth.
Gavin McCann	10.1.78 Blackpool	English	5-11	11-0	11	0	none.
Mitch Ward	19.6.71 Sheffield	English	5-8	10-2	160	7	Sheffield U, Crewe Alexandra.
FORWARDS							
Nick Barmby	11.2.74 Hull	English	5-7	11-4	174	33	Tottenham H, Middlesbrough.
Michael Branch	18.10.78 Liverpool	English	5-9	11-0	34	3	none.
Danny Cadermateri	2.10.79 Bradford	English	5-7	11-12	25	4	none.
Duncan Ferguson	27.12.71 Stirling	Scottish	6-4	13-8	193	63	Dundee U, Rangers.
Mickael Madar	8.5.68 Paris	French	6-3	13-6	17	6	Deportivo La Coruna (Spa).
John Oster	8.12.78 Skegness	Welsh	5-10	11-9	31	1	Grimsby T.
John Spencer	11.9.70 Glasgow	Scottish	5-6	11-7	145	39	QPR, Chelsea, Morton, Rangers.

Gareth Farelly

Republic of Ireland international Gareth Farelly is the man Everton fans have to thank for keeping them in the Premier League. His goal against Coventry in the last game of last season earned Howard Kendall's side a valuable point which moved Everton out of the relegation zone – at the expense of Bolton.

Farelly joined Everton last summer after five seasons on the fringes at Aston Villa. He had moved to Villa Park from Dublin club Home Park, who are famous for producing exciting young players, but was loaned out to Rotherham in the 1994–95 season to gain valuable experience. Farelly played a number of times for his country while in

Birmingham. He took time to adapt to life on Merseyside after his move from Villa, but his goal against Coventry has now established him. Manager Kendall said: "I think Gareth has been on edge here, but he will come back with a spring in his step for scoring that goal against Coventry. I believe he has got tremendous talent and that he will be all the better for the experience he has had with us so far."

Points make prizes: Gareth Farrelly's goal against Coventry earned Everton a priceless point that kept them in the Premiership.

Leeds United

Under George Graham, Leeds United finally have regained the confidence and discipline needed to succeed at the highest level. They are back in Europe and ready to challenge for honours again.

The former Arsenal boss has taken his time to build Leeds in his own image, but he now has the players he feels can deliver success to the Yorkshire giants. "We made a lot of changes in playing personnel last season," Graham says. "With ten players coming in and to finish in the top six, there's great satisfaction in that. There was a great team spirit among the boys here throughout the season."

Graham arrived at the club in September 1996 to replace Howard Wilkinson, who had paid the price for a 4–0 home thrashing by Manchester United. Wilkinson had been at the club since October 1988 when they were languishing in the old Second Division. He had steered United back to the top

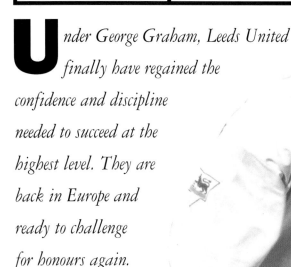

flight and within two years of promotion had won the League title, at the expense of Manchester United. It was Leeds' first championship since the 1970s, when Don Revie built a great side who won the title in 1974 and finished runners-up on no less than five occasions.

Leeds struggled after Revie left to manage England, and it was only under Wilkinson that they came close to emulating the successes of the side that featured the likes of Billy Bremner, Peter Lorimer, Allan Clarke, Norman Hunter and Jack Charlton. Wilkinson, a shrewd tactician but also a fierce disciplinarian, assembled a side in the early 1990s with an impressive midfield quartet: David Batty, Gary Speed, Gary McAllister and Gordon Strachan. Wilkinson was also responsible for introducing a Frenchman called Eric Cantona to English football, but was unable to sustain Leeds' success, either at home or in the European Cup. Cantona was sold to Manchester United, and Leeds finished 17th in the inaugural season of the Premier League. The arrival of Ghanaian striker Tony Yeboah revived Leeds' fortunes, and the signing of Swedish World Cup star Tomas Brolin promised great things. They made the 1996 Coca-Cola Cup final, but flopped at Wembley, losing 3–0 to Aston Villa.

Hassler: Jimmy Floyd tormented many an opposition defence with his direct style of play for Leeds.

LEEDS UNITED

Formed: 1919.
Nickname: United.
Stadium: Elland Road.
Capacity: 40,000.
Address: Elland Road, Leeds, LS11 0ES.
Telephone: 0113 2716037.
Clubcall: 0891 121180.
Fax: 0113 2720370.
Website: www.facarling.com/club/lu.fc
Manager: George Graham.

COLOURS

RECORDS

Record Premier League victory: 5–0 (v Tottenham, Aug 25, 1992; v Swindon May 7, 1994; v Derby, Mar 14, 1998).
Record Premier League defeat: 5–0 (v Liverpool, Jan 20, 1996).
Record transfer fee received: £3.5 million from Everton for Gary Speed, June 1996.
Record transfer fee paid: £4.5 million to Manchester U for Lee Sharpe, July 1997.
Record attendance: 57,892, v Sunderland, FA Cup fifth round replay, Mar 15, 1967.

HONOURS

League (3): 1968–69, 1973–74, 1991–92.
FA Cup (1): 1972.
League Cup (1): 1968.
Fairs Cup (2): 1969, 1971.

Stadium diagram: LOW FIELDS — Boxes — East Stand — Royal Stand — South Stand — Boxes — West Stand — ELLAND ROAD — L

FIXTURES 1998–99

Date	Opponent	H/A	Score
15 AUG	MIDDLESBROUGH	A	___ : ___
22 AUG	BLACKBURN ROVERS	H	___ : ___
29 AUG	WIMBLEDON	A	___ : ___
8 SEPT	SOUTHAMPTON	H	___ : ___
12 SEPT	EVERTON	A	___ : ___
19 SEPT	ASTON VILLA	H	___ : ___
26 SEPT	TOTTENHAM HOTSPUR	A	___ : ___
3 OCT	LEICESTER CITY	H	___ : ___
17 OCT	NOTTINGHAM FOREST	A	___ : ___
24 OCT	CHELSEA	H	___ : ___
31 OCT	DERBY COUNTY	A	___ : ___
7 NOV	SHEFFIELD WEDNESDAY	H	___ : ___
14 NOV	LIVERPOOL	A	___ : ___
21 NOV	CHARLTON ATHLETIC	H	___ : ___
28 NOV	MANCHESTER UNITED	A	___ : ___
5 DEC	WEST HAM UNITED	H	___ : ___
12 DEC	COVENTRY CITY	H	___ : ___
19 DEC	ARSENAL	A	___ : ___
26 DEC	NEWCASTLE UNITED	A	___ : ___
28 DEC	WIMBLEDON	H	___ : ___
9 JAN	BLACKBURN ROVERS	A	___ : ___
16 JAN	MIDDLESBROUGH	H	___ : ___
30 JAN	SOUTHAMPTON	A	___ : ___
6 FEB	NEWCASTLE UNITED	A	___ : ___
13 FEB	ASTON VILLA	A	___ : ___
20 FEB	EVERTON	H	___ : ___
27 FEB	LEICESTER CITY	A	___ : ___
6 MAR	TOTTENHAM HOTSPUR	H	___ : ___
13 MAR	SHEFFIELD WEDNESDAY	A	___ : ___
20 MAR	DERBY COUNTY	H	___ : ___
3 APR	NOTTINGHAM FOREST	H	___ : ___
5 APR	CHELSEA	A	___ : ___
10 APR	LIVERPOOL	H	___ : ___
17 APR	CHARLTON ATHLETIC	A	___ : ___
24 APR	MANCHESTER UNITED	H	___ : ___
1 MAY	WEST HAM UNITED	A	___ : ___
8 MAY	ARSENAL	H	___ : ___
16 MAY	COVENTRY CITY	A	___ : ___

Even before the sacking of Wilkinson, last season's priority was rebuilding. The departures from Elland Road of McAllister and Speed meant a big shake-up was on the cards and the new arrivals, goalkeeper Nigel Martyn and young midfielder Lee Bowyer, offered a useful basis for the future.

George Graham had been out of work for over a year following his worldwide suspension for allegedly receiving a transfer bung. He had received other offers, but had waited for what he thought was a big enough club. Leeds fitted the bill.

Graham's first season in charge, 1996–97, was pretty uneventful. The new manager concentrated on getting the defence sorted out – and there was precious little attacking football for the fans to enjoy. Brian Deane and Lee Sharpe finished as top scorers – with five goals each.

Last season, things improved dramatically. Graham's first signings – Gunnar Halle, Robert Molenaar and Alf-Inge Haaland – added defensive solidity. The arrival of David Hopkin added bite to midfield. And Dutch striker Jimmy Floyd Haisselbaink added goals. There were surprizes, too. Australian youngster Harry Kewell was a sensation in his first season at Elland Road and the impressive performances of Portuguese under-21 midfielder Bruno Robeiro were a big bonus.

Graham spent the summer scouring Europe for new signings – "I'll definitely be bringing in new players" was the message. Dutch striker Clyde Wijnhard was the first signing, to replace the departing Rod Wallace.

PREMIER LEAGUE TABLES

SEASON	POS.	P	W	D	L	F	A	PTS	TOP SCORER	AV. GATE
1993–94	5th	42	18	16	8	65	39	70	Wallace 17	34,493
1994–95	5th	42	20	13	9	59	38	73	Yeboah 12	32,925
1995–96	13th	38	12	7	19	40	57	43	Yeboah 12	32,580
1996–97	11th	38	11	13	14	28	38	46	Deane/Sharpe 5	32,117
1997–98	5th	38	17	8	13	57	46	59	Haisselbaink 16	34,641

Squad Info
KEY PLAYERS TO WATCH

Jimmy Floyd Hasselbaink

Few people had heard of Jimmy Floyd Hasselbaink when he was signed by Leeds manager George Graham before the start of last season. But the Dutch striker finished his first season at Leeds as the fans' Player of the Year after scoring 22 goals in all comepetitions. He even earned a call-up to the Dutch squad for the World Cup finals in France.

Hasselbaink, who was born in the former Dutch colony of Surinam, made a name for himself as top scorer in Portuguese football for Boavista. He made a slow start to his Premier League career, but even manager George Graham was surprized by his progress last season. Graham said: "Jimmy has done superbly for us. He has got more than 20 goals this season for us. He had a patchy start, but he has done superbly ever since.

"Jimmy has adapted superbly to our game both mentally and physically over the last few months. For a continental player to score so many goals in English football is a remarkable achievement.

Solid as a rock: Gunnar Halle has added solidity to the Leeds defence.

"I never set targets, neither for my club nor my players, but I think he has exceeded many people's expectations and I am absolutely delighted for him."

Graham was impressed by the partnerships established by Hasselbaink with Australian Harry Kewell and Rod Wallace. But the manager is planning to team Hasselbaink up in a Double-Dutch partnership with Clyde Wijnhard, a £1.5 million signing from Willem II. The 24-year-old Dutchman has signed a four-year contract after scoring 28 goals in 46 games in the last two seasons in Holland.

Nigel Martyn

Goalkeeper Nigel Martyn was all set to join Everton in the summer of 1996 from Crystal Palace, but had a last-minute change of heart and switched his allegiances to Elland Road, signing in a £2.25 million deal. Martyn is no stranger to million-pound deals. He became Britain's first million-pound goalkeeper when he joined Crystal Palace from Bristol Rovers in November 1989. He spent almost six seasons at Selhurst Park, where his performances earned him a call-up to the full England squad. He made his international debut against Germany in the 1993 US Cup, but was unable to dislodge David Seaman or Tim Flowers from the number one goalkeeping spot.

His move from First Division Palace in the summer of 1996 was a clear sign that Martyn wanted to be part of the England set-up again. The transfer to Leeds quickly paid off as his performances in the Premier League brought him to the attention of England coach Glenn Hoddle. Martyn got the call-up from Hoddle for the World Cup finals in France.

Unflappable under pressure and a superb shot-stopper, Martyn is now at the age (he turned 31 last August) when goalkeepers often reach their peak. Leeds manager George Graham, who says he has the best goalkeeper in the country, would certainly agree.

Second wind: Martyn has enjoyed a new lease of life with Leeds.

Gunnar Halle

When Gunnar Halle's on-off transfer from Oldham Athletic finally went through in December 1996, the Norwegian defender became George Graham's first signing as Leeds manager.

Leeds fans weren't particularly impressed by the signing of Halle for £400,000. They had

Player Records

	BORN	NATIONALITY	HEIGHT	WEIGHT	APPS	GOALS	PREVIOUS TEAMS
GOALKEEPERS							
Mark Beeney	30.12.67 Pembury	English	6-3	15-8	163	0	Gillingham, Maidstone U, Aldershot, Brighton & HA.
Nigel Martyn	11.8.66 St Austell	English	6-2	14-7	448	0	Bristol R, Crystal Palace.
DEFENDERS							
Gunnar Halle	11.8.65 Oslo	Norwegian	5-11	11-2	222	16	Lillestrom (Nor), Oldham Ath.
Ian Harte	31.7.77 Drogheda	Irish	5-9	11-8	16	0	none.
Martin Hiden	11.3.73 Verteidiger	Austrian	5-8	12-2	11	0	Rapid Vienna (Aut).
Mark Jackson	30.9.77 Leeds	English	6-1	11-13	19	0	none.
Gary Kelly	9.7.74 Drogheda	Irish	5-9	11-0	190	1	Home Farm (Ire).
Alan Maybury	8.8.78 Dublin	Irish	5-11	11-7	13	0	none.
Robert Molenaar	27.2.69 Holland	Dutch	5-10	11-5	35	3	Volendam (Hol).
Lucas Radebe	12.4.69 Johannesburg	South African	6-0	11-9	84	0	Kaiser Chiefs (SA).
David Robertson	17.10.68 Aberdeen	Scottish	5-11	12-7	344	17	Aberdeen, Rangers.
David Wetherall	14.3.71 Sheffield	English	6-3	13-11	180	12	Sheffield W.
MIDFIELDERS							
Jason Blunt	16.8.77 Penzance	English	5-8	11-7	4	0	none.
Lee Bowyer	3.1.77 London	English	5-9	9-9	105	15	Charlton Ath.
Andy Gray	15.11.77 Harrogate	English	6-1	14-6	21	1	none.
Alf-Inge Haaland	23.11.72 Stavanger	Norwegian	5-10	12-12	108	14	Young Boys (Swi), Nottingham F.
David Hopkin	21.8.70 Greenock	Scottish	5-9	10-3	166	24	Greenock Morton, Chelsea, Crystal P.
Lee Sharpe	27.5.71 Halesowen	English	6-0	12-6	235	29	Torquay U, Manchester U.
Harry Kewell	22.9.78 Smithfield, Australia	Australian	5-11	11-10	32	5	none.
FORWARDS							
Jimmy Floyd Hasselbaink	27.3.72 Surinam	Dutch	6-0	13-6	33	16	Boavista (Por).
Clyde Wijnhard	9.11.73 Holland	Dutch	5-11	12-8	75	36	Willem II, Ajax, FC Gronigen, Waalwijk
Bruno Ribeiro	22.10.75 Setubal, Portugal	Portugese	5-7	12-7	31	3	Vitoria Setubal (Por).

been expecting the arrival of centre-back John Scales from Liverpool, but Scales turned down United at the 11th hour in favour of a move south to Tottenham. So Halle it was.

Halle had joined Oldham from Lillestrom in 1991 for £280,000 and become a firm favourite at Boundary Park. He is an established international, with more than 50 caps for Norway, and a versatile defender to boot, although his preferred position is wide on the right.

Halle quickly established himself at Elland Road and, combined with other new signings such as David Robertson, Robert Molenaar and Austrian international Martin Hinden, provided the defensive solidity which allowed the attacking talents of Hasselbaink, Kewell and Ribeiro to shine.

Gary Kelly

Republic of Ireland international defender Gary Kelly is one of Leeds United's most consistent performers, having made his

debut for Leeds as a teenager in the 1991–92 season following his move from Dublin side Home Park.

Kelly demonstrated his versatility, performing in positions other than his favoured right-back when required. For the Republic of Ireland national side, Kelly plays in midfield and was captain in the friendly against Mexico last summer. The Ireland manager Mick McCarthy said: "It's a young Irish squad and Gary, with 27 caps, is the senior player. Since he came back into the side, Gary has been excellent on the right-hand side of midfield."

Kelly is in the strange position of playing in the same team as his nephew Ian Harte, three years his junior and also a full-back. But the youngster could wish for no better teacher than the man with the Emerald blood.

Part of the furniture: Kelly made his debut for Leeds way back in the 1991–92 season.

Leicester City

The Foxes

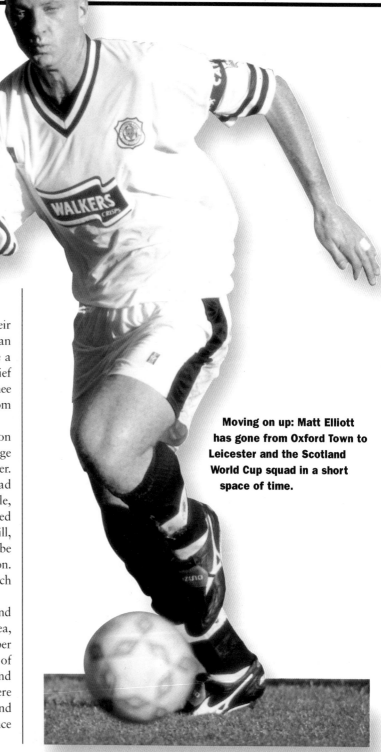

Last season was a momentous season for Leicester. They made the transition from Premier League wannabees to Premier League certainties, and competed in the UEFA Cup for the first time.

Martin O'Neill's side consolidated their success of the 1996–97 season – when they maintained their Premier League status and won the Coca-Cola League Cup – by maintaining their position in the top half of the table and putting up a decent fight in the UEFA Cup.

Under Martin O'Neill, Leicester have been moulded in their manager's own image; feisty, determined battlers with more than a little skill thrown in for good measure. That Leicester have a talented young manager who is committed to the cause is a relief for the fans. Recent experiences with Brian Little and Mark McGhee have taught the Leicester faithful to take oaths of loyalty from their manager with a pinch of salt.

Brian Little was a Leicester hero until he turned his back on the club during their first Premier League season to take charge at Aston Villa, the club where he had been a favourite as a player. Under Mark McGhee, the young Scottish manager who had done such a good job at Reading and who had replaced Little, Leicester failed to avoid the drop. In December 1995 he walked out of Filbert Street for Wolves. Leicester sent for Martin O'Neill, the former Nottingham Forest player who had taken Wycombe Wanderers from the Vauxhall Conference up to the Second Division. Under O'Neill, Leicester embarked on a late promotion push which culminated in that dramatic play-off final win at Wembley.

O'Neill was given £5 million to spend on new players, and he spent it wisely. Muzzy Izzet, who had been on loan from Chelsea, signed on a permanent basis. American international goalkeeper Kasey Keller arrived from Millwall. They joined a group of promising players that included midfielders Neil Lennon and Scott Taylor and strikers Steve Claridge and Emile Heskey. There were some old heads in the squad too, notably Garry Parker and club captain Steve Walsh, and even some Continental influence in Swedish defender Pontus Kaamark.

Moving on up: Matt Elliott has gone from Oxford Town to Leicester and the Scotland World Cup squad in a short space of time.

LEICESTER CITY

Formed: 1884.
Nickname: The Foxes.
Stadium: Filbert Street.
Capacity: 21,500.
Address: City Stadium, Filbert Street, Leicester LE3 7FL.
Telephone: 0116 2555000.
Clubcall: 0891 121185.
Fax: 0116 2470585.
Website: www.fa-carling.com/club/lc.fc
Manager: Martin O'Neill.

COLOURS

RECORDS

Record Premier League victory:
4–0 (v Derby C, April 25, 1998).
Record Premier League defeat:
4–0 (v Manchester U, April 15, 1996).
Record transfer fee received:
£3.25 million from Aston Villa for Mark Draper, July 1995.
Record transfer fee paid:
£1.6 million to Oxford U for Matt Elliott, January 1997.
Record attendance:
47,298, v Tottenham H, FA Cup fifth round, February 18, 1928.

HONOURS

League:
Runners-up, Division One, 1928–29.
FA Cup:
Runners-up 1949, 1961, 1963, 1969.
League Cup (2): 1969, 1997.

Stadium diagram: Carling Stand, Boxes, South Stand, North Stand, Boxes, East Stand, Filbert Street, Burnmoor Street.

FIXTURES 1998–99

Date	Opponent	H/A	Score
15 AUG	MANCHESTER UNITED	A	____ : ____
22 AUG	EVERTON	H	____ : ____
29 AUG	BLACKBURN ROVERS	A	____ : ____
9 SEPT	MIDDLESBROUGH	H	____ : ____
12 SEPT	ARSENAL	H	____ : ____
19 SEPT	DERBY COUNTY	A	____ : ____
26 SEPT	WIMBLEDON	H	____ : ____
3 OCT	LEEDS UNITED	A	____ : ____
17 OCT	TOTTENHAM HOTSPUR	H	____ : ____
24 OCT	ASTON VILLA	A	____ : ____
31 OCT	LIVERPOOL	H	____ : ____
7 NOV	CHARLTON ATHLETIC	A	____ : ____
14 NOV	WEST HAM UNITED	A	____ : ____
21 NOV	CHELSEA	H	____ : ____
28 NOV	COVENTRY CITY	A	____ : ____
5 DEC	SOUTHAMPTON	H	____ : ____
12 DEC	NOTTINGHAM FOREST	H	____ : ____
19 DEC	NEWCASTLE UNITED	A	____ : ____
26 DEC	SHEFFIELD WEDNESDAY	A	____ : ____
28 DEC	BLACKBURN ROVERS	H	____ : ____
9 JAN	EVERTON	A	____ : ____
16 JAN	MANCHESTER UNITED	H	____ : ____
30 JAN	MIDDLESBROUGH	A	____ : ____
6 FEB	SHEFFIELD WEDNESDAY	H	____ : ____
13 FEB	DERBY COUNTY	H	____ : ____
20 FEB	ARSENAL	A	____ : ____
27 FEB	LEEDS UNITED	H	____ : ____
6 MAR	WIMBLEDON	A	____ : ____
13 MAR	CHARLTON ATHLETIC	H	____ : ____
20 MAR	LIVERPOOL	A	____ : ____
3 APR	TOTTENHAM HOTSPUR	A	____ : ____
10 APR	WEST HAM UNITED	H	____ : ____
17 APR	CHELSEA	A	____ : ____
24 APR	COVENTRY CITY	H	____ : ____
1 MAY	SOUTHAMPTON	A	____ : ____
8 MAY	NEWCASTLE UNITED	H	____ : ____
16 MAY	NOTTINGHAM FOREST	A	____ : ____

Despite the new faces, though, players and fans knew they would be fighting for their lives in the Premier League. Good team spirit was going to be vital. Fortunately, Leicester had that in abundance. Important victories in the League were accompanied by some gutsy performances in the Cups. In the League Cup, Manchester United were beaten 2–0 on a memorable night at Filbert Street as the Foxes made it all the way to the final. In the FA Cup, victories over Southend and Norwich set up a fifth round tie at home to favourites Chelsea. A 2–2 draw at Filbert Street took the tie to Stamford Bridge and it needed a controversial penalty decision in Chelsea's favour to send the London side through to the next round. At the final whistle a fuming Martin O'Neill, unable to control his anger at the referee's decision, was forthright in his assessment of referee Mike Reid.

Then, in the League Cup final replay, played at Hillsborough after Emile Heskey had scrambled a last-minute equalizer at Wembley, Steve Claridge's goal gave the Foxes an historic win over Middlesbrough.

The Coca-Cola Cup victory sent Leicester into the UEFA Cup for the first time last season. They were handed a huge tie in the first round, against Spanish side Atletico Madrid. O'Neill's men put up a brave fight, but were ultimately undone by Spanish experience. Leicester carried on regardless in the League and showed last season why they are now one of the hardest teams in the Premier League to beat. There are few stars, but there is self-confidence, team spirit and determination in abundance.

PREMIER LEAGUE TABLES

SEASON	POS.	P	W	D	L	F	A	PTS	TOP SCORER	AV. GATE
1994–95	21st	42	6	11	25	45	80	29	Roberts 9	19,532
1996–97	9th	38	12	11	15	46	54	47	Claridge 12	20,184
1997–98	10th	38	13	14	11	51	41	53	Heskey 10	20,615

Squad Info

KEY PLAYERS TO WATCH

Matt Elliott

Central defender Matt Elliott's rise to prominence has been nothing short of sensational. Since arriving at Leicester from Oxford United two years ago in a £1.6 million transfer, Elliott has surpassed all expectations. He says: "It has been a long and winding road for me, but certainly everything has been on the up since I moved to Leicester."

Elliott did his time in the lower leagues with Oxford, Torquay, Scunthorpe and Charlton, but is now a rock of the Premier League defence at Filbert Street, and his adopted country Scotland.

He made his international debut for his country in November 1996 after being offered the chance of international football by Scotland manager Craig Brown. Elliott says: "I've taken a good deal of stick from the lads in the Leicester dressing room, mainly from Ian Marshall, but it has all been good-natured.

"I had never played in Scotland, not even on a club tour, so it was a first for me."

Leicester manager Martin O'Neill is a huge fan of the big centre-half. He says: "He is a quality player for us and he had a tremendous season last year. I love him. I would certainly put him up there with the likes of Tony Adams and Gary Pallister."

Steve Guppy

Because Leicester are not one of the wealthiest teams in the Premier League, they have to rely on picking up transfer bargains from the lower leagues.

Wing-back Steve Guppy is an example of how it is still possible to buy good players without having to spend millions on expensive foreigners. The Southampton-born wide man recently signed an extension to his contract which will keep him at Filbert Street until the year 2001. The deal was a recognition of the impact Guppy has made at Leicester since his £850,000 transfer from Port Vale. Guppy had experienced a high-profile move before, when he left his first club Wycombe Wanderers to join Kevin Keegan's Newcastle. But he spent only a few months with the Magpies before being sold to First Division Port Vale. Guppy, who came to professional football relatively late in life, was in excellent form for the Foxes last season and even earned a call-up to the England B team. Leicester manager Martin O'Neill said: "Steve has done so well for us that this new contract is simply due reward for all of his efforts."

Neil Lennon

Northern Ireland international midfielder Neil Lennon found himself in the headlines for the all the wrong reasons towards the end of last season. He was the victim of an unpleasant foul by Newcastle's Alan Shearer which the TV cameras caught, but which the FA inexplicably failed to punish.

Lennon was understandably upset by the all the furore surrounding Shearer's "kick that never was". He said: "I feel under pressure myself. It's almost as if I'm the guilty party and not the innocent party in all this. A lot of people have backed Alan Shearer's character, which is fair enough. But I keep seeing my name and picture in the papers for the wrong reasons.

"Everyone seems to have had their say, Glenn Hoddle, the Minister of Sport – I'll probably get a telegram from the Queen soon," he said. "It's becoming very wearing, because it keeps opening up again and it's been hard to focus on my football lately. It's obviously been distracting for myself

On song: Lennon has hit all the right notes since he arrived at Leicester from Crewe.

Player Records

	BORN	NATIONALITY	HEIGHT	WEIGHT	APPS	GOALS	PREVIOUS TEAMS
GOALKEEPERS							
Kasey Keller	27.1.69 Washington	American	6-1	12-7	239	0	Portland Univ (USA), Millwall.
Pegguy Arphaxad	18.5.73 France	French	6-0	13-0	6	0	Lens (Fra).
DEFENDERS							
Matt Elliott	1.11.68 Epsom	English	6-3	14-10	360	51	Charlton Ath, Torquay U, Scunthorpe U, Oxford U.
Pontus Kaamark	5.4.69 Sweden	Swedish	5-10	12-3	45	0	IFK Gothenburg (Swe).
Spencer Prior	22.4.71 Rochford	English	6--3	12-12	273	4	Southend U, Norwich C.
Steve Walsh	3.11.64 Fulwood	English	6-3	14-6	463	54	Wigan Ath.
Julian Watts	17.3.71 Sheffield	English	6-3	13-7	80	3	Rotherham U, Sheffield W, Shrewsbury T.
Theo Zagorakis	27.10.71 Greece	Greek	5-11	13-2	14	1	PAOK Salonika.
MIDFIELDERS							
Steve Guppy	29.3.69 Winchester	English	5-11	10-10	162	16	Wycombe W, Newcastle U, Port Vale.
Muzzy Izzet	31.10.74 Mile End	English	5-10	10-12	80	8	Chelsea.
Neil Lennon	25.6.71 Lurgan	Northern Irish	5-10	12-12	235	19	Manchester C, Crewe Alex.
Sam McMahon	10.2.76 Newark	English	5-10	11-6	5	1	none.
Garry Parker	7.9.65 Oxford	English	6-0	13-2	431	51	Luton, Hull C, Nottingham F, Aston Villa.
Rob Savage	18.10.74 Wrexham	Welsh	6-0	10-1	112	12	Crewe Alexandra.
Scott Taylor	28.11.70 Portsmouth	English	5-9	11-0	271	30	Reading.
Robert Ullathorne	11.10.71 Wakefield	English	5-8	11-3	100	8	Norwich C, Osasuna (Spa).
Stuart Wilson	16.9.77 Leicester	English	5-8	9-12	13	0	
FORWARDS							
Emile Heskey	11.1.78 Leicester	English	6-2	13-2	101	27	none.
Ian Marshall	20.3.66 Liverpool	English	6-1	12-12	318	84	Everton, Oldham Ath, Ipswich T.
Mark Robins	22.12.69 Ashton under Lyne	English	5-8	11-8	171	43	Manchester U, Norwich C.
Graham Fenton	22.5.74 Wallsend	English	5-10	12-10	88	16	Aston Villa, WBA, Blackburn R.
Tony Cottee	11.7.65 London	English	5-8	11-5	264	190	West Ham, Everton, Selangor (Mal).

and for the rest of the team."

The way the whole affair flared up, it was easy to forget what a good season Lennon had had for Leicester as the Foxes competed in the UEFA Cup for the first time. The red-haired midfielder remains a crucial player for club and country.

Emile Heskey

Big, burly striker Emile Heskey has all the qualities to be a striker of the highest order – pace, strength, technique and an eye for goal. No wonder people are talking about him as the best striker Leicester has produced since Gary Lineker – a comparison made even more striking by the fact that Heskey attended the same school as the former England legend.

It was a measure of Martin O'Neill's belief in Leicester-born Heskey's potential that the manager was prepared to sanction the sale of Iwan Roberts to Wolves in 1996 even though Leicester needed all the fire-power they could muster as they prepared for life back in the Premier League. The England under-21 striker, dubbed "Bruno" by his team-mates, did not let O'Neill down, scoring vital goals for Leicester, including the scrambled equaliser against Middlesbrough at Wembley in the 1997 Coca-Cola Cup final.

Although Heskey found goals harder to come by for Leicester in 1997–98, his reputation at England under–21 level won him a place in the England B squad where he made an instant impression with a goal against Chile.

YOU'LL NEVER WALK ALONE

LIVERPOOL FOOTBALL CLUB

EST. 1892

Liverpool
The Reds

This is Anfield. Three words that command respect from footballers and football fans everywhere. Although other clubs cast envious glances in the direction of Anfield and its proud and successful history, Liverpool feel the pressure to succeed more than any other club in the Premier League.

Liverpool are the most successful club in the history of English football. The roll of honours is impressive: 18 League titles (a record), runners-up on ten occasions, five FA Cups, five League Cups, two UEFA cups and four European Cups. It's some record, and current Liverpool manager Roy Evans is aware of the expectations that come with such a record.

Anfield has not celebrated a League title since 1990. That in itself is cause for serious concern. But when four of the last six championships have gone to deadly rivals Manchester United, it's easy to understand why feelings on Merseyside have reached fever pitch.

Last season was a failure for Liverpool, even though they finished third in the Premier League and reached the semi-finals of the Coca-Cola Cup and the third round of the UEFA Cup. For most clubs that sort of record would have been accepted if it had been offered before the season started. At Anfield, it was not good enough.

Liverpool were many people's favourites to win the Premier League last season. The signing of England international Paul Ince answered many of the critics who said that Roy Evans's side lacked a midfield "enforcer", a hard man who could win the ball for the more attacking players like Steve McManaman and Patrik Berger. The talented but troublesome striker Stan Collymore,

who had never really settled on Merseyside, was sold to Aston Villa. In Collymore's place came German striker Karleheinz Riedle, who had scored two goals for Borussia Dortmund in the 1997 European Champions League final, which suggested that Liverpool would not have to rely as much on Robbie Fowler for goals. And then, waiting in the wings, there was teenager Michael Owen, who had scored on his debut against Wimbledon at the end of the 1996–97 season and was being tipped for greatness.

Things did not start well for Liverpool. After a draw in their opening match at Wimbledon where, ironically, Michael Owen scored again, Leicester arrived at Anfield and walked away with a 2–1 victory. Things picked up in September and October with wins over Sheffield Wednesday, Aston Villa, Chelsea and Derby, but Manchester United and Arsenal were already showing greater consistency. The Reds stayed

Don't give an Ince: Paul Ince's never-say-die attitude has helped strengthen the Liverpool midfield.

LIVERPOOL

Formed: 1892.
Nickname: Reds or Pool.
Stadium: Anfield.
Capacity: 41,352.
Address: Anfield Road, Liverpool L4 0TH.
Telephone: 0151 263 2361.
Clubcall: 0891 121184.
Fax: 0151 260 8813.
Website: www.fa-carling.com/club.l.fc
Managers: Roy Evans, Gerard Houllier.

COLOURS

RECORDS

Record Premier League victory: 6–0 (v Manchester C, Oct 28, 1995).
Record Premier League defeat: 5–1 (v Coventry C, Dec 19, 1992).
Record transfer fee received: £7 million from Aston Villa for Stan Collymore, May 1997.
Record transfer fee paid: £8.5 million to Nottingham F for Stan Collymore, June 1995.
Record attendance: 61,905, v Wolves, FA Cup fourth round, Feb 2, 1952.

HONOURS

League (18): 1900–01, 1905–06, 1921–22, 1922–23, 1946–47, 1963–64, 1965–66, 1972–73, 1975–76, 1976–77, 1978–79, 1979–80, 1981–82, 1982–83, 1983–84, 1985–86, 1987–88, 1989–90.
FA Cup (5): 1965, 1974, 1986, 1989, 1992.
League Cup (5): 1981, 1982, 1983, 1984, 1995.
European Cup (4): 1977, 1978, 1981, 1984.
UEFA Cup (2): 1973, 1976.
European Super Cup: 1977.

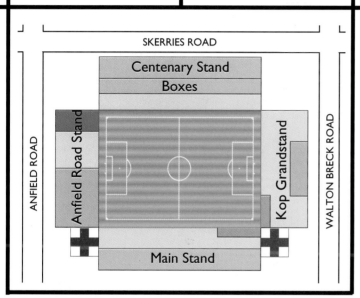

SKERRIES ROAD

Centenary Stand
Boxes
Anfield Road Stand
ANFIELD ROAD
Kop Grandstand
WALTON BRECK ROAD
Main Stand

FIXTURES 1998–99

Date	Opponent	H/A	Score
15 AUG	SOUTHAMPTON	H	____ : ____
22 AUG	ARSENAL	H	____ : ____
29 AUG	NEWCASTLE UNITED	A	____ : ____
9 SEPT	COVENTRY CITY	H	____ : ____
12 SEPT	WEST HAM UNITED	A	____ : ____
19 SEPT	CHARLTON ATHLETIC	H	____ : ____
26 SEPT	MANCHESTER UNITED	A	____ : ____
3 OCT	CHELSEA	H	____ : ____
17 OCT	EVERTON	A	____ : ____
24 OCT	NOTTINGHAM FOREST	H	____ : ____
31 OCT	LEICESTER CITY	A	____ : ____
7 NOV	DERBY COUNTY	H	____ : ____
14 NOV	LEEDS UNITED	H	____ : ____
21 NOV	ASTON VILLA	A	____ : ____
28 NOV	BLACKBURN ROVERS	H	____ : ____
5 DEC	TOTTENHAM HOTSPUR	A	____ : ____
12 DEC	WIMBLEDON	A	____ : ____
19 DEC	SHEFFIELD WEDNESDAY	H	____ : ____
26 DEC	MIDDLESBROUGH	A	____ : ____
28 DEC	NEWCASTLE UNITED	H	____ : ____
9 JAN	ARSENAL	A	____ : ____
16 JAN	SOUTHAMPTON	H	____ : ____
30 JAN	COVENTRY CITY	A	____ : ____
6 FEB	MIDDLESBROUGH	H	____ : ____
13 FEB	CHARLTON ATHLETIC	A	____ : ____
20 FEB	WEST HAM UNITED	H	____ : ____
27 FEB	CHELSEA	A	____ : ____
6 MAR	MANCHESTER UNITED	H	____ : ____
13 MAR	DERBY COUNTY	A	____ : ____
20 MAR	LEICESTER CITY	H	____ : ____
3 APR	EVERTON	H	____ : ____
5 APR	NOTTINGHAM FOREST	A	____ : ____
10 APR	LEEDS UNITED	H	____ : ____
17 APR	ASTON VILLA	H	____ : ____
24 APR	BLACKBURN ROVERS	A	____ : ____
1 MAY	TOTTENHAM HOTSPUR	H	____ : ____
8 MAY	SHEFFIELD WEDNESDAY	A	____ : ____
16 MAY	WIMBLEDON	H	____ : ____

in the top six all season, but never mounted a serious challenge for the title, especially after Manchester United won 3–1 at Anfield in early December.

There were fixed fortunes in the Cups too. There was an embarrassingly early exit from the FA Cup, when Coventry won at Anfield in the third round. There was better luck in the Coca-Cola Cup, and Liverpool were unlucky to lose to Middlesbrough over two legs in the semi-final. In the UEFA Cup, Liverpool won thr Battle of Britain against Celtic in the second round, but were outdone by French side Strasbourg in the third.

Evans is aware of the pressure on him to deliver success. "We've set the standards ourselves and we've got to live up to them," he said last season. "I don't think any manager of a club this size is going to get five years without winning major trophies."

Evans is an Anfield man through and through. His playing career with Liverpool was cut short through injury in the early 1970s, but he was immediately taken on to the coaching staff by manager Bill Shankly. Under Shankly and Bob Paisley, Evans learned the ways of the Anfield boot room – and much of that philosophy holds true today. Liverpool still play a "pass and move" style and in Michael Owen they have a goalscoring forward in the great Anfield tradition of Roger Hunt, Kevin Keegan and Ian Rush.

The pressure on Evans's players grows with every season that the League title ends up somewhere other than Anfield. Second place will not suffice for Liverpool this season. This is Anfield, after all.

PREMIER LEAGUE TABLES

SEASON	POS.	P	W	D	L	F	A	PTS	TOP SCORER	AV. GATE
1993–94	8th	42	17	9	16	59	55	60	Rush 14	38,503
1994–95	4th	42	21	11	10	65	37	74	Fowler 25	34,176
1995–96	3rd	38	20	11	7	70	34	71	Fowler 28	39,553
1996–97	4th	38	19	11	8	62	37	68	Fowler 18	39,776
1997–98	3rd	38	18	11	9	68	42	65	Owen 18	40,628

Squad Info

KEY PLAYERS TO WATCH

Robbie Fowler

Striker Robbie Fowler is expected to be out of the Liverpool side until after Christmas, but says he will come back from the biggest injury setback of his career as an improved player. Fowler damaged knee ligaments in last season's Merseyside derby match against Everton but says: "I am determined to come back from this a better player. The surgeon is pleased with the way things are going and I intend to play the best football of my life when I return."

Fowler certainly knows how to make a name for himself. Born in Liverpool, he was an Everton fan as a boy, scored on his debut for Liverpool, a Coca-Cola Cup game at Fulham in September 1993, and then scored all five Liverpool goals in the return leg at Anfield. He has not stopped scoring since and surely seems destined for a glittering career at the highest level.

Before his injury, Fowler, still only 23, had finished as Liverpool's top scorer for three successive seasons and had been hailed as the best striker in Britain. He scored his first goal for the full England side in 1997 against Mexico after a prolific career with the under-21s.

Fowler's goal scoring style has been compared to the master goal-poacher, Jimmy Greaves, and there is something uncanny about the way he makes it look so easy. The comparisons with Greaves and Ian Rush, the Liverpool legend Fowler has now replaced, would be enough to knock many strikers off their stride, but goals just come naturally to Robbie Fowler.

Michael Owen

Few teenagers in the history of English football have made more of a sensational impact than 18-year-old Michael Owen. The Liverpool striker's arrival in English football last season was simply awesome. He started the campaign as just another wannabee striker and finished it as a key member of England's World Cup team after becoming the youngest player to appear for England this century and became his country's youngest-ever goalscorer with his goal against Morocco in a World Cup warm up in Casablanca. He then followed that with arguably *the* goal of the World Cup – a sensational strike against Argentina in the second round.

Owen is not short of admirers. England's 1966 World Cup hero Geoff Hurst says: "He's scored

Reasons to be cheerful: Michael Owen could be Liverpool's key.

Robbie who?: Robbie Fowler is the forgotten man of English football after a year out with injury.

Player Records

	BORN	NATIONALITY	HEIGHT	WEIGHT	APPS	GOALS	PREVIOUS TEAMS
GOALKEEPERS							
David James	1.8.70 Welwyn	English	6-5	14-2	177	0	Watford.
Tony Warner	11.5.74 Liverpool	English	6-4	13-9	0	0	none.
Brad Friedel	18.5.71 Lakewood, Ohio	American	6-4	14-4	11	0	Galatasaray (Tur), Columbus Crew (USA).
DEFENDERS							
Phil Babb	30.11.70 Lambeth	English	6-0	12-3	260	18	Millwall, Bradford C, Coventry C.
Stig Inge Bjornebye	11.12.69 Norway	Norwegian	5-10	11-9	116	2	Rosenborg (Nor).
Steve Harkness	27.8.71 Carlisle	English	5-10	11-2	125	2	Carlisle U, Huddersfield T, Southend U.
Rob Jones	5.11.71 Wrexham	English	5-8	11-0	258	2	Crewe Alex.
Bjorn Tore Kvarme	17.7.72 Trondheim	Norwegian	6-1	12-3	38	0	Elverum (Nor), Kongsvinger (Nor), Rosenborg (Nor).
Dominic Matteo	24.4.74 Dumfries	English	6-1	11-10	75	0	Sunderland.
Mark Wright	1.8.63 Dorchester	English	6-2	13-3	482	22	Oxford U, Southampton, Derby Co.
MIDFIELDERS							
Jamie Carragher	28.1.78 Liverpool	English	6-0	11-3	22	1	none.
Jamie Cassidy	21.11.77 Liverpool	English	5-9	10-7	0	0	none.
Paul Ince	21.10.67 Ilford	English	5-10	12-2	304	43	West Ham, Manchester U, Inter (Ita).
Oyvind Leonhardsen	17.8.70 Norway	Norwegian	5-10	11-13	104	18	Rosenborg (Nor), Wimbledon.
Jason McAteer	18.6.71 Birkenhead	English	5-11	11-10	201	11	Bolton W.
Steve McManaman	11.2.72 Liverpool	English	6-0	10-6	244	42	none.
Danny Murphy	18.3.77 Chester	English	5-9	10-8	16	0	Crewe A.
Jamie Redknapp	25.6.73 Barton on Sea	English	6-0	12-10	190	19	Bournemouth.
Michael Thomas	24.8.67 Lambeth	English	5-9	12-6	288	33	Arsenal, Portsmouth.
David Thompson	12.9.77 Liverpool	English	5-7	10-0	6	1	none.
FORWARDS							
Patrik Berger	10.11.73 Czech Rep	Czech	6-1	12-10	45	9	Slavia Prague (Cze), Sparta Prague (Cze), Borussia Dortmund (Ger).
Sean Dundee	7.12.72 South Africa	German	5-11	11-5	0	0	Karlsruhe (Ger).
Robbie Fowler	9.4.75 Liverpool	English	5-11	11-10	160	92	none.
Michael Owen	14.12.79 Liverpool	English	5-7	10-4	38	19	none.
Karlheinz Reidle	16.9.65 Simmerberg-Weiler	German	6-0	11-2	25	6	Werder Bremen (Ger), Lazio (Ita), Borussia Dortmund (Ger).

goals at every level and he is easily the most consistent striker in the Premiership. His pace is electric and he frightens defenders." And Peter Shilton, England's most-capped international adds: "He reminds me very much of Gary Lineker and he could be just as successful. He's got pace that frightens keepers and is also a great finisher."

The young striker had been scoring goals at such a prolific rate in Liverpool's youth and reserve sides that manager Roy Evans was under pressure to introduce him to first-team action. Evans bowed to the inevitable with two games of the the 1996–97 season to go. With Fowler suspended, Owen was given his chance against Wimbledon at Selhurst Park. The youngster made a dramatic impact, scoring his first League goal, with a coolly taken finish. He has been in the spotlight ever since.

Sean Dundee

Stand aside Robbie Fowler, Sean "Crocodile" Dundee is in town

and determined to prove his worth after his £2-million transfer from German club Karlsruhe.

Liverpool manager Roy Evans moved quickly to sign 25-year-old Dundee after he learned that Fowler's knee injury would keep him out until after Christmas.

Dundee has a big point to prove with Liverpool. The South African-born striker burst onto the scene two years ago and could do no wrong for Karlsruhe. His goals even brought him to the attentions of German national coach Berti Vogts. Dundee took German nationality as commentators in Germany predicted he would eventually inherit Jürgen Klinsmann's role as chief goalscorer in the German national side. But last season, things went horribly wrong. He had missed Euro 96 through injury, and scored only three times as Karlsruhe's miserable season ended in relegation.

If he can put his recent troubles behind him, Liverpool could just have another striking sensation on their hands.

Manchester United

The Red Devils

On the charge: Ryan Giggs will provide the main focus for the Reds this season.

Under manager Alex Ferguson, Manchester United have become the undisputed heavy-weight champions of the Premier League. They may have missed out on last season's title to Arsenal, but the feeling at Old Trafford is that the Premier League trophy is only on loan to Highbury.

Despite the amazing success of recent seasons, it's easy to forget that Ferguson was nearly forced out of Old Trafford in 1990. Only a late Mark Robins goal against Nottingham Forest kept United in the FA Cup third round. Later that year, Lee Martin scored the winner as United beat Crystal Palace at Wembley to secure Ferguson's first trophy.

While many fans turned against Fergie, Bobby Charlton and the other United directors did not. They knew something that few were aware of – that Ferguson was completely overhauling the youth team at Old Trafford, sowing the seeds of future success. In 1992, two years after the FA Cup triumph and a year after winning the European Cup-winners' Cup in Rotterdam, United won the FA Youth Cup. Ryan Giggs, already a first-team regular at the age of 17, turned out for the winning side, which also contained David Beckham, Nicky Butt and Gary Neville.

Those players now form the backbone of the United first team which has won so much in such a short space of time. Ferguson is keen to credit his home-grown youngsters, notably David Beckham, and he believes the best is yet to come from them. "We are still a young club," he says. "The players are still learning and have still got their hunger. With that hunger you can achieve things."

For all the League and Cup triumphs, one prize still eludes Ferguson's United – the European Cup. United's finest hour came in 1968, when they beat Benfica at Wembley in the European Cup final. It was a personal triumph for manager Matt Busby, a survivor of the 1958 Munich air disaster. Busby remains the most successful manager in United's history. Ferguson is not far behind, with four Leagues, three Cups (including two Doubles) and the European Cup-winners' Cup, but until he guides United to the European Cup, comparisons are pointless. For the last two seasons, United have come mighty close. In 1997, they lost to eventual winners Borussia Dortmund in the semi-finals. Last season, after being tipped as one of the favourites, United were

MANCHESTER UTD

Formed: 1878.
Nickname: The Red Devils.
Stadium: Old Trafford.
Capacity: 55,500.
Address: Sir Matt Busby Way,
Old Trafford, Manchester,
M16 0RA.
Telephone: 0161 872 1661.
0161 930 1968.
Clubcall: 0891 121161.
Fax: 0161 876 5502.
Website: www.fa-carling/club/com/mu.fc
Manager: Alex Ferguson.

COLOURS

RECORDS

Record Premier League victory:
9–0 (v Ipswich T, Mar 4, 1995).
Record Premier League defeat:
5–0 (v Newcastle U, Oct 20, 1996).
Record transfer fee received:
£7 million from Internazionale for
Paul Ince, June 1995.
Record transfer fee paid:
£10.75 million to PSV Eindhoven for
Jaap Stam, May 1998.
Record attendance:
70,504, v Aston Villa, Division One,
Dec 27, 1920.

HONOURS

League (11):
1907–08, 1910–11, 1951–52, 1955–56,
1956–57, 1964–65, 1966–67,
1992–93, 1993–94, 1995–96, 1996–97.
FA Cup (9):
1909, 1948, 1963, 1977, 1983, 1985,
1990, 1994, 1996.
League Cup (1): 1992.
European Cup (1): 1968.
European Cup-winners' Cup (1):
1991.

UNITED ROAD

North Stand

STRETFORD END | West Stand | East Stand | SIR MATT BUSBY WAY

South Stand

FIXTURES 1998–99

Date	Opponent	H/A	Score
15 AUG	LEICESTER CITY	H	___ : ___
22 AUG	WEST HAM UNITED	A	___ : ___
8 SEPT	CHARLTON ATHLETIC	A	___ : ___
12 SEPT	COVENTRY CITY	H	___ : ___
19 SEPT	ARSENAL	A	___ : ___
23 SEPT	CHELSEA	H	___ : ___
26 SEPT	LIVERPOOL	H	___ : ___
3 OCT	SOUTHAMPTON	A	___ : ___
17 OCT	WIMBLEDON	H	___ : ___
24 OCT	DERBY COUNTY	A	___ : ___
31 OCT	EVERTON	A	___ : ___
7 NOV	NEWCASTLE UNITED	H	___ : ___
14 NOV	BLACKBURN ROVERS	H	___ : ___
21 NOV	SHEFFIELD WEDNESDAY	A	___ : ___
28 NOV	LEEDS UNITED	H	___ : ___
5 DEC	ASTON VILLA	A	___ : ___
12 DEC	TOTTENHAM HOTSPUR	A	___ : ___
19 DEC	MIDDLESBROUGH	H	___ : ___
26 DEC	NOTTINGHAM FOREST	H	___ : ___
28 DEC	CHELSEA	A	___ : ___
9 JAN	WEST HAM UNITED	H	___ : ___
16 JAN	LEICESTER CITY	A	___ : ___
30 JAN	CHARLTON ATHLETIC	H	___ : ___
6 FEB	NOTTINGHAM FOREST	A	___ : ___
13 FEB	ARSENAL	H	___ : ___
20 FEB	COVENTRY CITY	A	___ : ___
27 FEB	SOUTHAMPTON	H	___ : ___
6 MAR	LIVERPOOL	A	___ : ___
13 MAR	NEWCASTLE UNITED	A	___ : ___
20 MAR	LIVERPOOL	A	___ : ___
3 APR	WIMBLEDON	A	___ : ___
5 APR	DERBY COUNTY	H	___ : ___
10 APR	BLACKBURN ROVERS	A	___ : ___
17 APR	SHEFFIELD WEDNESDAY	H	___ : ___
24 APR	LEEDS UNITED	A	___ : ___
1 MAY	ASTON VILLA	H	___ : ___
8 MAY	MIDDLESBROUGH	A	___ : ___
16 MAY	TOTTENHAMM HOTSPUR	H	___ : ___

---

unexpectedly beaten by Monaco in the quarter-finals after they had topped their opening round group, ahead of Italian champions Juventus.

The defeat by Monaco seemed to knock the stuffing out of United's season. They were beaten by Arsenal at Old Trafford in the League and did not have enough in the final straight to overhaul the eventual Double winners.

The biggest criticism of United last season was that the board of directors did not spend enough money on big-name players, despite the loss of Eric Cantona through retirement and captain Roy Keane through injury. United quickly rectified that before the season had even finished with the £10.75 million signing of Dutch defender Jaap Stam, a record signing for United and a world record for a defender.

Ferguson also played youngters Phil Mulryne, John Curtis, Wes Brown and Michael Clegg in the last game of the season, a 2–0 win at Barnsley – proof that there will still be space for the home-grown talent among the expensive foreign stars.

"It's disappointing for us not to have won [the Premiership]," said Ferguson. "But there's a lot of good things at the club. There's a very good structure, we've got everything in place and a formula we are happy with. We just have to get a pool of players who can stay fit all the time and then I think maybe we've got a chance this year."

PREMIER LEAGUE TABLES

SEASON	POS.	P	W	D	L	F	A	PTS	TOP SCORER	AV. GATE
1993–94	1st	42	27	11	4	80	38	92	Cantona 18	44,244
1994–95	2nd	42	26	10	6	77	28	88	Kanchelskis 14	43,681
1995–96	1st	38	25	7	6	73	35	82	Cantona 14	41,700
1996–97	1st	38	21	12	5	76	44	75	Solskjaer 18	55,081
1997–98	2nd	38	23	8	7	73	26	77	Cole 15	55,164

Grand Stam: Dutch defender Jaap Stam is Man Utd's new boy.

Jaap Stam

Alex Ferguson identified United's need for a world-class defender at the start of last season when he tried to buy Brazil's Celio Silva and Germany's Markus Babbel. Neither transfer came off, but United did land Jaap Stam last May.

Stam moved to Old Trafford in a staggering £10.75 million transfer – a world record amount for a defender, and easily beating United's previous highest transfer of £6 million for Andy Cole in January 1995.

Predictably Stam claimed that his move to Manchester was a "dream come true". He said: "It's a great feeling. As a little kid I adored Manchester United." Manager Alex Ferguson was also delighted to have signed Stam. He said: "It's a major signing for us and he's a fantastic player. We're really delighted to get him."

Stam joined United from PSV Eindhoven after coming to professional football relatively late in life. He joined Dutch Second Division side FC Zwolle aged 19 and quickly moved on to Cambuur Leeuwarden and Willem II, before moving to PSV in 1995. Stam won the Dutch League, Cup and Supercup under Dick Advocaat, now boss of Glasgow Rangers, and earned international recogi-

tion just before Euro 96, against Germany. Stam started out as a midfielder and was converted to right-back at Willem II. He made the switch to centre-back after an injury crisis at PSV.

Stam has some experience of English football. He had a trial with Sheffield Wednesday when he was with FC Zwolle. "I felt small being on the same pitch as Trevor Francis and Chris Waddle," he says. "Apparently they wanted to sign me, but I decided to stay in Holland. At that time I still lived with my parents and had never been abroad. It all came too soon."

David Beckham

With his stunning lobbed goal on the opening day of the 1996–97 season against Wimbledon, David Beckham confirmed what many at Old Trafford already knew – that he is one of the most gifted midfielders English football has produced for a long time.

Beckham has come a long way in a short space of time. A "Cockney Red" who supported United as a boy, Beckham initially found first-team opportunities hard to come by at Old

Red Devil: But Beckham needs to keep his demons in check.

Player Records

	BORN	NATIONALITY	HEIGHT	WEIGHT	APPS	GOALS	PREVIOUS TEAMS
GOALKEEPERS							
Peter Schmeichel	18.11.63 Gladsaxe	Danish	6-4	15-13	258	0	Hvidore (Den), Brondby (Den).
Raimond Van Der Gouw	24.3.63 Odenzaal	Dutch	6-5	13-0	7	0	Go Ahead Eagles (Hol), Vitesse Arnhem (Hol).
DEFENDERS							
Henning Berg	1.9.68 Eidsvoll	Norwegian	6-0	12-4	186	5	Lillestrom, Blackburn R.
Chris Casper	28.4.75 Burnley	English	6-0	11-11	18	1	Bournemouth.
Michael Clegg	3.7.77 Tameside	English	5-8	11-8	7	0	none.
John Curtis	3.9.78 Nuneaton	English	5-10	1-7	7	0	none.
Dennis Irwin	31.10.65 Cork	Irish	5-8	10-8	500	22	Leeds U, Oldham Ath.
Ronnie Johnsen	10.6.69 Norway	Norwegian	6-1	13-0	53	2	Lillestrom (Nor), Besiktas (Tur).
David May	24.6.70 Oldham	English	6-0	12-10	196	8	Blackburn R.
Gary Neville	18.2.75 Bury	English	5-10	11-11	115	1	none.
Philip Neville	21.1.77 Bury	English	5-10	11-10	74	1	none.
Jaap Stam	17.7.72 Holland	Dutch	6-2	12-6	0	0	FC Zwolle, Cambuur, Willem II, PSV Eindhoven (Hol).
Ronnie Wallwork	10.9.77 Manchester	English	5-10	12-12	1	0	none.
MIDFIELDERS							
David Beckham	2.5.75 Leytonstone	English	6-0	11-2	115	26	Preston NE.
Nicky Butt	21.5.75 Manchester	English	5-10	11-3	117	11	none.
Terry Cooke	5.8.76 Birmingham	English	5-7	9-9	14	0	Sunderland, Birmingham C.
Jordi Cruyff	9.2.74 Barcelona	Dutch	6-0	11-0	21	3	Barcelona (Spa).
Ryan Giggs	29.11.73 Cardiff	Welsh	5-11	10-7	236	50	Cobh Ramblers (Ire), Nottingham F.
Roy Keane	10.8.71 Cork	Irish	5-10	12-10	237	39	Cobh Ramblers (Ire), Nottingham F.
FORWARDS							
Andy Cole	15.10.71 Nottingham	English	5-11	11-2	230	123	Arsenal, Fulham, Bristol C, Newcastle U.
Erik Nevland	10.11.77 Norway	Norwegian	5-10	11-10	1	0	Viking Stavangar (Nor).
Paul Scholes	16.11.74 Salford	English	5-7	11-0	98	26	none.
Ole Gunnar Solskjaer	26.2.73 Norway	Norwegian	5-10	11-10	53	24	Molde (Nor).
Teddy Sheringham	2.4.66 Highams Park	English	6-0	12-5	464	192	Millwall, Nottingham F, Tottenham H.
Graeme Tomlinson	10.12.75 Keighley	English	5-9	11-7	24	6	Bradford C, Luton T.

Trafford after his elevation from United's youth team. He went on loan to Preston North End towards the end of the 1994–95 season and returned a changed man, winning a regular place in United's double-winning team of 1995–96.

The spectacular goals just kept on coming and Beckham became an integral part of England's World Cup squad. However, once in France, the 23-year-old experienced the ups and downs of the sport: omitted from the opener against Tunisia, Beckham then scored a screaming free-kick which eliminated the Colombians and set up a second-round clash with Argentina. In that match, a moment of stupidity when he lashed out after being fouled, earned him a red card. He remains not quite the finished article.

Roy Keane

Republic of Ireland midfielder Roy Keane is back after missing most of last season with a cruciate knee injury and he is ready to resume his role as the unsung hero of the United team. His drive and determination inspire his team-mates and scare the living daylights out of opponents. Keane cost United a then British record £3.75 million in the summer of 1993 when they signed him from Nottingham Forest. Since then, along with Peter Schmeichel and Gary Pallister, Keane has formed the backbone of United's League- and Cup-winning teams.

Ryan Giggs

With all the attention being paid to England players like David Beckham and Paul Scholes and the Neville brothers, it is easy to forget just what an important player Ryan Giggs is to Alex Ferguson's team. The Welsh international showed a return to some of his best form last season and rediscovered his goalscoring touch, especially against Juventus in the Champions League at Old Trafford.

Giggs seems to have been around forever, but he is still only 24. He was on the books of Manchester City as a schoolboy, but made his debut for United at the age of 17. He was the star of the United team which won the 1991 FA Youth Cup final and has since clocked up more than 200 League appearances.

The inevitable comparisons with George Best which surfaced early in Giggs' career have not hindered his progress. The emergence of other young stars in United's first team has helped to take the pressure off Giggs. We are already seeing a more mature Ryan Giggs, and the best could be yet to come.

Middlesbrough

Bryan Robson's Boro are back in the big time after a record third promotion to the Premier League – and this time they are determined to stay up.

Middlesbrough are the original see-saw merchants. They have gone up and down between the top division more times than they would care to remember. This season manager Bryan Robson will be quite happy if he stays out of the headlines. He says: "There has never been a dull moment since I took over – three Wembley Cup finals, one promotion, one relegation and now another promotion. I've got to admit that now that we are back in the Premiership I would settle for mid-table safety – it would at least make for a quieter life."

Middlesbrough have only won one major trophy – the 1994–95 Division One League championship – but their history has been far from uneventful. Formed in 1876, Boro entered the Football League in 1899 and won promotion to the First Division in 1902. They made the headlines in the 1904 when they paid the first four-figure transfer fee – £1,000 for Sunderland's Alf Common. They stayed in the top flight until 1924, but were back up again in 1927 and stayed up until 1954.

Boro were revived in the 1970s by Jack Charlton, who steered them back into the First Division and to four FA Cup quarter-finals and a League Cup semi-final. However, in the 1980s, the club fell into decline. Between 1982 and 1986 they fell from the First to the Third Division and almost went out of business. They climbed back up to the First Division, then went back down again in 1989 and only escaped relegation to the Third Division in 1990 by two points.

Things looked up under Colin Todd in 1991, but Boro lost the First Division play-off semi-finals. The next season, under Lennie Lawrence, Boro made it to last 16 of the FA Cup, the League Cup semi-finals – and were promoted to the Premier League.

Boro found it tough going in the first season of the new League. Paul Wilkinson, who had scored 24 goals in the 1991–92 promotion campaign, could only manage 14. Boro finished second from bottom and were relegated. It was not all doom and gloom, though.

Bryan Robson, who was coming to the end of a hugely successful career as a midfielder and captain of Manchester United and England, moved to Middlesbrough in the summer of 1994 to take over as player-manager. He had been impressed by Boro's plans for buying new players and the proposals for a brand new stadium. Robson brought in a host of new players, including Norwegian striker Jan-Aage Fjortoft from Swindon, whose goals in the final games of the 1994–95 season clinched promotion for Boro as champions.

The next season was a special one for Boro. They moved into their new home – the 30,000 all-seater, £13 million Riverside stadium – and brought in some big names. England forward Nick Barmby signed from Tottenham in a record £5.25 million deal, and Brazilian international midfielder Juninho shunned offers from Italy and Spain to move to the Riverside in a £4.75 million transfer. Boro meant business and they finished the season in a respectable seventh place in the Premier League, just

The future's bright: Paul Merson has put his problems behind him and is having a ball.

MIDDLESBROUGH

Formed: 1876.
Nickname: Boro.
Stadium: The Riverside.
Capacity: 30,000.
Address: Cellnet Rverside Stadium, Middlesbrough TS3 6RS.
Telephone: 01642 877700.
Fax: 01642 877840.
Website: www.fa-carling.com/club/m.fc
Manager: Bryan Robson.

COLOURS

RECORDS

Record Premier League victory:
6–1 v Derby County, 5 March, 1997.
Record Premier League defeat:
5–0 v Chelsea, 4 February, 1996.
Record transfer fee received:
£5.75 million from Everton for Nick Barmby, November 1996.
Record transfer fee paid:
£7 million to Juventus for Fabrizio Ravanelli, July 1996.
Record attendance:
53,596, Newcastle, Division One, 27 December, 1949 (Ayresome Park).

HONOURS

League: Best finish third 1913–14. Champions Division One, 1994–95.
FA Cup: Runners-up 1997.
League Cup: Runners-up 1997, 1998.

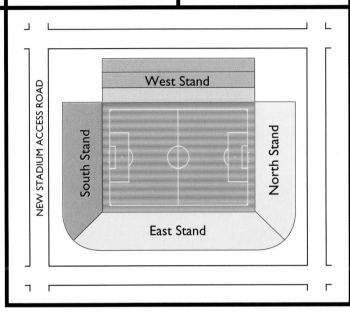

West Stand
South Stand
North Stand
East Stand
NEW STADIUM ACCESS ROAD

FIXTURES 1998–99

Date	Opponent	H/A	Score
15 AUG	LEEDS UNITED	H	____ : ____
22 AUG	ASTON VILLA	A	____ : ____
29 AUG	DERBY COUNTY	H	____ : ____
9 SEPT	LEICESTER CITY	A	____ : ____
12 SEPT	TOTTENHAM HOTSPUR	A	____ : ____
19 SEPT	EVERTON	H	____ : ____
26 SEPT	CHELSEA	A	____ : ____
3 OCT	SHEFFIELD WEDNESDAY	H	____ : ____
17 OCT	BLACKBURN ROVERS	H	____ : ____
24 OCT	WIMBLEDON	A	____ : ____
31 OCT	NOTTINGHAM FOREST	H	____ : ____
7 NOV	SOUTHAMPTON	A	____ : ____
14 NOV	CHARLTON ATHLETIC	A	____ : ____
21 NOV	COVENTRY CITY	H	____ : ____
28 NOV	ARSENAL	A	____ : ____
5 DEC	NEWCASTLE UNITED	H	____ : ____
12 DEC	WEST HAM UNITED	H	____ : ____
19 DEC	MANCHESTER UNITED	A	____ : ____
26 DEC	LIVERPOOL	H	____ : ____
28 DEC	DERBY COUNTY	A	____ : ____
9 JAN	ASTON VILLA	H	____ : ____
16 JAN	LEEDS UNITED	A	____ : ____
30 JAN	LEICESTER CITY	H	____ : ____
6 FEB	LIVERPOOL	A	____ : ____
13 FEB	EVERTON	A	____ : ____
20 FEB	TOTTENHAM HOTSPUR	H	____ : ____
27 FEB	SHEFFIELD WEDNESDAY	A	____ : ____
6 MAR	CHELSEA	H	____ : ____
13 MAR	SOUTHAMPTON	H	____ : ____
29 MAR	NOTTINGHAM FOREST	A	____ : ____
3 APR	BLACKBURN ROVERS	A	____ : ____
5 APR	WIMBLEDON	H	____ : ____
10 APR	CHARLTON ATHLETIC	H	____ : ____
17 APR	COVENTRY CITY	A	____ : ____
24 APR	ARSENAL	H	____ : ____
1 MAY	NEWCASTLE UNITED	A	____ : ____
8 MAY	MANCHESTER UNITED	H	____ : ____
16 MAY	WEST HAM UNITED	A	____ : ____

missing out on a lucrative place in Europe.

The summer of 1996 saw the arrival of Italian striker Fabrizio Ravanelli, fresh from a European Cup triumph with Juventus, and Brazilan midfielder Emerson. Their combined cost was £11 million. At times in the 1996–97 season Boro played some delightful football. They progressed in both Cup competitions – all the way to both finals – but ultimately the campaign was a terrible disappointment. Beaten by Leicester in the Coca-Cola Cup final and by Chelsea in the FA Cup final, Robson's men suffered the torment of relegation on the final day of the season.

That summer, Juninho left in a £12 million transfer to Atletico Madrid. Ravanelli and Emerson stayed for the opening games of Boro's life back in the First Division, but soon jumped ship, to Marseille and Tenerife respectively. Robson was quick to bring in reinforcements. Paul Merson arrived from Arsenal in a £5 million deal, and there were further forays into the foreign market. Italian striker Marco Branca was signed from Internazionale and he was joined by Colombian World Cup forward Hamilton Ricard.

Boro surged up the First Division table, eventually finishing in the second automatic promotion slot. They also reached the Coca-Cola Cup final again, but lost to Chelsea 2–0 in a repeat of the 1997 FA Cup final.

Robson will not mind if his players miss out on the Cups again this year's – his goal is Premier League survival.

PREMIER LEAGUE TABLES

SEASON	POS.	P	W	D	L	F	A	PTS	TOP SCORER	AV. GATE
1992–93	21st	42	11	11	20	54	75	44	Wilkinson 14	18,724
1995–96	12th	38	11	10	17	35	59	41	Barmby 7	29,283
1996–97	19th	38	10	12	16	51	60	39	Ravanelli 16	29,875

Paul Merson

Paul Merson stunned football in the summer of 1997 when he left Arsenal, the team he had been with since his schooldays, for a £5 million move north to Middlesbrough. But he answered his critics in the best possible way – on the pitch. His performances for Boro last season earned him the north-East footballer of the Year award – and even a recall to Glenn Hoddle's squad, and he scored in his first game back, against Switzerland.

Last summer, Merson committed himself to Boro for the rest of his career. He says, "This is going to be my last club. My aim is to carry on for the four years left on my contract and then finish as a player. Maybe after that I could get fixed up with something else at Boro. I love it here. I can't wait for my wife and kids to move up and join me full time." Merson planned to move his family into a luxury house at Wynyard, where his neighbours include former Newcastle chairman Sir John Hall.

The move up north has definitely been worth it for Merson and he is looking forward to life back in the Premier League. "The fans will turn around now and tell you that I've been worth the transfer fee. They might have thought after the first game against Charlton 'what have we bought here?' We probably need a couple of big-name signings to strengthen our squad. You have to start well in the Premiership. You look at the teams who eventually go down, like Barnsley, and they always seem to lose about eight of their opening ten matches."

The return to the England team was a personal triumph for Merson and capped a remarkable comeback from his much-publicized drug, alcohol and gambling addictions. "I thought my time with England had gone," he says. "I had my chances at international level and I blew them."

Merson won the League, FA Cup, League Cup and Cup-winners' Cup with Arsenal, but admits he doesn't remember much about the victories because of his drink and drug problems. "I just want to enjoy playing football now because when I stop enjoying it, I think I will pack it in," he says. "For so many years I couldn't enjoy it, so now I just want to play with a smile on my face."

Marco Branca

Bryan Robson knew what he was getting when he signed Marco Branca last season – a top-class striker with bags of experience. Branca signed for Boro after losing out in the fight for first-team places at Internazionale of Milan. Apparently, there was a little-known Brazilian called Ronaldo ahead of him in the pecking order.

The 33-year-old striker was keen to move to England after spending his entire career in Italy playing for a host of top clubs. He made his League debut back in the 1984–85 season for Calgiari and he went on to play for Udinese, Sampdoria, Fiorentina, Parma, Roma and Inter, scoring more than 70 goals in just over 300 League appreareances.

Branca was an immediate hit at 'Boro, scoring with almost his first touch of the ball against Liverpool in the Coca-Cola Cup semi-final at the Riverside Stadium.

Paul Gascoigne

Was is there left to say about Paul Gascoigne? How about that he is facing the toughest season of his career. Gazza is back in the top flight of English football for the first time in seven years and he has a big point to prove.

Glenn Hoddle's decision to leave him out of England's World Cup plans was a huge blow for Gazza and it left him angry and devastated, but determined to do well with Boro this season. Gazza joined Boro from Rangers at the tail end of last season and helped them win promotion to the Premier League and even played a part in the Coca-Cola Cup final.

Boro manager Bryan Robson is in no doubt as to what Gazza can bring to the Premier League. "He's the one player whose got that little bit of genius and that's why everybody talks about him," says Robson. "He's got that little bit of something which is different to everybody else."

Robson thinks that Gazza has a chance of playing for England again. "Paul is very upset. I said to him it is a big disappointment, but he has

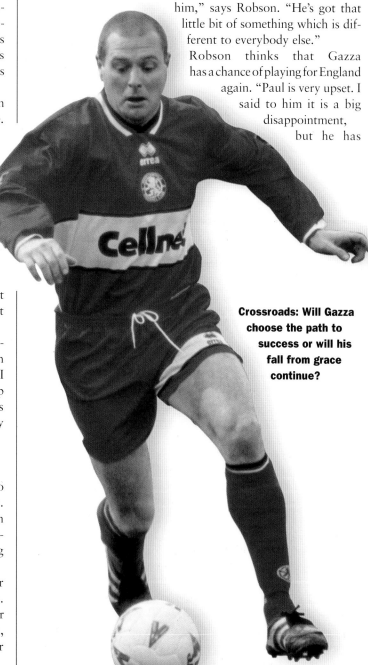

Crossroads: Will Gazza choose the path to success or will his fall from grace continue?

Player Records

	BORN	NATIONALITY	HEIGHT	WEIGHT	APPS	GOALS	PREVIOUS TEAMS
GOALKEEPERS							
Marion Beresford	2.9.69 Lincoln	English	6-1	13-5	3	0	Burnley.
Ben Roberts	22.6.75 Bishop Auckland	English	6-0	13-3	37	0	Hartlepool, Wycombe, Bradford (loans)
Mark Schwarzer	6.10.72 Sydney	Australia	6-4	13-8	55	0	Kaiserslautern, Bradford.
DEFENDERS							
Clayton Blackmore	23.9.64 Neath	Welsh	5-8	11-13	244	24	Manchester United, Bristol City (loan).
Curtis Fleming	8.10.68 Manchester	Irish	5-10	12-8	185	2	Swindon Town.
Steve Vickers	13.10.67 Bishop Auckland	English	6-2	13-2	471	18	Tranmere Rovers.
Craig Liddle	21.10.71 Chester-le-Street	English	5-11	12-5	25	0	none.
Vladimir Kinder	9.3.69 Bratislava	Czech	5-10	13-0	166	22	Slovan Bratislava.
Gianluca Festa	15.3.69 Cagliari, Sardinia	Italian	6-0	13-6	317	8	Cagliari, Fersuicis (loan) Inter, Roma (loan).
Craig Harrison	10.11.77 Gateshead	English	6-0	11-13	19	0	none.
Dean Gordon	10.2.73 Thornton Heath	English	6-0	13-4	0	0	Crystal Palace.
Gary Pallister	30.6.65 Ramsgate	English	6-4	15-0	0	0	Middlesbrough, Darlington, Man Utd.
MIDFIELDERS							
Robbie Mustoe	28.8.68 Oxford	English	5-10	11-10	330	29	Oxford United.
Phil Stamp	12.12.75 Middlesbrough	English	5-10	13-5	59	3	none.
Alan Moore	25.11.74 Dublin	Irish	5-10	11-4	114	14	none.
Paul Merson	20.3.68 London	English	6-0	13-0	375	90	Arsenal, Brentford (loan).
Andy Townsend	27.7.63 Maidstone	Irish	5-11	13-8	430	35	Southampton, Norwich, Chelsea, Aston Villa.
Neil Maddison	2.10.69 Darlington	English	5-9	11-11	182	21	Southampton.
Anthony Ormerod	31.3.79 Middlesbrough	English	5-10	11-5	18	3	none.
Paul Gascoigne	27.5.67 Gateshead	English	5-10	12-2	7	0	Newcastle, Tottenham, Lazio, Rangers
Mark Summerbell	30.10.76 Durham	English	5-10	10-3	12	0	none.
FORWARDS							
Mikkel Beck	12.5.73 Aarhus	Danish	6-2	12-9	151	47	B 1909, Fortuna Cologne.
Alun Armstrong	22.2.75 Blaydon	English	6-0	10-5	140	43	Newcastle, Stockport.
Marco Branca	4.4.64 Grosetto	Italy	5-11	12-5	19	9	Udinese, Sampdoria, Fiorentina, Parma, Roma, Inter.
Andy Campbell	18.4.69 Middlesbrough	English	6-1	13-2	10	0	none.

only just turned 31 and he has still got plenty of football left in him. He has got to enjoy his football next season and prove his fitness because the European Championships are coming up."

We have waited a long time to see Gazza back in English football. His spells in Italy and Scotland with Lazio and Rangers produced mixed results, but now he is back where he belongs.

Gary Pallister

The big man is back at 'Boro. After a spectacularly successful spell at Manchester United, Gary Pallister is back at the club where he started out.

Things were a little different when Pallister moved from Middlesbrough to Manchester United in the summer of 1989. His £2.3

million was a British record. Boro were still playing at Ayresome Park. And Manchester United had not won the League for 22 years! Pallister's move to Old Trafford coincided with United's recent run of success. Within a year of the big defender's arrival, United had won the FA Cup. A year later they lifted the European Cup-winners' Cup and then the first of four Premier League titles in five years.

Last season, injuries affected Pallister's performances on the pitch and hampered his chances of a place in the England sqaud. The arrival of Dutch international Jaap Stam reduced Pallister's chances of a first-team place – and he leapt at the chance of a return to Boro.

Back to his roots: Pallister is back at 'Boro.

Newcastle United
The Magpies

Life is never boring if you're a Newcastle United fan. Over the last 18 months on Tyneside, St James' Park regulars have witnessed the resgination of Kevin Keegan, the arrival of Kenny Dalglish, a first-ever European Champions League campaign, a flirtation with relegation and, to round it all off, an FA Cup final.

Keegan's resignation in January 1997 took everybody by surprise. He was, and still is, a hero on Tyneside. Perhaps only Keegan, a hero as a player during his short time at St James' Park in the early 1980s, was capable of reviving such a slumbering giant. Because, make no mistake, back in early 1992, when Keegan got the call to return to Tyneside, Newcastle were in serious danger of going under. They were slipping slowly but surely into the old Third Division. Attendances were down, morale was at rock bottom, and things couldn't get much worse.

Keegan performed a miracle in rescuing the Magpies from relegation, the purchase of Arsenal reject Andy Cole from Bristol City proved inspired. Next season, a combination of Keegan's leadership, chairman Sir John Hall's money and Cole's goals fired Newcastle in the Premier League as Division One champions.

Keegan had always said he did not want to be a manager, preferring life in retirement in sunny Spain. But after his instant success in management on Tyneside, he was already being talked about as a future manager of England. It seemed Keegan

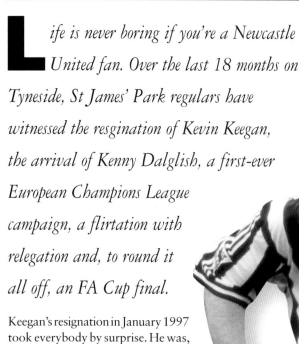

could do no wrong – he took Newcastle into the UEFA Cup in their first season back in the top flight.

The 1995–96 season promised great things at St James' Park. Andy Cole had been sold to Manchester United in a staggering £7 million deal that brought young Northern Ireland winger Keith Gillespie to St James'. The Cole deal upset a lot of people on Tyneside, but Keegan had two words for the fans outside St James' Park when he explained why he had sold his prolific striker – "trust me".

The Cole cash and a little more besides was spent in the summer of 1995 on Les Ferdinand (QPR), French winger David Ginola (from Paris St Germain), Warren Barton (Wimbledon) and Shaka Hislop (Reading). The previous two seasons had seen Newcastle challenging at the right end of the League table, but not quite good enough for the final push. This season promised to be different. And so it almost was.

With Gillespie and Ginola supplying the bullets, Ferdinand and Peter Beardsley fired Newcastle into what, by the spring, seemed like an unbeatable lead. Unfortunately Keegan let his attacking instincts get the better of him, signing Colombian striker Faustino Asprilla from Italy for another Newcastle record, £6.7 million. Asprilla's arrival seemed to knock Keegan's side out of their stride, and they finished the season in second place to Manchester United.

Perhaps that summer Keegan decided he had done all he could for the Magpies. Not even the world-record signing of Alan Shearer could prevent Keegan from calling it quits. With the twin strike force of Shearer and Ferdinand, Keegan's side notched up notable victories – the 5–0 thrashing of Manchester United, a 7–1 demolition of Tottenham – but the end was in sight.

Those who thought Kenny Dalglish's arrival

Toon idol: Alan Shearer must lead by example in the new season.

NEWCASTLE UNITED

Formed: 1881.
Nickname: The Magpies.
Stadium: St. James' Park.
Capacity: 36,610.
Address: St James' Park,
Newcastle-upon-Tyne,
NE1 4ST.
Telephone: 0191 201 8400.
Clubcall: 0891 121 190.
Fax: 0191 201 8600.
Email: nufc@dila.pipex.com.
Manager: Kenny Dalglish.

COLOURS

RECORDS

Premier League victory:
7–1 v Tottenham H, 28 December, 1996.
Premier League defeat:
5–1 v Coventry City, 19 December, 1992.
Transfer fee received:
£6,000,000 from Manchester Utd for Andy
Cole, January 1995 (plus Keith Gillespie
valued at £1,000,000).
Transfer fee paid:
£15,000,000 to Blackburn Rovers for Alan
Shearer, July 1996.
Attendance:
68,386 v Chelsea, Division One, 3 September
1930.

HONOURS

FA Premier League:
1993–94; runners-up 1995–96.
Football League: Champions 1904–05,
1906–07, 1908–09, 1926–27.
Division Two: Champions 1964–65,
1992–93 (as Division One); runners-up
1897–98, 1947–48.
FA Cup: Winners 1910, 1924, 1932,
1951, 1952, 1955; runners-up 1905, 1906,
1908, 1911, 1974, 1998.
Football League Cup:
Runners-up 1976.
Fairs (UEFA) Cup: Winners 1969.

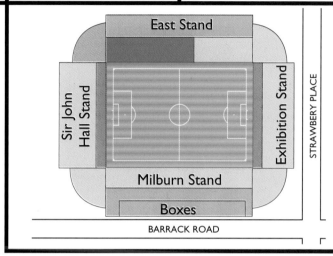

FIXTURES 1998–99

15 AUG	CHARLTON ATHLETIC	H	___	:	___
22 AUG	CHELSEA	A	___	:	___
29 AUG	LIVERPOOL	H	___	:	___
9 SEPT	ASTON VILLA	A	___	:	___
12 SEPT	SOUTHAMPTON	H	___	:	___
19 SEPT	COVENTRY CITY	A	___	:	___
26 SEPT	NOTTINGHAM FOREST	H	___	:	___
3 OCT	ARSENAL	A	___	:	___
17 OCT	DERBY COUNTY	H	___	:	___
24 OCT	TOTTENHAM HOTSPUR	A	___	:	___
31 OCT	WEST HAM UNITED	H	___	:	___
7 NOV	MANCHESTER UNITED	A	___	:	___
14 NOV	SHEFFIELD WEDNESDAY	H	___	:	___
21 NOV	EVERTON	A	___	:	___
28 NOV	WIMBLEDON	H	___	:	___
5 DEC	MIDDLESBROUGH	A	___	:	___
12 DEC	BLACKBURN ROVERS	A	___	:	___
19 DEC	LEICESTER CITY	H	___	:	___
26 DEC	LEEDS UNITED	H	___	:	___
28 DEC	LIVERPOOL	A	___	:	___
9 JAN	CHELSEA	H	___	:	___
16 JAN	CHARLTON ATHLETIC	A	___	:	___
30 JAN	ASTON VILLA	H	___	:	___
6 FEB	LEEDS UNITED	H	___	:	___
13 FEB	COVENTRY CITY	H	___	:	___
20 FEB	SOUTHAMPTON	A	___	:	___
27 FEB	ARSENAL	H	___	:	___
6 MAR	NOTTINGHAM FOREST	A	___	:	___
13 MAR	MANCHESTER UNITED	H	___	:	___
20 MAR	WEST HAM UNITED	A	___	:	___
3 APR	DERBY COUNTY	A	___	:	___
5 APR	TOTTENHAM HOTSPUR	H	___	:	___
10 APR	SHEFFIELD WEDNESDAY	A	___	:	___
17 APR	EVERTON	H	___	:	___
24 APR	WIMBLEDON	A	___	:	___
1 MAY	MIDDLESBROUGH	H	___	:	___
8 MAY	LEICESTER CITY	A	___	:	___
16 MAY	BLACKBURN ROVERS	H	___	:	___

at St James' Park would put end to the rollercoaster rides of the Keegan years were mistaken. The former Liverpool and Blackburn boss steadied the ship after Keegan left and guided United into second place in the Premier League – and a place in the European Champions League.

Just as things seemed to be going well, disaster struck. Alan Shearer was injured in a pre-season friendly tournament, and put out of action for six months – just days after Les Ferdinand had been sold to Tottenham for £6 million. There were other high-profile departures from St James' Park: David Ginola also joined Spurs, Peter Beardsley moved to Bolton and Faustino Asprilla rejoined Italian side Parma. The sales left Newcastle with money in the bank, but little flair on the pitch. The team muddled through the season, not helped by off-the-pitch allegations about club directors Freddie Sheppard and Douglas Hall. Only the return of Alan Shearer ahead of schedule in January helped Dalglish's men avoid an embarrassing defeat at the hands of non-League Stevenage in the FA Cup. Dalglish finally brought in reinforcements in the form of midfielder Gary Speed, Greek defender Nicos Dabizas and Swedish striker Andreas Andersson.

They arrived too late to prevent Newcastle getting caught up in a relegation dogfight, but the FA Cup remained a realistic target – especially after the Magpies beat Sheffield United in the semi-final at Old Trafford. In their first Wembley final for 24 years, Newcastle went down 2–0 to Arsenal, but their phenomenonly loyal fans will be back for more at St James' this season as Dalglish once again tries to steady the ship and steer Newcastle towards the promised land.

PREMIER LEAGUE TABLES

SEASON	POS.	P	W	D	L	F	A	PTS	TOP SCORER	AV. GATE
1994–95	6th	42	20	12	10	67	47	72	Beardsley 13	34,690
1995–96	2nd	38	24	6	8	68	37	78	Ferdinand 25	36,507
1996–97	4th	38	19	10	9	70	42	67	Shearer 25	36,578
1997–98	15th	38	11	11	16	35	44	44	Barnes 6	36,672

Alan Shearer

Jackie Milburn, Malcolm MacDonald, Andy Cole, Alan Shearer. The number nine shirt at Newcastle United has always been special, but for many on Tyneside Alan Shearer is the best centre-forward ever to have worn the black-and-white stripes.

When Newcastle paid Blackburn Rovers a then world record £15 million in the summer of 1996 to bring Alan Shearer to Tyneside, they knew they were buying a world-class striker. Shearer had just finished as top scorer at Euro 96 and had been wanted by some of the world's top clubs, including Barcelona and Juventus.

The move to Newcastle was a move back home to his roots for Shearer. The England striker had stood on the terraces at St James' Park as a boy and cheered on his heroes, including one Kevin Keegan. Ironically, Shearer had to go all the way down south to Southampton to make a name as a professional footballer after being rejected by Newcastle as a youngster. An horrific ankle injury sustained in a pre-season friendly last summer sidelined Shearer for much of last season, but he returned to play a crucial role in England's World Cup plans.

England coach Glenn Hoddle says he wouldn't swap the Newcastle man for any other striker. "Alan's a better all-round finisher, with his head, left and right foot, than Ronaldo, Batistuta or Klinsmann," he said. "Alan gives you that added ingredient that means you can win games. Not just the ones you deserve to win, but sometimes the ones you don't. In a tight game he can make the difference."

Hoddle adds: "As well as the goals, he's the captain and leads by example. Hard work isn't a dirty word to him. There's nothing flash about him. You're secure in your mind that he won't do anything to set alarm bells ringing. He's got that terrific mentality about him." Praise indeed.

David Batty

When Leeds United decided to sell midfielder David Batty to Blackburn Rovers, fans at Elland Road were so incensed that they displayed a banner at home games with the slogan "Batty is God" in protest at the transfer.

The move to Blackburn provoked strong feelings at Leeds, and it was easy to see why. David Batty is a passionate, committed player and fans have always been quick to respond to his dedication to the cause.

It was a wrench for Batty to leave Leeds, the team he had supported as a boy and with whom he had won the League title in 1992, but at Blackburn, under Kenny Dalglish, Batty continued to collect silverware, winning the Premier League in 1995.

Kevin Keegan was quick to recognize Batty's battling qualities in midfield and brought him to Newcastle in the spring of 1996. Batty quickly settled in at St James' where he began to be seen as more than just a midfield "enforcer". England coach Glenn Hoddle, like Terry Venables before him, recognized the

Batty-ring ram: David Batty's uncompromising style of play wears down the opposition.

Player Records

	BORN	NATIONALITY	HEIGHT	WEIGHT	APPS	GOALS	PREVIOUS TEAMS
GOALKEEPERS							
Shay Given	20.4.76 Lifford	Irish	6-1	12-10	48	0	Blackburn R, Sunderland.
Pavel Srnicek	10.3.68 Ostrava	Czech	6-2	14-7	149	0	Banik Ostrava (Cze).
DEFENDERS							
Philippe Albert	10.8.67 Bouillon	Belgian	6-3	13-0	93	8	Charleroi (Bel), Mechelen (Bel), Anderlecht (Bel).
Warren Barton	19.3.69 Stoke Newington	English	5-11	12-00	293	14	Maidstone U, Wimbledon.
Nicos Dabizas	3.8.72 Greece	Greek	6-0	12-1	11	1	Olympiakos (Gre).
Andrew Griffin	7.3.79 Billinge	English	5-9	10-10	38	0	Stoke C.
Steve Howey	26.10.71 Sunderland	English	6-1	11-12	168	6	none.
Aaron Hughes	8.11.79 Magherafelt	Irish	6-0	11-2	4	0	none.
Stuart Pearce	24.4.62 Hammersmith	English	5-10	13-0	384	57	Coventry C, Nottingham F.
Alessandro Pistone	27.7.75 Milan	Italian	5-11	12-2	28	0	Inter Milan.
Steve Watson	1.4.74 North Shields	English	6-1	12-7	201	12	none.
MIDFIELDERS							
John Barnes	7.11.63 Jamaica	English	5-11	12-07	573	155	Watford, Liverpool.
David Batty	2.12.68 Leeds	English	5-8	12-0	340	8	Leeds U, Blackburn R.
James Crawford	1.5.73 Chicago	Irish	5-11	11-6	13	0	Rotherham U.
Keith Gillespie	18.2.75 Larne	Northern Irish	5-9	11-5	123	16	Manchester U, Wigan Ath.
Des Hamilton	15.8.76 Bradford	English	5-11	12-9	100	5	Bradford C.
Temuri Ketsbaia	18.3.68 Georgia	Georgian	5-11	11-12	31	3	AEK Athens (Gre).
Robert Lee	1.2.66 West Ham	English	5-10	11-13	406	102	Charlton Ath.
Gary Speed	8.9.69 Mancot	Welsh	5-10	12-10	319	56	Leeds, Everton.
FORWARDS							
Andreas Andersson	10.4.74 Stockholm	Swedish	6-0	12-7	13	3	Tidaholms, Degerfors, Gothenburg, Milan.
Bjarni Gudjonsson	26.2.79 Iceland	Icelandic	5-10	12-0	0	0	IA Arkanes (Ice).
Alan Shearer	13.8.70 Newcastle	English	5-11	12-6	304	160	Southampton, Blackburn R.

qualities Batty brings to the national side, and the Newcastle midfielder played a significant part in the World Cup.

He brought solidity to the England midfield in the game against Argentina when England had been reduced to ten men, but when the match moved to a penalty shoot-out, he was one of two men to miss from the spot as England crashed out.

Nicos Dabizas

One of the biggest transformations that has taken place under Kenny Dalglish at St James' Park is in defence. Newcastle were, under Kevin Keegan, one of the Premier League's most exciting outfits, but they were also one of the weakest at the back.

Dalglish has changed all that, and their defensive play is now much stronger. One player who has contributed more than most to the defensive strength on Tyneside is Greek international Nicos

Dabizas. The centre-back arrived in Newcastle last February following a £2 million transfer from Olympiakos. He admits it was hard to adapt to speed and style of Premier League football, saying: "It has been difficult for me to pick up the pattern and pace of the game here, but things will get better as I gain more experience. I hope to be more positive and then be more comfortable on the ball.

"But I like the physical nature of the game here. It is more physical than in Greece and I enjoy this."

Dabizas played an important role in Newcastle's run to the FA Cup final last season – and hopes to go one stage further and win a trophy with the Toon this year. He is not short of silverware experience – he won the Greek championship with Olympiakos before the big-money move to England.

Solid: Dabizas is a rock of a defender.

Nottingham Forest

The Reds

Under Dave Bassett, Nottingham Forest bounced back from the disappointment of relegation at the first attempt. They are back in the Premier League after winning the First Division last season.

Bassett is the king of the promotion battle. He's seen success with Wimbledon, Sheffield United, Crystal Palace and now Forest. However, he will have to go a long, long way before he is talked about even in the same breath as the club's greatest manager, Brian Clough.

Under Clough, Forest scaled the heights of English and European football. They won the League in 1978 and the European Cup twice, in 1979 and 1980. Clough took charge at the City Ground in 1975 and the club's destiny was changed forever. He steered Forest out of the old Second Division in 1977 and, amazingly, to the First Division title and the League Cup a year later.

Clough was a charismatic man with a phenomenal ability to motivate his players, who at the time included England goalkeeper Peter Shilton, Tony Woodcock, Archie Gemmill and Martin O'Neill. Trevor Francis became English football's first million pound player when Clough signed him from Birmingham City in February 1979. Three months later in Munich, Francis scored the winner against Malmo as Forest won the European Cup.

Forest performed the amazing feat of retaining the European Cup when they beat Kevin Keegan's Hamburg in May 1980. Forest went on to finish third in the League on four occasions in the 1980s and also won the League Cup again, in 1989. By now Clough had completely rebuilt the side around the defensive talents of England internationals Stuart Pearce and Des Walker.

Up front, Clough's own son Nigel featured in a side which went to Wembley four years in a row. In 1989, they beat Luton Town 3–1 to win the League Cup and retained the trophy a year later by beating Oldham 1–0. In the 1991 FA Cup final, Forest lost out to Spurs, despite Paul Gascoigne's early exit. Forest were again the losers in 1992, when Manchester United beat them in the League Cup final.

The following season was Clough's last – and one Forest fans will want to forget. Forest never recovered from the sales of Des Walker to Sampdoria and Teddy Sheringham to Spurs and Clough's men spent all but seven weeks of the season in bottom place, and were relegated.

Clough was replaced at the City Ground by Frank Clark, a former player and European Cup winner in 1979 who had impressed as manager of Leyton Orient. Forest had lost Roy Keane to Manchester United and

Back on the Forest track: Steve Stone has played a large part in the club's revival.

NOTTINGHAM FORREST

Formed: 1865.
Nickname: Reds.
Stadium: The City Ground.
Capacity: 30,557.
Address: City Ground, Nottingham NG2 5FJ.
Telephone: 0115 952 6000.
Fax: 0115 952 6003.
Website: www.fa-carlingcom/club/nf.fc
Manager: Dave Bassett.

COLOURS

RECORDS

Record Premier League victory:
7–1 v Sheffield Wednesday, 1 April 1995.
Record Premier League defeat:
7–0 v Blackburn Rovers, 18 November 1995.
Record transfer fee received:
£8.5 million from Liverpool for Stan Collymore, June 1995.
Record transfer fee paid:
£4.5 million to Celtic for Pierre Van Hooijdonk, March 1997.
Record attendance:
49, 946 V Manchester United, Division One, 28 October, 1967.

HONOURS

League (1): 1977–78.
FA Cup (2): 1898, 1959.
Runners-up 1991.
League Cup (4): 1978, 1979, 1989, 1990. Runners-up 1980, 1992.
European Cup (2): 1979, 1980.

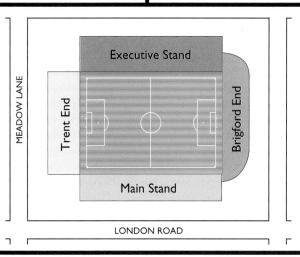

FIXTURES 1998–99

15 AUG	ARSENAL	A	____	:	____
22 AUG	COVENTRY CITY	H	____	:	____
29 AUG	SOUTHAMPTON	A	____	:	____
9 SEPT	EVERTON	H	____	:	____
12 SEPT	CHELSEA	A	____	:	____
19 SEPT	WEST HAM UNITED	H	____	:	____
26 SEPT	NEWCASTLE UNITED	A	____	:	____
3 OCT	CHARLTON ATHLETIC	H	____	:	____
17 OCT	LEEDS UNITED	H	____	:	____
24 OCT	LIVERPOOL	A	____	:	____
31 OCT	MIDDLESBROUGH	A	____	:	____
7 NOV	WIMBLEDON	H	____	:	____
14 NOV	DERBY COUNTY	H	____	:	____
21 NOV	TOTTENHAM HOTSPUR	A	____	:	____
28 NOV	ASTON VILLA	H	____	:	____
5 DEC	SHEFFIELD WEDNESDAY	A	____	:	____
12 DEC	LEICESTER CITY	A	____	:	____
19 DEC	BLACKBURN ROVERS	H	____	:	____
26 DEC	MANCHESTER UNITED	A	____	:	____
28 DEC	SOUTHAMPTON	H	____	:	____
9 JAN	COVENTRY CITY	A	____	:	____
16 JAN	ARSENAL	H	____	:	____
30 JAN	EVERTON	A	____	:	____
6 FEB	MANCHESTER UNITED	H	____	:	____
13 FEB	WEST HAM UNITED	A	____	:	____
20 FEB	CHELSEA	H	____	:	____
27 FEB	CHARLTON ATHLETIC	A	____	:	____
6 MAR	NEWCASTLE UNITED	H	____	:	____
13 MAR	WIMBLEDON	A	____	:	____
20 MAR	MIDDLESBROUGH	H	____	:	____
3 APR	LEEDS UNITED	A	____	:	____
5 APR	LIVERPOOL	H	____	:	____
10 APR	DERBY COUNTY	A	____	:	____
17 APR	TOTTENHAM HOTSPUR	H	____	:	____
24 APR	ASTON VILLA	A	____	:	____
1 MAY	SHEFFIELD WEDNESDAY	H	____	:	____
8 MAY	BLACKBURN ROVERS	A	____	:	____
16 MAY	LEICESTER CITY	H	____	:	____

Nigel Clough to Liverpool, but Clark spent the money wisely, bringing in Colin Cooper from Millwall and Stan Collymore from Southend. Collymore scored 19 goals in a campaign which ended in promotion to the Premier League.

Collymore was in even better form in the Premier League, forming a lucrative partnership with Dutch international Bryan Roy and scoring 22 League goals as Forest finished third to gain a place in the UEFA Cup. Forest were unable to hold on to Collymore for the 1995–96 season, selling him for a club record £8.5 million to Liverpool. They did well enough without Collymore in the UEFA Cup, losing to eventual winners Bayern Munich in the quarter-finals, but with new signings Kevin Campbell and Chris Bart-Williams, Forest were unable to repeat the previous season's feats, and they finished ninth.

Midfielder Steve Stone had been one of the stars of Forest's UEFA Cup run, even earning England recognition and playing for Terry Venables's side at Euro 96. However, Stone was injured early on in the 1996–97 campaign, and Forest never recovered. Clark left the City Ground and was replaced by Dave Bassett. But neither Bassett's experience at fighting the drop, nor the signing of Dutch striker Pierre Van Hooijdonk could save Forest from relegation.

Last season, Bassett quickly rallied the troops. With Stone back in action, and nearing the sort of form that caught Terry Venables's eye three years ago, Van Hoojdonk in great form and exciting young signings such as Alan Rogers and Andy Johnson to complement older campaigners like Ian Woan and Colin Cooper, Forest were promoted as champions.

PREMIER LEAGUE TABLES

SEASON	POS.	P	W	D	L	F	A	PTS	TOP SCORER	AV. GATE
1992–93	22nd	42	10	10	22	41	62	40	Clough 10	21,910
1994–95	3rd	42	22	11	9	72	43	77	Collymore 22	23,633
1995–96	9th	38	15	13	10	50	54	58	Lee/Roy/Woan 8	26,083
1996–97	20th	38	6	16	16	31	59	34	Campbell/Haarland 6	24,587

Scot Gemmill

Scot Gemmill has a lot to live up to. As the son of former Forest favourite Archie, he is following in the family tradition of starring for Forest, although his dad now works as a scout for local rivals Derby!

Scot is now in his eighth season with Forest, making 289 appearances in League and Cups. He has also become an established international with Scotland and was a regular in the Scottish campaign to qualify for the 1998 World Cup in France.

Scot's dad Archie, although playing his club football south of the border, was keen for his son to retain his Scottish roots – hence the name Scot, not Scott, and he insisted that Scot was born north of the border, in Paisley.

Steve Stone

It is easy to forget that just over two years ago, Steve Stone was a regular in the England side making nine appearances in the 1996 season. But a horrific knee injury, sustained in the fifth game of the 1996–97 season, put him out of action – and was a major factor in Forest's relegation that season. Stone had been one of the stars of Terry Venables's England team in the run-up to Euro 96 and appeared twice in the finals, as a substitute against Scotland and Spain.

But now Stone is back and ready to challenge again for international honours after the misery of having to watch England's World Cup campaign on the television. His bustling, up-'em-and-at-'em style was evident last season as Forest claimed the First Division title.

Back in action: Bart-Williams will be hoping to stay injury free.

Chris Bart-Williams

Midfielder Chris Bart-Williams returned to action last season after missing much of Forest's last Premier League campaign through injury. He played a key role in midfield as Forest bounced back to the top flight after just one season away.

Bart-Williams has long been tipped for glory. As a 16-year-old with Leyton Orient, he played for England under-21 and was signed by Sheffield Wednesday a year later. He was on the losing side in the 1992 FA and League Cup finals, as Wednesday lost both matches to Arsenal, and was a regular with Wednesday until a £2.5 million to Forest in the summer of 1995. Former Forest manager Frank Clark was Bart-Williams's mentor at Orient and he was re-united with his protégé for two Premier League campaigns. Clark did not play Bart-Williams in such an attacking role at Forest – and the midfielder had to wait nearly two seasons before scoring his first goal for Forest.

Last season, Bart-Williams started to regain the form and fitness which made him such an exciting talent as a teenager.

Like father, like son: Scot Gemmill is following in dad's footsteps

Player Records

	BORN	NATIONALITY	HEIGHT	WEIGHT	APPS	GOALS	PREVIOUS TEAMS
GOALKEEPERS							
Mark Crossley	16.6.69 Barnsley	Welsh	6-0	16-0	261	0	none.
Marco Pascolo	2.5.66 Switzerland	Swiss	6-1	12-10	3	0	Cagliari (Ita).
DEFENDERS							
Craig Armstrong	23.5.75 South Shields	English	5-11	12-10	37	0	Burnley, Bristol Rovers, Gillingham, Watford.
Thierry Bonalair	14.6.66 Paris	French	5-9	10-8	31	2	Neuchatel Xamax (Swi).
Colin Cooper	28.2.67 Durham	English	5-9	11-9	445	32	Millwall.
Steve Chettle	27.9.68 Nottingham	English	6-1	13-1	370	8	none.
Christian Edwards	23.11.75 Caerphilly	Welsh	6-3	11-9	83	1	Swansea C.
Jon Olav Hjelde	30.7.72 Levanger	Norwegian	6-2	12-5	28	1	Rosenborg (Nor).
Des Lyttle	24.9.71 Wolverhampton	English	5-8	12-13	220	4	Swansea C.
Alan Rogers	3.1.77 Liverpool	Englisjh	5-10	11-9	103	1	Tranmere R.
MIDFIELDERS							
Chris Bart-Williams	16.6.74 Sierra Leone	English	5-11	11-0	242	23	Sheffield Wed, Leyton Orient.
Scot Gemmill	2.1.71 Paisley	Scottish	5-11	11-6	225	21	none.
Andy Johnson	2.5.74 Bristol	English	6-1	12-2	100	17	Norwich C.
Steve Stone	20.8.71 Gateshead	English	5-8	12-5	168	20	none.
Geoff Thomas	5.8.64 Manchester	English	5-10	10-7	397	58	Wolves, Crystal Palace, Crewe Alexandra, Rochdale.
Ian Woan	14.12.67 Wirral	English	5-10	12-2	208	31	Runcorn.
FORWARDS							
Kevin Campbell	4.2.70 Lambeth	English	6-1	13-8	273	92	Arsenal, Leyton Orient, Leicester C.
Steve Guinan	24.12.75 Birmingham	English	6-1	13-7	3	0	none.
Paul McGregor	17.12.74 Liverpool	English	5-10	11-6	30	3	none.
Ian Moore	24.8.76 Birkenhead	English	5-11	12-2	52	10	Tranmere Rovers.
Pierre Van Hooijdonk	29.11.69 Steenbergen	Dutch	6-5	13-13	98	60	Celtic (Sco), NAC Breda (Hol).

Pierre Van Hooijdonk

Dutch international striker Pierre Van Hooijdonk was a wanted man last summer. He was linked to a number of big-money transfers as clubs tried to tempt Forest manager Dave Bassett into cashing in on his biggest asset.

Van Hooijdonk is a classy frontman with excellent control and technique despite his height (6ft 4ins) and his goalscoring record in British football is impressive. Van Hooijdonk was a big hit at Celtic after a £1 million move from Dutch side NAC Breda. He notched 46 goals in 66 League appearances in Scotland, before falling out with the Glasgow club over a new contract and deciding to move south of the border. West Ham were the favourites to sign the big Dutchman, but he opted for a move to the City Ground in March 1997 and a £4.5 million transfer which made him Forest's most expensive player. Van

Hooijdonk took his time finding his feet at Forest and could do little to prevent Forest's relegation from the Premier League. Last season he was on target 29 times in 42 League games, a record which was good enough to earn a recall to the Dutch national team and a place in their World Cup squad.

Although Van Hooijdonk started most games on the bench during Holland's World Cup campaign, he nonetheless scored a well-worked goal in the 5–0 thrashing of South Korea in the group stages, and also made an appearance in the thrilling semi-final clash with Brazil, which Holland eventually lost after a penalty shoot-out.

Despite that cruel setback, Van Hooijdonk will undoubtedly return to Forest eager to put into practice all he learned during France '98.

Target man: Van Hooijdonk's height is a target for crosses from his Forest teammates.

Sheffield Wednesday
The Owls

Sheffield Wednesday have all the qualities needed to be one of England's leading clubs: strong support, a famous stadium and top-quality players, but no silverware. Last season was again a disappointment, with managers David Pleat and Ron Atkinson both failing to make it to the new season. With the summer appointment of Danny Wilson, however, the club has chosen one of the best young managers in England as the new boss.

Handy Andy: Wednesday's dynamic England star Andy Hinchcliffe will be hoping for a better season at Hillsborough in 1998–99.

Wednesday have not won the League for 67 years, when they collected back-to-back titles in 1929 and 1930; the last time they won the FA Cup was in 1935. In fact, the only major honour Wednesday have won since the Second World War was the League Cup, in 1991. They lived a yo-yo existence in the 1950s, being relegated three times and promoted on four occasions. The 1960s were spent in Division One, but with limited success; the high point was reaching the 1966 FA Cup final, which they lost to Everton.

Things took a turn for the worse in the 1970s with relegation to Division Two and worse still, in 1975, Division Three. However, under the management of Jack Charlton and then Howard Wilkinson, Wednesday climbed back towards the big time. Promotion to the top division was secured in 1984.

Wilkinson had moved on to Leeds United in 1988 and Ron Atkinson moved in at Hillsborough. Wednesday lost their top-flight status in 1990 on goal difference, but bounced back after just one season while also winning the League Cup following a Wembley win over Atkinson's former club Manchester United.

Atkinson was succeeded in 1991 by Trevor Francis who took Wednesday to third place in the League in his first season in charge. The following year Francis's men reached two Wembley finals, but lost both to Arsenal. Francis was building an impressive side, with Chris Waddle joined by fellow England internationals Des Walker and Andy Sinton in 1994, along with Romanian Dan Petrescu and Swede Klas Ingesson. But the expensively assembled side could finish the 1994–95 season in only 13th place, and Francis was sacked.

Wednesday then turned to former Tottenham manager David Pleat, who experienced mixed

SHEFFIELD WEDS

Formed: 1905.
Nickname: The Owls.
Stadium: Hillsborough.
Capacity: 39,814.
Address: Hillsborough, Sheffield S6 1SW.
Telephone: 0114 2343122.
Clubcall: 0891 121186.
Fax: 0114 2337145.
Website: www.fa-carling.com/club/sw.fc
Manager: Danny Wilson

COLOURS

RECORDS

Record Premier League victory:
5–0 (v West Ham, Dec 18, 1993; v Ipswich, April 24, 1994; v Bolton, Nov 97).
Record Premier League defeat:
7–1 (v Nottingham F, April 1, 1995).
Record transfer fee received:
£2.65 million from Blackburn R for Paul Warhurst, Sept 1993.
Record transfer fee paid:
£3 million to Internazionale for Benito Carbone, Oct 1996.
Record attendance:
72,841, v Manchester C, FA Cup fifth round, 17 Feb, 1934.

HONOURS

League (4): 1903, 1904, 1929, 1930.
FA Cup (3): 1896, 1907, 1935.
League Cup (1): 1991.

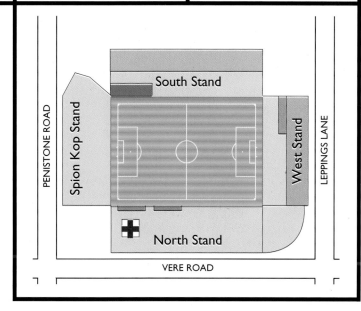

FIXTURES 1998–99

15 AUG	WEST HAM UNITED	H	____ : ____
22 AUG	TOTTENHAM HOTSPUR	A	____ : ____
29 AUG	ASTON VILLA	H	____ : ____
9 SEPT	DERBY COUNTY	A	____ : ____
12 SEPT	BLACKBURN ROVERS	H	____ : ____
19 SEPT	WIMBLEDON	A	____ : ____
26 SEPT	ARSENAL	H	____ : ____
3 OCT	MIDDLESBROUGH	A	____ : ____
17 OCT	COVENTRY CITY	A	____ : ____
24 OCT	EVERTON	H	____ : ____
31 OCT	SOUTHAMPTON	H	____ : ____
7 NOV	LEEDS UNITED	A	____ : ____
14 NOV	NEWCASTLE UNITED	A	____ : ____
21 NOV	MANCHESTER UNITED	H	____ : ____
28 NOV	CHELSEA	A	____ : ____
5 DEC	NOTTINGHAM FOREST	H	____ : ____
12 DEC	CHARLTON ATHLETIC	H	____ : ____
19 DEC	LIVERPOOL	A	____ : ____
26 DEC	LEICESTER CITY	H	____ : ____
28 DEC	ASTON VILLA	A	____ : ____
9 JAN	TOTTENHAM HOTSPUR	H	____ : ____
16 JAN	WEST HAM UNITED	A	____ : ____
30 JAN	DERBY COUNTY	H	____ : ____
6 FEB	LEICESTER CITY	A	____ : ____
13 FEB	WIMBLEDON	H	____ : ____
20 FEB	BLACKBURN ROVERS	A	____ : ____
27 FEB	MIDDLESBROUGH	H	____ : ____
6 MAR	ARSENAL	A	____ : ____
13 MAR	LEEDS UNITED	H	____ : ____
20 MAR	SOUTHAMPTON	A	____ : ____
3 APR	COVENTRY CITY	H	____ : ____
5 APR	EVERTON	A	____ : ____
10 APR	NEWCASTLE UNITED	H	____ : ____
17 APR	MANCHESTER UNITED	A	____ : ____
24 APR	CHELSEA	H	____ : ____
1 MAY	NOTTINGHAM FOREST	A	____ : ____
8 MAY	LIVERPOOL	H	____ : ____
16 MAY	CHARLTON ATHLETIC	A	____ : ____

fortunes with the foreign legion. Ingesson and Petrescu soon left and Yugoslav Darko Kovacevic and Belgian Marc Degryse barely lasted the 1995–96 season, which ended with Wednesday needing a point on the last day to be sure of avoiding relegation.

In 1996–97 a mixture of foreign flair and English grit saw Wednesday as the early leaders of the Premier League. Andy Booth, a £2.8 million capture from Huddersfield, and Italian midfielder Benito Carbone, a club record buy from Internazionale, were the outstanding performers as Pleat's side finished seventh.

Last season, Pleat strengthened the side with Italian forward Paolo Di Canio, who was joined later in the season by Norwegian international Petter Rudi and Everton defenders Andy Hinchcliffe and Earl Barrett.

By now Ron Atkinson was back in charge at Hillsbrough. Pleat had been sacked after a string of poor results, including a 6–1 thrashing by Manchester United. Everyone rallied around Atkinson as Wednesday moved into mid-table, even though memories of Atkinson's departure in 1991 for Aston Villa were still fresh in some fans' minds.

But there was no disguising that it was a poor season at Hillsborough and, as many people predicted, Atkinson's contract wasn't renewed during the summer. Instead, the club appointed Barnsley's manager Danny Wilson as the new boss. He arrives at the club with a strong reputation for man-management and good football.

PREMIER LEAGUE TABLES

SEASON	POS.	P	W	D	L	F	A	PTS	TOP SCORER	AV. GATE
1993–94	7th	42	16	16	10	76	54	64	Bright 19	27,191
1994–95	13th	42	13	12	17	49	57	51	Bright 11	26,570
1995–96	15th	38	10	10	18	48	61	40	Hirst 13	24,577
1996–97	7th	38	14	15	9	50	41	57	Booth 10	25,714
1997–98	16th	38	12	8	18	52	67	44	Di Canio 12	26,697

Andy Booth

England under-21 striker Andy Booth arrived at Hillsborough in July 1996 with a reputation for scoring goals. He had managed a goal every other game for his home-town club Huddersfield, hence the fee – a then club record £2.8 million.

Wednesday had won the race with a number of other Premier League clubs for Booth's signature and the 24-year-old forward did not disappoint, finishing the 1996–97 season as Wednesday's top scorer and weighing in with seven goals last season.

Strike-force: Andy Booth's goals will make Danny Wilson happy.

Welsh Owl: Midfielder Pembridge is a Wednesday mainstay.

Mark Pembridge

For all the foreign stars Sheffield Wednesday have had among their ranks in recent years, one of the Owls' most effective midfield performers has been British. Welsh international Mark Pembridge is now well established on the left side of Wednesday's midfield following his £900,000 move in July 1995 from Derby County.

The switch to Sheffield reunited Pembridge with his old Luton manager David Pleat, who had signed the Merthyr Tydfil-born player as a 14-year-old. Pembridge gained international recognition while at Luton, making his Wales debut in 1991 against Brazil. Within a year he had joined Derby County in a £1.3 million deal.

Benito Carbone

Italian Benito Carbone has impressed everyone at Sheffield Wednesday following his transfer from Internazionale in October 1996 for a club record £3 million.

Carbone had been surplus to requirements at Inter under English coach Roy Hodgson, now manager of Blackburn Rovers, but quickly established himself in the Wednesday first team. He announced his arrival in England to a live TV audience when he scored one of the goals of the 1996–97 season against Nottingham Forest at Hillsborough.

Carbone started his career with Torino, and played for six different clubs in eight years in Italy. The former Italian under-21 international was seen by Wednesday as a natural successor to Chris Waddle. Carbone says: "I think my best position is on the right side of midfield, but really I just want to play. It doesn't matter where."

Player Records

	BORN	NATIONALITY	HEIGHT	WEIGHT	APPS	GOALS	PREVIOUS TEAMS
GOALKEEPERS							
Matt Clarke	3.11.73 Sheffield	English	6-3	11-7	128	0	Rotherham U.
Kevin Pressman	6.11.67 Fareham	English	6-1	14-13	232	0	Stoke C.
DEFENDERS							
Peter Atherton	6.4.70 Wigan	English	5-7	13-7	404	7	Wigan Ath, Coventry C.
Earl Barrett	28.4.67 Rochdale	English	5-10	11-2	434	8	Manchester C, Chester C, Oldham, Aston Villa, Everton.
Lee Briscoe	30.9.75 Pontefract	English	5-11	11-5	46	0	none.
Andy Hinchcliffe	5.2.69 Manchester	English	5-10	13-7	192	15	Manchester C, Everton.
Jon Newsome	6.9.70 Sheffield	English	6-3	13-10	188	14	Sheffield W, Leeds U, Norwich C.
Steve Nicol	11.12.61 Irvine	Scottish	5-10	12-6	494	45	Ayr U, Liverpool, Notts Co.
Ian Nolan	9.7.70 Liverpool	Northern Irish	5-11	11-11	224	5	Tranmere R.
Goce Sedlowski	10.4.74 Macedonia	Macedonian	6-1	13-4	4	0	Pobeda Prilep, Hajduk Split (Cro).
Dejan Stefanovic	28.10.74 Yugoslavia	Yugoslav	6-2	12-10	55	4	Red Star Belgrade (Yug).
Des Walker	26.11.65 Hackney	English	5-11	11-11	484	1	Nottingham F, Sampdoria (Ita).
MIDFIELDERS							
Niclas Alexandersson	29.12.71 Vessigebro	Swedish	5-11	12-5	6	0	IFK Gothenburg (Swe).
Benito Carbone	14.8.71 Bagnara Calabra	Italian	5-6	1-7	68	15	Torino (Ita), Reggina (Ita), Casertara (Ita), Ascoli (Ita), Torino (Ita), Napoli (Ita), Internazionale (Ita).
Graham Hyde	10.11.70 Doncaster	English	5-8	11-11	172	11	none.
Jim Magilton	6.5.69 Belfast	Northern Irish	6-0	14-12	294	48	Liverpool, Oxford U, Southampton.
Scott Oakes	5.8.72 Leicester	English	5-11	11-11	197	29	Leicester C, Luton T.
Mark Pembridge	29.11.70 Merthyr Tydfil	Welsh	5-7	11-11	267	45	Luton T, Derby Co.
Petter Rudi	17.9.73 Norway	Norwegian	6-1	12-4	22	0	Molde (Nor).
Guy Whittingham	10.11.64 Evesham	English	5-10	12-0	308	122	Portsmouth, Aston Villa, Wolverhampton W.
FORWARDS							
Andy Booth	17.3.73 Huddersfield	English	6-1	12-6	181	71	Huddersfield T.
Richie Humphreys	30.11.77 Sheffield	English	5-10	11-3	41	3	none.
Paolo Di Canio	14.4.69 Italy	Italian	5-10	12-5	35	12	Celtic, Milan (Ita).

Paolo Di Canio

Italian forward Paolo Di Canio can look back on his first season with Sheffield Wednesday with a great deal of satisfaction. He made a major impact up front for the Owls, often alongside his fellow Italian Benito Carbone, and finished as Wednesday's top scorer in the League with 12 goals and two in the Cups.

"It's not been easy," he says. "But for my first season in the Premiership, I think I have done well. I've scored 14 goals, which isn't bad. I hope the fans have been happy with me and they've realized that I've always given 100 per cent when I play for Sheffield Wednesday."

This season, though, Di Canio is determined to do better. "Now that I understand the Premiership and with a stronger team I know I can give a lot more and show all of my qualities. It's terrible when you've so many good players and such good fans to be struggling at the bottom of the table," Di Canio admitted. "We had a very bad start, winning just one of our first nine matches and it put a lot of pressure on us from the media, the fans and our manager. In other leagues you can maybe get away with winning a couple and losing a couple of your first few games, but not in the Premier League."

Di Canio joined Wednesday after an impressive season for Celtic in Scotland, where he was voted Footballer of the Year.

With Danny Wilson now in charge of the Owls, Di Canio will be able to work with a manager who will make him the focus of Wednesday's attacks.

Canny Di Canio: The Italian forward is growing in confidence after finding his feet in the Premiership.

Southampton
The Saints

Southampton are living proof that small clubs can survive in the Premier League. They have been in the top division since 1978 and last season, under new manager Dave Jones, they cruised along comfortably in mid-table after putting a shaky start behind them.

Matt Black: Le Tissier's omission from the England World Cup squad cast a dark cloud over the Channel Islander. He'll be out to prove Hoddle wrong in 1999.

Southampton went against the vogue for employing foreign managers when they appointed Dave Jones in the summer of 1997. Jones is a manager of the old school. He still uses the dieticians and fitness trainers so favoured by the likes of Arsène Wenger, but Jones learned his trade in the lower reaches of the Football League. He became the Saints' fifth manager in less than four years when he took over at the Dell from Graeme Souness. "It was too good an opportuity to turn down," said Jones. "When I was in charge of Stockport I gave myself three or four years to get into the Premiership, and it has been two and a bit."

Jones first came to Southampton's attention in the 1996–97 season when his Stockport team knocked the Saints out of the Coca-Cola Cup. That season Jones steered Stockport to promotion to the First Division before taking up the Saints' offer of a permanent job.

Last season, Jones, who played as a centre-half for Everton and Coventry, made sweeping changes at the Dell. He got rid of more than half of the first-team squad. In came Kevin Davies, Paul Jones and Lee Todd from Stockport, as well as experienced campaigners such as midfielders Carlton Palmer and Kevin Richardson and stiker David Hirst.

After a difficult start, which saw Southampton in the bottom three in August and September, the Saints established themselves in mid-table. Manchester United, Liverpool, Leeds and Chelsea were all beaten as Southampton eventually finished 12th, eight points clear of the relegation zone.

It was a far cry from the previous season, when the Saints

SOUTHAMPTON

Formed: 1885.
Nickname: The Saints.
Stadium: The Dell.
Capacity: 15,000.
Address: Milton Road, Southampton SO15 2XH.
Telephone: 01703 220505.
Clubcall: 0891121178.
Fax: 01703 330360.
Website: www.fa-carling.com/club.s.fc
Manager: Dave Jones.

COLOURS

RECORDS

Record Premier League victory:
6–3 (v Manchester U, Oct 26, 1996).
Record Premier League defeat:
7–1 (v Everton, Nov 16, 1996).
Record transfer fee received:
£7.5 million from Blackburn for Kevin Davies, June 1998.
Record transfer fee paid:
£2 million to Sheffield Wednesday for David Hirst, Oct 1997.
Record attendance:
31,044, v Manchester United, Division One, 8 October, 1969.

HONOURS

League: Runners-up, 1983–84.
FA Cup (1): 1976.
League Cup: Runners-up, 1979.

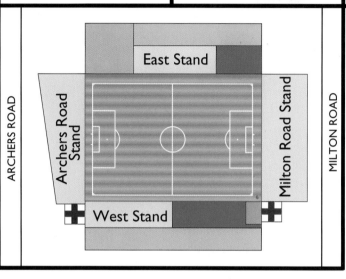

FIXTURES 1998–99

15 AUG	LIVERPOOL	H	____ : ____
22 AUG	CHARLTON ATHLETIC	A	____ : ____
29 AUG	NOTTINGHAM FOREST	H	____ : ____
8 SEPT	LEEDS UNITED	A	____ : ____
12 SEPT	NEWCASTLE UNITED	A	____ : ____
19 SEPT	TOTTENHAM HOTSPUR	H	____ : ____
26 SEPT	WEST HAM UNITED	A	____ : ____
3 OCT	MANCHESTER UNITED	H	____ : ____
17 OCT	ARSENAL	A	____ : ____
24 OCT	COVENTRY CITY	H	____ : ____
31 OCT	SHEFFIELD WEDNESDAY	A	____ : ____
7 NOV	MIDDLESBROUGH	H	____ : ____
14 NOV	ASTON VILLA	H	____ : ____
21 NOV	BLACKBURN ROVERS	A	____ : ____
28 NOV	DERBY COUNTY	H	____ : ____
5 DEC	LEICESTER CITY	A	____ : ____
12 DEC	EVERTON	A	____ : ____
19 DEC	WIMBLEDON	H	____ : ____
26 DEC	CHELSEA	H	____ : ____
28 NOV	NOTTINGHAM FOREST	A	____ : ____
9 JAN	CHARLTON ATHLETIC	H	____ : ____
16 JAN	LIVERPOOL	A	____ : ____
30 JAN	LEEDS UNITED	H	____ : ____
6 FEB	CHELSEA	A	____ : ____
13 FEB	TOTTENHAM HOTSPUR	A	____ : ____
20 FEB	NEWCASTLE UNITED	H	____ : ____
27 FEB	MANCHESTER UNITED	A	____ : ____
6 MAR	WEST HAM UNITED	H	____ : ____
13 MAR	MIDDLESBROUGH	A	____ : ____
20 MAR	SHEFFIELD WEDNESDAY	H	____ : ____
3 APR	ARSENAL	H	____ : ____
5 APR	COVENTRY CITY	A	____ : ____
10 APR	ASTON VILLA	A	____ : ____
17 APR	BLACKBURN ROVERS	H	____ : ____
24 APR	DERBY COUNTY	A	____ : ____
1 MAY	LEICESTER CITY	H	____ : ____
8 MAY	WIMBLEDON	A	____ : ____
16 MAY	EVERTON	H	____ : ____

avoided the drop on the last day. However, delight at avoiding relegation turned to frustration in the summer of 1997 following the resignation of Souness and, worse still, of Director of Football Lawrie McMenemy, the most successful manager in the club's history. It was under McMenemy that Southampton won their only major honour to date when, as Second-Division underdogs, the Saints beat Manchester United 1–0 to win the 1976 FA Cup. McMenemy steered Southampton to promotion two years later and in 1983–84 guided the club through their best-ever season. They finished a close second behind Liverpool in the League and reached the semi-finals of the FA Cup.

Under successive managers Chris Nicholl, Ian Branfoot and Alan Ball, Southampton flirted with success in the Cups, but struggled to make an impression in the top division. In the 1990s, only the goals of Alan Shearer (before his £3.3 million move to Blackburn) and Matthew Le Tissier have saved the Saints from relegation. The Channel Islander remains crucial to their future, although the club continues to scour the lower leagues for talent.

Kevin Davies was one such bargain. Signed from Stockport for £700,000 in the summer of 1997 – despite interest from a host of other Premier League clubs – the young forward scored some awesome goals in his first Premiership season as he displayed a natural aptitude for top-flight football. Although he was sold to Blackburn last summer for £7.5 million, the money from Davies's sale will enable Dave Jones to buy players to strengthen the existing squad.

PREMIER LEAGUE TABLES

SEASON	POS.	P	W	D	L	F	A	PTS	TOP SCORER	AV. GATE
1993–94	18th	42	12	7	23	49	66	43	Le Tissier 25	14,751
1994–95	10th	42	12	18	12	61	63	54	Le Tissier 19	14,685
1995–96	17th	38	9	11	18	34	52	38	Le Tissier/Shipperley 7	14,819
1996–97	16th	38	10	11	17	50	56	41	Le Tissier 13	15,105
1997–98	12th	38	14	6	18	50	55	48	Ostenstad/Le Tissier 11	15,159

Matthew Le Tissier

There have been some great players who have graced The Dell over the years – Alan Ball, Mick Channon, Kevin Keegan, Alan Shearer – but none has been more talented than Matthew Le Tissier.

No other player comes close to Le Tissier in the eyes of Saints supporters. Le Tissier's defence-splitting passes, breathtaking goals and match-winning free-kicks make him one of the most gifted players of his generation. For many it is a mystery why Le Tissier has never moved to a bigger club, but for Southampton fans it is a cause for celebration. His goals – 151 in 383 League games – are the main reason the Saints are still in the Premier League.

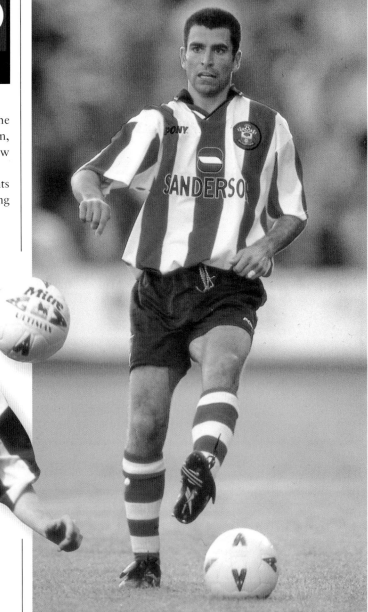

St Francis: Benali wants to put his hard man days behind him.

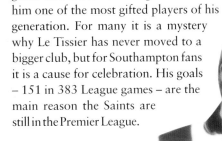

Golden Egil: The Norwegian was a member of his country's 1998 World Cup squad.

As a professional, Guernsey-born Le Tissier has always been a one-club man, but as a boy he played for Guernsey side Vale Recreation. He began his association with Southampton more than 14 years ago, signing schoolboy forms in 1984 and becoming an apprentice a year later. He made his debut in August 1986, two months before turning fully professional. Le Tissier scored six goals in 24 games during his first season, but then suffered through injuries during 1987–88 and failed to score in 19 outings. He returned to form and fitness the following year and in 1989–90, his 20 goals in 35 games earned him the PFA Young Player of the Season award.

Since then, Le Tissier's form and goals have been crucial to Southampton's survival in the top flight. 19 League goals in 1990–91, 15 in 1992–93, 25 in 1993–94, 20 in 1994–95 – and no ordinary goals either. His spectacular long-range effort against Blackburn was goal of the 1994–95 season and last season he was again top scorer.

Player Records

	BORN	NATIONALITY	HEIGHT	WEIGHT	APPS	GOALS	PREVIOUS TEAMS
GOALKEEPERS							
Paul Jones	18.4.67 Chirk	Welsh	6-3	14-0	117	0	Stockport C, Wolverhampton W.
Neil Moss	10.5.75 New Milton	English	6-2	13-3	25	0	Bournemouth.
Darryl Flahavan	28.11.78 Southampton	English	5-10	11-4	0	0	none.
DEFENDERS							
Francis Benali	30.12.68 Southampton	English	5-10	10-13	253	1	none.
John Beresford	4.9.66 Sheffield	English	5-6	10-12	378	14	Manchester C, Barnsley, Portsmouth, Newcastle U.
Richard Dryden	14.6.69 Stroud	English	6-0	13-0	227	11	Bristol R, Exeter C, Manchester C, Notts Co, Plymouth Argyle, Birmingham C, Bristol C.
Claus Lundekvam	22.2.73 Norway	Norwegian	6-1	13-6	60	0	SK Brann (Nor).
Ken Monkou	29.11.64 Surinam	Dutch	6-3	14-5	269	11	Feyenoord (Hol), Chelsea.
Duncan Spedding	7.9.77 Camberley	English	6-1	11-1	7	0	none.
MIDFIELDERS							
Steven Basham	2.12.77 Southampton	English	5-11	11-3	15	0	none.
Jason Bowen	24.12.72 Merthyr Tydfil	Welsh	5-0	9-0	175	30	Swansea, Birmingham C.
David Hughes	30.12.72 St Albans	English	5-10	11-8	30	3	none.
Matt Oakley	17.8.77 Peterborough	English	5-10	12-1	39	3	none.
Carlton Palmer	5.12.65 Rowley Regis	English	6-2	12-4	359	26	West Bromwich Albion, Sheffield W, Leeds U.
Kevin Richardson	4.12.62 Newcastle	English	5-7	11-7	415	36	Everton, Watford, Arsenal, Real Sociedad, Aston Villa, Coventry C.
Stuart Ripley	20.11.67 Middlesbrough	English	6-0	13-0	441	40	Middlesbrough, Bolton, Blackburn.
Matt Robinson	23.12.74 Exeter	English	5-11	11-2	14	0	none.
FORWARDS							
David Hirst	7.12.67 Cudworth	English	5-11	13-10	365	146	Barnsley, Sheffield W.
Stig Johansen	13.6.73 Norway	Norwegian	5-9	12-0	6	0	Bodo/Glimt (Nor)
Matt Le Tissier	14.10.68 Guernsey	English	6-1	13-8	383	151	none
Egil Ostenstad	2.10.66 Haugesund	Norwegian	6-0	12-8	57	21	Viking Stavanger (Nor).
Andy Williams	8.10.77 Bristol	English	5-10	10-10	20	0	none

As a Channel Islander, Le Tissier was eligible to play for any of the home countries – England, Wales, Scotland and Northern Ireland – as well as France. He turned down an offer to play for the French as his dream was always to play for England. He made his debut for England as a substitute against Denmark in Terry Venables's first game as England coach, but failed to make the squad for Euro 96.

Glenn Hoddle played Le Tissier against Italy in England's World Cup qualifier at Wembley, but ignored him for the World Cup finals in France.

Egil Ostenstad

Matthew Le Tissier may be the Saints' most gifted player, but Egil Ostenstad is the most successful at international level. The Norwegian striker collected the Saints' Player of the Season award after an impressive first season on the south coast. Ostenstad joined Southampton for £900,000 in October 1996 after scoring 23 goals in 24 games for Norwegian side Viking Stavanger. He made his debut against Coventry and soon established a good relationship with another new arrival from abroad, Eyal Berkovic. The two foreigners combined with devastating effect in the Saints' 6–3 humiliation of Manchester United.

Ostenstad was a busy man last summer. He was a key member of the Norwegian squad which competed in the World Cup finals in France after finishing the 1997–98 season as the Saints' joint top scorer.

Francis Benali

Hard-man defender Francis Benali may not be one of the Premier League's most gifted or glamorous players, but he is a living legend in Southampton. Benali, who has been sent off 11 times in his career, signed a new contract with the Saints last summer following a memorable season.

He was booked just three times in 22 appearances in the 1997–98 campaign while only being sent off once. He even scored the first-ever goal of his career in the 2–1 victory against Leicester. He insists he has cleaned up his act in recent months. He says: "I know I've had my problems in the past, but I tried really hard last season. I'm fed up with people thinking I'm some kind of nutter… I've only ever wanted to play for Southampton and I'm so very pleased the club have decided to offer me a new contract."

Tottenham Hotspur Spurs

Sol Man: After the departure of Gary Mabbutt, Campbell is now "Mr Spurs".

Tottenham Hotspur are one of English football's most high-profile clubs, but have won only one trophy, the 1991 FA Cup, in the past 14 years. Despite that lack of recent success, Spurs are rarely out of the headlines for long.

Last season was a torrid one for Spurs. Not only did they spend much of the campaign flirting with relegation, but they also had to put up with the sight of their great rivals Arsenal doing the League and Cup Double. Gerry Francis paid the price for poor results and quit as manager, to be replaced by the little-known Swiss coach Christian Gross. But the fans still endured another disappointing season in which Spurs' hopes were dashed by further injuries to key players.

Spurs supporters have come to expect success – and stylish football, too. The club have won the League twice, in 1951 and 1961, when the team managed by Bill Nicholson and featuring such talented players as Danny Blanchflower, John White and Dave Mackay did the League and FA Cup Double.

They retained the FA Cup a year later and then, with striker Jimmy Greaves in the ranks, they won the 1963 Cup-winners' Cup, making Spurs the first British team to win a European trophy.

Since then, Spurs' finest hours have been in the Cups. In 1967, they were FA Cup-winners again, launching the club into a successful new era. With a side that featured the likes of Pat Jennings, Mike England, Alan Gilzean and Alan Mullery, Tottenham won two League Cups (1971 and 1973) and a second European prize, the 1972 UEFA Cup.

Their Cup tradition continued in the 1980s with a side built by manager Keith Burkinshaw around the current England manager Glenn Hoddle. Foreign players were rare in England at the time, so Tottenham's signing of two World Cup winners, the Argentinians Ossie Ardiles and Ricardo Villa, made the team which won the 1981 and 1982 FA Cups a special side for many reasons.

The club fell into decline in the late 1980s, but remained headline news as a battle took place for control of Tottenham's finances, with businessman Alan Sugar eventually winning. No sooner had Terry Venables guided a side featuring Gary Lineker and Paul Gascoigne to a then-record eighth FA Cup in 1991 than everything fell apart. An acrimonious dispute with Sugar led to Venables's departure and his eventual replacement by Ossie Ardiles.

TOTTENHAM HOTSPUR

Formed: 1882.
Nickname: Spurs.
Stadium: White Hart Lane.
Capacity: 33,083.
Address: 748 High Rd, London
N17 0AP.
Telephone: 0181 365 5000.
Clubcall: 0891 335555.
Fax: 0181 365 5005.
Website: www.fa-carling.com/club/th.fc
Manager: Christian Gross.

COLOURS

RECORDS

Record Premier League victory:
5–0 (v Oldham Ath Sept 18, 1993).
Record Premier League defeat:
7–1 (v Newcastle U, Dec 28, 1996).
Record transfer fee received:
£5.5 million from Lazio for Paul
Gascoigne, May 1992.
Record transfer fee paid:
£4.5 million to Crystal Palace for Chris
Armstrong, June 1995.
Record attendance:
75,038, v Sunderland, FA Cup sixth round,
Mar 5, 1938.

HONOURS

League (2): 1951, 1961.
FA Cup (8): 1901, 1921, 1961, 1962,
1967, 1981, 1982, 1991.
League Cup (2): 1971, 1973.
European Cup-winners' Cup (1):
1963.
Fairs Cup (2): 1972, 1984.

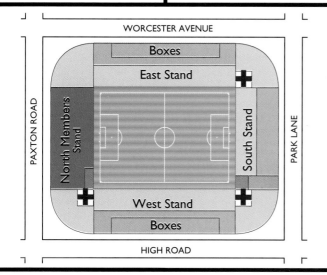

FIXTURES 1998–99

15 AUG	WIMBLEDON	A	___ : ___
22 AUG	SHEFFIELD WEDNESDAY	H	___ : ___
29 AUG	EVERTON	A	___ : ___
9 SEPT	BLACKBURN ROVERS	H	___ : ___
12 SEPT	MIDDLESBROUGH	H	___ : ___
19 SEPT	SOUTHAMPTON	A	___ : ___
26 SEPT	LEEDS UNITED	H	___ : ___
3 OCT	DERBY COUNTY	A	___ : ___
17 OCT	LEICESTER CITY	A	___ : ___
24 OCT	NEWCASTLE UNITED	H	___ : ___
31 OCT	CHARLTON ATHLETIC	H	___ : ___
7 NOV	ASTON VILLA	A	___ : ___
14 NOV	ARSENAL	A	___ : ___
21 NOV	NOTTINGHAM FOREST	H	___ : ___
28 NOV	WEST HAM UNITED	A	___ : ___
5 DEC	LIVERPOOL	H	___ : ___
12 DEC	MANCHESTER UNITED	H	___ : ___
19 DEC	CHELSEA	A	___ : ___
26 DEC	COVENTRY CITY	A	___ : ___
28 DEC	EVERTON	H	___ : ___
9 JAN	SHEFFIELD WEDNESDAY	A	___ : ___
16 JAN	WIMBLEDON	H	___ : ___
30 JAN	BLACKBURN ROVERS	A	___ : ___
6 FEB	COVENTRY CITY	H	___ : ___
13 FEB	SOUTHAMPTON	H	___ : ___
20 FEB	MIDDLESBROUGH	A	___ : ___
27 FEB	DERBY COUNTY	H	___ : ___
6 MAR	LEEDS UNITED	A	___ : ___
13 MAR	ASTON VILLA	H	___ : ___
20 MAR	CHARLTON ATHLETIC	A	___ : ___
3 APR	LEICESTER CITY	H	___ : ___
5 APR	NEWCASTLE UNITED	A	___ : ___
10 APR	ARSENAL	H	___ : ___
17 APR	NOTTINGHAM FOREST	A	___ : ___
24 APR	WEST HAM UNITED	H	___ : ___
1 MAY	LIVERPOOL	A	___ : ___
8 MAY	CHELSEA	H	___ : ___
16 MAY	MANCHESTER UNITED	A	___ : ___

Under Ardiles, the Spurs tradition of stylish attacking football continued. But not even the shock signing of German World Cup striker Jürgen Klinsmann could prevent Ardiles from getting the sack as Spurs' "famous five" attack scored goals by the bucketful, but conceded just as many.

Gerry Francis replaced the sacked Ardiles in November 1994 and adopted a more pragmatic approach. Klinsmann scored 20 League goals, but by the summer the German had left for Bayern Munich. In a matter of months Spurs also lost homesick youngster Nicky Barmby to Middlesbrough, and two other foreign stars, Romanians Gica Popescu and Ilie Dumitrescu.

In came Chris Armstrong and Ruel Fox, but injuries to key midfielder Darren Anderton hampered Spurs' progress. The signing of David Ginola and Les Ferdinand from Newcastle in the summer of 1997 raised hopes that things might improve. But the injury jinx struck again. Darren Anderton, Chris Armstrong, John Scales, Steffen Iversen and Ferdinand all missed sizeable sections of the season and Spurs spent the season in or around the relegation zone. The arrival of Christian Gross did little to ease the worries, and not even the signing on loan of former favourite Jürgen Klinsmann lifted the gloom – the German was struck by injury.

In the end Spurs secured their Premier League status on the penultimate Saturday of the season with a 6–2 win at Wimbledon, with Klinsmann scoring four goals. This season, more will be expected of White Hart Lane's well-paid stars. But with Spurs, you never know what will happen.

PREMIER LEAGUE TABLES

SEASON	POS.	P	W	D	L	F	A	PTS	TOP SCORER	AV. GATE
1993–94	15th	42	11	12	19	54	59	45	Sheringham 14	27,150
1994–95	7th	42	16	14	12	66	58	62	Klinsmann 20	27,259
1995–96	8th	38	16	13	9	50	38	61	Sheringham 16	30,510
1996–97	10th	38	13	7	18	44	51	46	Sheringham 7	31,067
1997–98	14th	38	11	11	16	44	56	44	Klinsmann 7	29,153

Squad Info
KEY PLAYERS TO WATCH

Sol Campbell

Central defender Sol Campbell was one of the best things in a poor season for Spurs last year. The England international kept things together at the back after signing a new contract which will keep him at White Hart Lane until 2001. Campbell says it was "a gut feeling" which led him to agree the new deal, despite reported interest from Manchester United and Liverpool.

A move north never seemed attractive for Londoner Sol, who is now a regular in the England side. Campbell, who has been at Spurs since the age of 14, is still only 23 and said: "Because I've been around so long people think I'm 26 or 27, but I'm not. I'll only be that age when I come out of the new contract, and that's not old these days."

Campbell first came to prominence in the 1993–94 season when injuries forced the then manager Ossie Ardiles to use the youngster as an emergency striker. Campbell was also playing as a full-back, but said at the time that his favourite position was in central midfield. However, current Spurs boss Gerry Francis was quick to spot that Campbell's qualities would be best used in central defence.

It is as a centre-back that Campbell became established as an England international. Terry Venables called Campbell into the national squad for Euro 96 and current England coach Glenn Hoddle is a big fan – particularly after his barnstorming performances during the World Cup. As solid as ever in defence – he was simply awesome against Argentina – it was Campbell's counter-attacking skills that most impressed the public.

Darren Anderton

Last season, midfielder Darren Anderton made a spectacular return to prominence after a dramatic recall by England coach Glenn Hoddle in time for the World Cup finals in France. During the tournament, Anderton shrugged off some early criticism, to emerge as one of his side's most influential players. His stunning goal against Colombia securing England's place in the second round, was just reward for his hard work.

One of the Lions: Anderton returned from France with an enhanced reputation.

Anderton's Spurs' career has been blighted by injury. He had returned from injury in the late spring of 1996 to reclaim his place in the England side. But no sooner had he helped his country reach the semi-finals of Euro 96 than Anderton suffered from a recurrence of a long-term hernia injury. He made 15 appearances in the 1996–97 season, and even fewer last season – and Spurs suffered without him. But just as his England career appeared on hold, Anderton was called up for a pre-World Cup friendly against Saudi Arabia and he duly went to France in the final party of 22.

Tricky winger Anderton has never been one to grab the limelight. He reportedly burst out laughing when he heard how much the then Tottenham manager Terry Venables was going to pay for him in May 1992 – £1.75 million.

Moussa Saib

Moussa Saib is a classic Spurs player – a creative midfielder who can dazzle and delight with his skill and enterprise. The Algerian midfielder was signed by Spurs in January 1998 after captaining his country at the African Nations Cup finals in Burkina Faso. He moved to White Hart Lane in a £3.5-million transfer from Spanish club Valencia, where there had been a change in coach and Saib had been allowed to leave. The Algerian had been linked with Arsenal the previous summer, but chose to move to Spain from Auxerre in France, where he had won the French League and Cup Double and competed in the Champions League.

Christian Gross was impressed with Saib's peformances when he broke into the Spurs side last season. "He is an excellent player," said Gross. "Technically he is very good, he is a fast-thinking player and he can create chances and score goals, and he works very hard."

Player Records

	BORN	NATIONALITY	HEIGHT	WEIGHT	APPS	GOALS	PREVIOUS TEAMS
GOALKEEPERS							
Espen Baardsen	7.12.77 Norway	Norwegian	6-1	13-2	11	0	Major league soccer (USA).
Ian Walker	31.10.71 Watford	English	6-1	12-9	194	0	Oxford U, Ipswich T.
Frode Grodas	24.10.69 Sognal	Norwegian	6-2	14-7	21	0	Lillestrom, Chelsea.
DEFENDERS							
Colin Calderwood	20.1.65 Glasgow	Scottish	6-0	12-12	581	28	Mansfield T, Swindon T.
Sol Campbell	18.9.74 Newham	English	6-1	14-1	168	2	none.
Stephen Carr	29.8.76 Dublin	Irish	5-7	12-2	65	0	none.
John Scales	4.7.66 Harrogate	English	6-2	13-5	399	15	Bristol R, Wimbledon, Liverpool.
Ramon Vega	14.6.71 Olten	Swiss	6-2	13-6	33	4	Trimbach (Swi), Olten (Swi), Grasshopper (Swi), Cagliari (Ita).
Clive Wilson	13.11.62 Manchester	English	5-7	10-0	461	29	Manchester C, Chester, Chelsea, Manchester C, QPR.
MIDFIELDERS							
Darren Anderton	3.3.72 Southampton	English	6-1	12-0	205	29	Portsmouth.
Nicola Berti	14.4.67 Salsomaggione	Italian	6-1	12-3	17	3	Fiorentina, Internazionale (Ita).
Stephen Clemence	31.3.78 Liverpool	English	5-11	11-7	17	0	none.
Garry Brady	7.9.76 Glasgow	Scottish	5-10	10-10	11	0	none.
Ruel Fox	14.1.68 Ipswich	English	5-6	10-0	313	44	Norwich C, Newcastle U.
David Ginola	25.1.67 Gossin	French	6-0	11-10	86	10	Brest (Fra), Paris SG (Fra) Newcastle U.
Allan Nielsen	13.3.71 Denmark	Danish	5-10	11-6	55	9	Brondby (Den).
Moussa Saib	6.3.68 Theniet	Algerian	5-8	11-8	9	1	Auxerre (Fra), Valencia (Spa).
Andy Sinton	19.3.66 Newcastle	English	5-8	11-5	523	72	Cambs. U, Brentford, QPR, Sheffield W.
FORWARDS							
Rory Allen	17.10.77 Beckenham	English	5-11	11-2	16	2	none.
Chris Armstrong	19.6.71 Newcastle	English	6-0	13-3	274	88	Wrexham, Millwall, Crystal Palace.
Jose Dominguez	16.2.74, Lisbon, Portugal	Portugese	5-3	10-0	18	2	Benfica (Por), Birmingham C, Sporting Lisbon (Por).
Neale Fenn	18.1.77 Edmonton	English	5-10	11-6	8	0	none.
Les Ferdinand	18.12.66 Acton	English	5-11	13-5	255	126	QPR, Brentford, Besiktas, Newcastle U.
Steffen Iversen	13.7.75 Trondheim	Norwegian	6-2	13-6	29	6	Rosenborg (Nor).
Paul Mahorn	13.8.73 Whipps Cross	English	5-10	13-1	13	1	Fulham, Burnley.

Nicola Berti

When former Italian international arrived at White Hart Lane in January on a free transfer from Serie A side Internazionale, it was assumed by everybody that he would just be staying until the end of the season and then would leave, just like his close friend Jurgen Klinsmann. But last summer he agreed a new one-year deal with Spurs and was set to be a key player for Tottenham this season.

The 30-year-old midfielder asked Inter chiefs if he could leave Milan when he was told of Spurs' interest last season. Spurs bought up the remaining months of Berti's contract (worth £360,000) and the Italian moved to England.

Berti took the decision to extend his contract with Spurs after deciding that English football was to his liking. He made 312 appearances and scored 41 goals for Inter over ten seasons after joining in 1988 from Fiorentina and was a member of the Italian squad which finished runners-up at the 1994 World Cup in the USA. But last season, he watched most of the action from the substitutes bench at the San Siro, and he jumped at the chance of a move to England.

Earning his Spurs: Berti has warmed to life at White Hart Lane.

West Ham United The Hammers

West Ham United may be small when compared with the likes of Liverpool and Manchester United, but they continue to play skilful, attractive soccer in the great tradition of the East End "Academy" of football.

Tradition remains important in E13. West Ham have had only eight managers in their history (six since the war), fewer than any other Premier League club. The current boss, Harry Redknapp, was a former player, as was his predecessor Billy Bonds.

The most successful period in the club's history came in the 1960s when,

under manager Ron Greenwood, they won the FA Cup for the first time in 1964, followed a year later by the European Cup-winners' Cup. By beating German side 1860 Munich, the Hammers became only the second British club to win a European trophy.

At that time three West Ham players – Bobby Moore, Geoff Hurst and Martin Peters – were established members of the English national team, and they were Wembley winners again in 1966 when England won the World Cup after famously beating West Germany 4–2 in extra time.

Greenwood became general manager in 1974, before going on to manage England, and was succeeded by John Lyall. In Lyall's first season in charge the Hammers reached the FA Cup final, where they beat Second Division Fulham 2–0. A year later Lyall's side reached the Cup-winners' Cup final, but could not repeat the heroics of 1965, losing to Belgian side Anderlecht.

West Ham were relegated from the old First Division in 1978, but reached the FA Cup final as a Second Division side in 1980, beating Arsenal 1–0. Promotion back to the top flight followed in 1981, along with a League Cup final appearance (they lost the replay to Liverpool) and in 1985–86 the Hammers had their best season yet, finishing third in the League behind Everton and champions Liverpool.

Lyall stayed in charge until 1989, when West Ham were relegated. Lou Macari spent a short, unpopular time as manager before the club turned to the services of former captain Billy Bonds. Under Bonds, the Hammers won promotion, but were relegated again in 1992 and spent a season outside the new Premier League before returning a year later.

Bonds gave way to his assistant and former team-mate Harry Redknapp in August 1994. Redknapp has been a sharp operator in the transfer market, particularly overseas. Croatian defender Slaven Bilic arrived from Germany and formed a solid partnership with Danish defender Marc Rieper, and midfielder John Moncur brought his passing ability from Swindon. Julian Dicks returned from his short spell at Liverpool and another former Hammers' favourite, Tony Cottee, arrived from Everton.

Other signings were not so successful. Don Hutchison, a record £1.5-million buy from Liverpool, was sold to Sheffield United after failing to settle, and the money was used to buy Romanian World Cup star Ilie Dumitrescu. Fellow Romanian Florin Raducioiu arrived in the summer of 1996 from Spain but fell out with Redknapp. With Portuguese stars Paulo Futre and Hugo Porfirio, Northern

Rio Grand: The young West Ham and England star has put in some fine performances since making his Hammers' debut.

WEST HAM UNITED

Formed: 1895.
Nickname: The Hammers.
Stadium: Boleyn Ground.
Capacity: 25,985.
Address: Green Street, Upton Park, London E13 9AZ.
Phone: 0181 548 2748.
Clubcall: 0891 121165.
Fax: 0181 548 2758.
Website: www.fa-carling.com/club.wh.fc
Manager: Harry Redknapp.

COLOURS

RECORDS

Record Premier League victory:
6–0 (v Barnsley, Jan 10, 1998).
Record Premier League defeat:
5–0 (v Sheffield Wednesday, Dec 18, 1993; v Liverpool May 2, 1998).
Record transfer fee received:
£4.5 million from Everton for Slaven Bilic, May 1997.
Record transfer fee paid:
£5 million to Arsenal for John Hartson, Feb 1997.
Record attendance:
42,322, v Tottenham Hotspur, Division One, Oct 17, 1970.

HONOURS

League: Third place 1985–86.
FA Cup (3): 1964, 1975, 1980.
League Cup: runners-up 1966, 1981.
European Cup-winners' Cup (1): 1965.

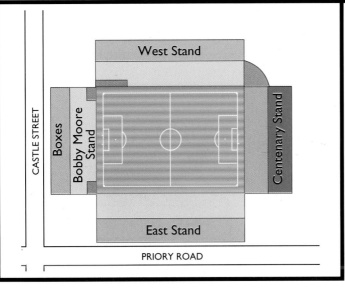

FIXTURES 1998–99

15 AUG	SHEFFIELD WEDNESDAY	A	____ : ____
22 AUG	MANCHESTER UNITED	H	____ : ____
29 AUG	COVENTRY CITY	A	____ : ____
9 SEPT	WIMBLEDON	H	____ : ____
12 SEPT	LIVERPOOL	H	____ : ____
19 SEPT	NOTTINGHAM FOREST	A	____ : ____
26 SEPT	SOUTHAMPTON	H	____ : ____
3 OCT	BLACKBURN ROVERS	A	____ : ____
17 OCT	ASTON VILLA	H	____ : ____
24 OCT	CHARLTON ATHLETIC	A	____ : ____
31 OCT	NEWCASTLE UNITED	A	____ : ____
7 NOV	CHELSEA	H	____ : ____
14 NOV	LEICESTER CITY	H	____ : ____
21 NOV	DERBY COUNTY	A	____ : ____
28 NOV	TOTTENHAM HOTSPUR	H	____ : ____
5 DEC	LEEDS UNITED	A	____ : ____
12 DEC	MIDDLESBROUGH	A	____ : ____
19 DEC	EVERTON	H	____ : ____
26 DEC	ARSENAL	A	____ : ____
28 DEC	COVENTRY CITY	H	____ : ____
9 JAN	MANCHESTER UNITED	A	____ : ____
16 JAN	SHEFFIELD WEDNESDAY	H	____ : ____
30 JAN	WIMBLEDON	A	____ : ____
6 FEB	ARSENAL	H	____ : ____
13 FEB	NOTTINGHAM FOREST	H	____ : ____
20 FEB	LIVERPOOL	A	____ : ____
27 FEB	BLACKBURN ROVERS	H	____ : ____
6 MAR	SOUTHAMPTON	A	____ : ____
13 MAR	CHELSEA	A	____ : ____
20 MAR	NEWCASTLE UNITED	H	____ : ____
3 APR	ASTON VILLA	A	____ : ____
5 APR	CHARLTON ATHLETIC	H	____ : ____
10 APR	LEICESTER CITY	A	____ : ____
17 APR	DERBY COUNTY	H	____ : ____
24 APR	TOTTENHAM HOTSPUR	A	____ : ____
1 MAY	LEEDS UNITED	H	____ : ____
8 MAY	EVERTON	A	____ : ____
16 MAY	MIDDLESBROUGH	H	____ : ____

Ireland's Michael Hughes and Australians Robbie Slater and Stan Lazaridis joining veteran Czech goalkeeper Ludek Miklosko, the Hammers had a seriously cosmopolitan feel to them.

However, the foreign influence failed to yield the desired results, especially on the goalscoring front, and by Christmas Redknapp had offloaded a number of his foreign legion and later splashed out a club record £7 million on strikers John Hartson (from Arsenal) and Paul Kitson (from Newcastle). Redknapp was criticized for paying so much money for two reserve team players, but the gamble paid off. The duo's goals didn't dry up and the Hammers lived to fight another day in the Premier League.

In the summer of 1997, Redknapp used the money from Slaven Bilic's £4.5-million transfer to Everton to bring in new players. Israeli international Eyal Berkovic arrived from Southampton, and later in the season Andrew Impey and Trevor Sinclair were signed from QPR. French striker Samassi Abou joined from Cannes, along with his fellow countryman Bernard Lama, France's international goalkeeper. The changes did the trick and the Hammers cruised through the season in mid-table and, for the first time in years, with European ambitions. In the end, Redknapp's men finished the season in eighth place, just one point behind Aston Villa, who claimed the final UEFA Cup place.

Upton Park was a fearsome place to visit last season – West Ham lost just two home games all season – and as long as the Hammers maintain their rich tradition for good fooballing habits, it will remain so for many years to come.

PREMIER LEAGUE TABLES

SEASON	POS.	P	W	D	L	F	A	PTS	TOP SCORER	AV. GATE
1993–94	13th	42	13	13	16	47	58	52	Morley 13	20,572
1994–95	14th	42	13	11	18	44	48	50	Cottee 13	20,118
1995–96	10th	38	14	9	15	48	52	51	Cottee/Dicks 10	22,340
1996–97	14th	38	10	12	16	39	48	42	Kitson 8	26,578
1997–98	8th	38	16	8	14	56	57	56	Hartson 15	25,075

John Hartson

More than a few eyebrows were raised in February 1997 when Harry Redknapp smashed West Ham's transfer record to sign striker John Hartson from Arsenal. Yet the £5 million turned out to be money well spent. West Ham were stuck in the relegation zone before Hartson arrived, but his five goals, and those of Paul Kitson, helped the Hammers to finish the season comfortably clear of trouble.

The 22-year-old Welshman was languishing in Arsenal's reserves following the arrival of Dennis Bergkamp. New manager Arsène Wenger had given him few first-team opportunities, so he jumped at the chance to revive his career in East London.

Hartson has always been a promising player. He was Britain's most expensive teenager when George Graham signed him from Luton Town for £2.5 million in January 1995. The move to West Ham has also revived ginger-haired Hartson's international career – he scored the only goal in Wales's friendly win over Scotland last May.

Partners: Paul Kitson and John Hartson are a dangerous duo.

Gold top: John Hartson has become a popular figure at Upton Park after scoring 15 League goals last season.

Paul Kitson

Just as John Hartson was edged out of Highbury by Dennis Bergkamp, so the arrival of Alan Shearer at St James' Park reduced Paul Kitson's first-team opportunities at Newcastle United. In almost two-and-a-half years in the north-east, Kitson made just 26 first-team starts.

Kitson was signed by Kevin Keegan from Derby County for £2.25 million in September 1994, having started his career with Leicester City. But with Shearer, Asprilla and Les Ferdinand ahead of him in the pecking order, 26-year-old Kitson found himself on the bench… if he was lucky. New manager Kenny Dalglish even dropped him from the first-team squad.

So the £2.3 million move south to London in 1997 made sense for Kitson, who quickly established an effective partnership with Hartson, and Newcastle were later to rue his departure when they lost strikers through injury.

With Hartson acting as a more traditional target man, Kitson grabbed eight League goals to finish the season as the Hammers' top scorer. Last season, injury robbed Kitson of the opportunity to add to his reputation, but he remains a key weapon in West Ham's armoury.

Player Records

	BORN	NATIONALITY	HEIGHT	WEIGHT	APPS	GOALS	PREVIOUS TEAMS
GOALKEEPERS							
Ludek Miklosko	9.12.61 Ostrava	Czech	6-5	14-0	315	0	Banik Ostrava (Cze).
Craig Forrest	20.9.67 Vancouver	Canadian	6-4	14-4	13	0	Ipswich T, Colchester U.
Shaka Hislop	22.2.69 London	Trinidad & Tobago	6-3	14-4	157	0	Howard Univ (US), Reading, Newcastle
DEFENDERS							
Tim Breacker	2.7.65 Bicester	English	5-11	13-0	447	11	Luton T.
Julian Dicks	8.8.68 Bristol	English	5-10	13-0	366	54	Birmingham C, West Ham U, Liverpool.
Rio Ferdinand	7.11.78 London	English	6-2	12-0	51	2	none
Richard Hall	14.3.72 Ipswich	English	6-2	13-11	155	15	Scunthorpe U, Southampton.
Marc Keller	14.1.68 France	French	5-11	11-12	-	-	Racing Strasbourg, Karlsruhe
Steve Potts	7.5.67 Hartford, Connecticut	English	5-7	10-11	377	27	none
David Unsworth	16.10.73 Chorley	English	6-0	13-0	148	13	Everton
Ian Pearce	7.5.74 Bury St. Edmonds	English	6-4	14-3	34	2	Chelsea, Blackburn
MIDFIELDERS							
Eyal Berkovic	2.4.72 Haifa	Israeli	5-8	10-6	63	11	Southampton, Maccabi Haifa (Isr)
Andrew Impey	13.9.71 London	English	5-8	11-2	206	13	Queens Park Rangers.
John Moncur	22.9.66 Stepney	English	5-7	9-10	201	12	Tottenham H, Swindon T.
Frank Lampard	21.6.78 Romford	English	6-0	13-7	65	5	Swansea C.
Stan Lazaridis	16.8.72 Perth	Australian	5-9	11-12	54	3	West Adelaide (Aus).
Steve Lomas	18.1.74 Hanover	Northern Irish	6-0	11-9	151	10	Manchester C.
FORWARDS							
John Hartson	5.4.75 Swansea	Welsh	6-1	14-6	150	45	Luton T, Arsenal.
Paul Kitson	9.1.71 Murton	English	5-10	10-12	218	64	Leicester C, Derby Co, Newcastle U.
Samassi Abou	4.4.73 Ivory Coast	French	5-10	12-2	19	5	Cannes
Trevor Sinclair	2.3.73 Dulwich	English	5-10	12-5	267	32	Blackpool, QPR

Marc Keller

France international Marc Keller is one of the latest foreign signings to arrive at Upton Park. Manager Harry Redknapp has had mixed luck with his forays into the foreign transfer market. Florin Raudcioiu, Narco Boogers and Paulo Futre are some of the names who did not work out; Eyal Berkovic, Stan Laziridis and Slaven Bilic are some of the names that did. West Ham took advantage of the Bosman ruling to snap up Keller on a free transfer from German side Karlsruhe.

The 29-year-old, who was unlucky not to be inlcuded in France's World Cup squad, said: "I think more French players will come here this summer, and, of course, I know Bernard Lama. He told me all about the club. He had nice things to say and that helped me make up my mind.'

Hammers managing director Peter Storrie was delighted with the deal and said: "There aren't too many players of Marc's calibre who will be available on free transfers under the Bosman ruling. We're glad we've got one of them. I'm just delighted he's chosen to join the Hammers. We think our fans will take to him."

Rio Ferdinand

West Ham have always have had a knack for producing talented young players. Some of England's finest – Bobby Moore, Geoff Hurst, Trevor Brooking – have graduated from West Ham's Academy down the years.

However, in recent times the Hammers have lost out to North London rivals Arsenal and Tottenham in the race to recruit local schoolboy talent. Rio Ferdinand is proof that the production line is up and running again. Rio, a second cousin of Spurs striker Les, made the breakthrough into West Ham's first team last season after serving a brief apprenticeship in the youth and reserve teams at Upton Park. His impressive performances in central defence brought him to the attention of England coach Glenn Hoddle and he made his full international debut, aged just 19, against Cameroon in November 1997.

Rio was named in a preliminary squad of 30 for England's World Cup squad, but few expected the youngster to be named in the final 22. However, Hoddle sprang a major surprize when he named Rio in his squad for the World Cup in France. The Hammers' defender was naturally delighted. "You can't put into words what it means to wear the England shirt and it exceeds all the expectations of when you dream of such things as a young lad." He says he was prepared to fight for his right to go to the World Cup. "I believe in myself and am confident," he says. "You have got to be single minded and selfish to achieve things like that. I like to think I'm a nice guy off the pitch, but if you are not mean and selfish on the field then you won't get to the heights you want to achieve. You've got to close off a lot of things off the pitch as well."

Comparisons with the late, great Bobby Moore are inevitable, but ultimately pointless when talking about the future of Rio Ferdinand. Nevertheless, he has the talent and the ability to be one of England's great defenders. Watch this space.

Wimbledon
The Dons

Wimbledon are one of the most dramatic success stories to have gripped English football in the past 20 years. Since they entered the Football League in 1977, the south London side have surpassed all the wildest dreams of their supporters, winning the FA Cup in 1988 and surviving in the top division for more than a decade.

Hero: Robbie Earle scored for Jamaica in the World Cup.

Despite their humble beginnings, Wimbledon's history goes back more than 100 years to the days of the Wimbledon Old Centrals, who played their home games on Wimbledon Common. For 75 years Wimbledon were one of London's top amateur sides. They beat Sutton United at Wembley to win the 1962 Amateur Cup and came to national prominence in 1975 when they beat First Division Burnley in the third round of the FA Cup and took Leeds United to a replay in the fourth round.

Following three straight Southern League titles, the Dons gained election to the Football League in 1977 and entered the old Fourth Division. Under manager Dario Gradi, Wimbledon won promotion to the third division in 1979, only to be relegated immediately. The same fate awaited new manager Dave "Harry" Bassett, as the Dons went up in 1981, down in 1982, but then, crucially, up again in 1983. Since then, there has been no stopping them.

Bassett's men won promotion to the Second Division in 1984, and by 1986 they had made it to the top flight. From non-League to First Division in nine years was a remarkable achievement which will probably never be equalled.

Bassett moved on in 1987, by which time Lebanese businessman Sam Hammam was the club's chairman. It was love at first sight for Hammam, who had not been interested in football before he visited Plough Lane. Under Bassett, Wimbledon's long-ball style attracted more than its fair share of critics, but the "Crazy Gang" tag which replaced the Wombles image only spurred the club on to greater things. New manager Bobby Gould led the Dons to their proudest moment, the 1988 FA Cup final. At Wembley, the Crazy Gang famously overcame Liverpool's "Culture Club" thanks to Lawrie Sanchez, who scored the only goal of the game, and goalkeeper and captain Dave Beasant, who saved a penalty from John Aldridge. Gould was succeeded by Ray Harford, Peter Withe and then Joe Kinnear, but Wimbledon continued to hold their own in the top flight, despite a move from their cramped Plough Lane home to share Selhurst Park with Crystal Palace in 1991. However, attendances at their temporary home are such that money was often tight. Dennis Wise, Vinnie Jones, Dave Beasant, Terry Phelan, John Scales, Keith Curle and Warren Barton were just some of the players sold to make ends meet. In came cut-price replacements like Robbie Earle, Oyvind Leonhardsen and Marcus Gayle, as well as such home-grown talents as defender Chris Perry. The 1996–97 season was

WIMBLEDON

Formed: 1889.
Nickname: The Dons.
Stadium: Selhurst Park.
Address: Selhurst Park, South Norwood, London SE25 6PY.
Telephone: 0181 771 2233.
Clubcall: 0891 121175.
Fax: 0181 768 0640.
Email: www.fa-carling.com/club.w.fc
Manager: Joe Kinnear.

COLOURS

RECORDS

Record Premier League victory: 4–0 (v Crystal Palace, April 9, 1993; v Everton, Sept 7, 1996).
Record Premier League defeat: 7–1 (v Aston Villa, Feb 11, 1995).
Record transfer fee received: £4 million from Newcastle for Warren Barton, June 1995.
Record transfer fee paid: £2 million to Millwall for Ben Thatcher, June 1996.
Record attendance: 30,115 v Manchester United, FA Premier League, May 9, 1993.

HONOURS

League: best season sixth, 1993–94.
FA Cup (1): 1988.
League Cup: semi-finalists 1997.

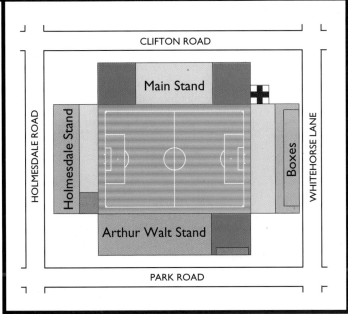

CLIFTON ROAD

Main Stand

HOLMESDALE ROAD

Holmesdale Stand

WHITEHORSE LANE

Boxes

Arthur Walt Stand

PARK ROAD

FIXTURES 1998–99

15 AUG	TOTTENHAM HOTSPUR	H	____ : ____
22 AUG	DERBY COUNTY	A	____ : ____
29 AUG	LEEDS UNITED	H	____ : ____
9 SEPT	WEST HAM UNITED	A	____ : ____
12 SEPT	ASTON VILLA	A	____ : ____
19 SEPT	SHEFFIELD WEDNESDAY	H	____ : ____
26 SEPT	LEICESTER CITY	A	____ : ____
3 OCT	EVERTON	H	____ : ____
17 OCT	MANCHESTER UNITED	A	____ : ____
24 OCT	MIDDLESBROUGH	H	____ : ____
31 OCT	BLACKBURN ROVERS	H	____ : ____
7 NOV	NOTTINGHAM FOREST	A	____ : ____
14 NOV	CHELSEA	A	____ : ____
21 NOV	ARSENAL	H	____ : ____
28 NOV	NEWCASTLE UNITED	A	____ : ____
5 DEC	COVENTRY CITY	H	____ : ____
12 DEC	LIVERPOOL	H	____ : ____
19 DEC	SOUTHAMPTON	A	____ : ____
26 DEC	CHARLTON ATHLETIC	H	____ : ____
28 DEC	LEEDS UNITED	A	____ : ____
9 JAN	DERBY COUNTY	H	____ : ____
16 JAN	TOTTENHAM HOTSPUR	A	____ : ____
30 JAN	WEST HAM UNITED	H	____ : ____
6 FEB	CHARLTON ATHLETIC	A	____ : ____
13 FEB	SHEFFIELD WEDNESDAY	A	____ : ____
20 FEB	ASTON VILLA	H	____ : ____
27 FEB	EVERTON	A	____ : ____
6 MAR	LEICESTER CITY	H	____ : ____
13 MAR	NOTTINGHAM FOREST	H	____ : ____
20 MAR	BLACKBURN ROVERS	A	____ : ____
3 APR	MANCHESTER UNITED	H	____ : ____
5 APR	MIDDLESBROUGH	A	____ : ____
10 APR	CHELSEA	H	____ : ____
17 APR	ARSENAL	A	____ : ____
24 APR	NEWCASTLE UNITED	H	____ : ____
1 MAY	COVENTRY CITY	A	____ : ____
8 MAY	SOUTHAMPTON	H	____ : ____
16 MAY	LIVERPOOL	A	____ : ____

a watershed for the Dons. The club did not have to sell any players in the summer of 1996 and instead splashed out a record £1.84 million on Ben Thatcher. Defeats in their opening three League games had the critics claiming that this would be the season that Wimbledon would be found out, but Joe Kinnear's men surprized everyone and by Christmas it was clear that they would be challenging for honours come the end of the season.

Kinnear's men finished eighth in the League, a remarkable achievement for a club with such limited resources. The Dons reached two Cup semi-finals (beating holders Aston Villa on the way in the Coca-Cola Cup and Manchester United in the FA Cup), but were swamped by fixtures and their good chance of a first European campaign through a high League placing or a Cup win was missed after looking probable for much of the season. The fighting spirit was still there, but the direct route football had been replaced by a more thoughtful, passing game.

Last season, the critics were again out in force when the Dons struggled in their opening League matches. Oyvind Leonhardsen, who had been sold to Liverpool for £3.5 million had been missed, but Kinnear's men rallied. An era ended when Vinnie Jones, the original Crazy Gang member, was sold to QPR, but new signings Andy Roberts and Mark Kennedy helped to ensure that the Wimbledon success story continues for at least another year.

PREMIER LEAGUE TABLES

SEASON	POS.	P	W	D	L	F	A	PTS	TOP SCORER	AV. GATE
1993–94	6th	42	18	11	13	56	53	65	Holdsworth 17	10,474
1994–95	9th	42	15	11	16	48	65	56	Ekoku 9	10,230
1995–96	14th	38	10	11	17	55	70	41	Earle 11	13,246
1996–97	8th	38	15	11	12	49	46	56	Ekoku 11	15,141
1997–98	17th	38	10	14	14	34	46	44	Ekoku/Euell/Cort/M Hughes/Leaburn 4	16,666

Flower of Scotland: Sullivan is a Scotland international.

Robbie Earle

By today's prices, the £775,000 Wimbledon paid Port Vale to sign Robbie Earle in July 1991 seems like an absolute bargain. The attacking midfielder has been one of the most impressive performers in Wimbledon's League and Cup exploits of recent seasons and it was a mystery to many why Glenn Hoddle did not call Earle up to the England squad.

It is possible that if he was playing for a more glamorous club, Robbie Earle would have received the international call-up long ago. He looked all set to move to a bigger club in 1994, but injury wiped out the 1994–95 season and he was restricted to just nine appearances.

He returned to form the following season, scoring 11 League goals from midfield. Goals are one of 32-year-old Earle's major strengths – he finished his first season with the Dons as top scorer and his powerful, well-timed runs from midfield have been a major source of goals for Wimbledon ever since. Earle looks set to stay at Wimbledon for the rest of his playing career, and he is busy carving out a future for himself as a media pundit.

Robbie has long since put the snub by England behind him. He was more than happy to accept an invitation from Jamaica to join their World Cup campaign and he teamed up with Portsmouth's Paul Hall and Fitzroy Simpson and Derby's Deon Burton to help the Reggae Boyz qualify for France 98. It was an historic achievement – and Earle was praised by Jamaica coach Rene Simoes for the professionalism which he brought to the squad.

His finest hour came during Jamaica's opening match in the tournament when he headed home his country's first-ever World Cup goal in the 3–1 defeat against eventual semi-finalists, Croatia. Although the Reggae Boyz were heavily beaten by Argentina, they finished on a high, with a defeat of Japan.

Chris Perry

Over the years Wimbledon have had to sell their best players to wealthier clubs just to make ends meet. But their survival in the top flight has owed as much to their unnerving ability to unearth stars in their own ranks. Defender Chris Perry is one such case.

Perry, a local lad from nearby Carshalton, supported the Dons as a boy and chose to train with them as an associated

Local lad: Chris Perry was born just down the road in Carshalton.

Player Records

	BORN	NATIONALITY	HEIGHT	WEIGHT	APPS	GOALS	PREVIOUS TEAMS
GOALKEEPERS							
Paul Heald	20.9.68 Wath on Dearne	English	6-2	12-5	200	0	Sheffield U, Leyton Orient, Coventry C., Crystal Palace, Swindon T.
Neil Sullivan	24.2.70 Sutton	Scottish	6-0	12-1	107	0	Crystal Palace.
DEFENDERS							
Dean Blackwell	5.12.69 Camden	English	6-1	12-10	161	1	Plymouth Argyle.
Kenny Cunningham	28.6.71 Dublin	Irish	5-11	11-2	265	1	Millwall.
Gary Elkins	4.5.66 Wallingford	English	5-9	11-13	219	5	Fulham, Exeter C.
Duncan Jupp	25.1.75 Guildford	English	6-0	12-11	114	2	Fulham.
Alan Kimble	6.8.66 Poole	English	5-10	12-4	433	24	Charlton Ath, Exeter C, Cambridge U.
Brian McAllister	30.11.70 Glasgow	Scottish	5-11	12-5	99	1	Plymouth Argyle, Crewe Alex.
Chris Perry	26.4.73 London	English	5-8	10-8	98	1	none.
Ben Thatcher	30.11.75 Swindon	English	5-11	12-7	125	1	Millwall.
MIDFIELDERS							
Neil Ardley	1.9.72 Epsom	English	5-11	11-9	139	8	none.
Stewart Castledine	22.1.73 Wandsworth	English	6-1	12-13	34	7	Wycombe W.
Andy Clarke	22.7.67 Islington	English	5-10	11-7	167	17	Barnet.
Robbie Earle	27.1.65 Newcastle-under-Lyme	English	5-9	10-10	417	128	Port Vale.
Peter Fear	10.9.73 London	English	5-10	11-7	70	4	none.
Ceri Hughes	26.2.71 Pontypridd	Welsh	5-10	11-6	174	19	Luton T.
Michael Hughes	2.8.71 Larne	Northern Irish	5-7	10-13	148	23	Manchester C, Strasbourg (Fra), West Ham U.
Andy Roberts	20.3.74 Dartford	English	5-10	13-0	250	8	Millwall, Crystal Palace.
Mark Kennedy	15.5.76 Dublin	Irish	5-11	11-0	63	9	Millwall, Liverpool.
FORWARDS							
Carl Cort	1.11.77 London	English	6-2	12-0	30	4	Lincoln C.
Efan Ekoku	8.6.67 Manchester	Nigerian	6-1	12-0	199	67	Bournemouth, Norwich C.
Jason Euell	6.2.77 South London	English	5-11	11-2	34	8	none.
Marcus Gayle	27.9.70 Hammersmith	English	6-1	12-9	288	39	Brentford.
Jon Goodman	2.6.71 Walthamstow	English	6-0	12-3	168	46	Millwall.
Carl Leaburn	30.3.69 Lewisham	English	6-3	13-0	292	52	Charlton A, Northampton T

schoolboy in 1987 despite interest from other, bigger clubs. He became a trainee in 1989 and signed as a professional in 1991. Perry broke into the first team towards the end of the 1993–94 season and soon became a regular choice for manager Joe Kinnear.

Perry has attracted praise from all quarters for his performances for the Dons. There have been calls for him to be included in the England squad, and he was shortlisted for the PFA Young Player of the Year award in 1997.

Marcus Gayle

Wimbledon have made a habit of taking players from the lower leagues and turning them into accomplished Premier League performers. Forward Marcus Gayle is the latest to get the Wimbledon career-enhancing treatment.

Hammersmith-born Gayle, a former England youth international, spent six seasons with Brentford before joining Wimbledon for £250,000 in March 1994. At first the Dons used 27-year-old Gayle as a winger without any great success, but in the 1996–97 season he came into his own as a striker. He scored a memorable goal against Chelsea and played well enough to keep first-choice forward Dean Holdsworth out of the side.

His performances last season brought him to the attention of Jamaica's national coach Rene Simoes, who was keen to add a tall, physical striker to his squad.

Gayle force: From England B to Jamaica, Marcus Gayle has always had the look of an international player.

F.A. Premier League Records

Not surprisingly, Manchester United are the most successful club in the history of the Premier League. United, champions four times in six Premier League seasons, also hold the record for the most points in a season, most wins, fewest goals conceded, biggest win and most goals for.

Single Season Records

MOST GOALS FOR:	Newcastle United (1993–94): 82
FEWEST GOALS FOR:	Leeds United (1996–97): 28
MOST GOALS AGAINST:	Swindon Town (1993–94): 100
FEWEST GOALS AGAINST:	Manchester United (1997–98): 26
MOST POINTS:	Manchester United (1993–94): 92
FEWEST POINTS:	Ipswich Town (1994–95): 27
BEST START:	Nottingham Forest (1995–96): 12 games undefeated
WORST START:	Swindon Town (1993–94): 15 games without a win
MOST WINS:	Manchester United (1993–94), Blackburn Rovers (1994-95): 27
FEWEST WINS:	Swindon Town (1993–94): 5
MOST DEFEATS:	Ipswich Town (1994–95): 29
FEWEST DEFEATS:	Manchester United (1993–94): 4
MOST CLEAN SHEETS:	Manchester United (1994–95): 24
FEWEST CLEAN SHEETS:	Ipswich Town (1994–95): 3
BEST AVERAGE ATTENDANCE:	Manchester United (1997–98): 55,164
WORST AVERAGE ATTENDANCE:	Wimbledon (1992–93): 8,405
FIRST SIDE TO FINISH SEASON UNBEATEN AT HOME:	Manchester United (1995–96)

Overall Records

BIGGEST WIN:	Manchester United v Ipswich Town (March 4, 1995): 9–0
BIGGEST AWAY WIN:	Sheffield Wednesday v Blackburn Rovers (March 2, 1995): 1–7
MOST GOALS FOR:	Manchester United: 446
FEWEST GOALS FOR:	Barnsley: 37
MOST GOALS AGAINST:	Southampton: 356
MOST POINTS:	Manchester United: 498
FEWEST POINTS:	Swindon Town: 30
MOST WINS:	Manchester United: 146
MOST DRAWS:	Coventry City: 85
MOST DEFEATS:	Southampton: 106
LONGEST UNBEATEN RUN:	Nottingham Forest (February 21, 1995 – November 18, 1995): 25 games
LONGEST UNBEATEN HOME RUN:	Manchester United (December 17, 1994 – November 2, 1996): 36 games
LONGEST UNBEATEN AWAY RUN:	Manchester United (October 8, 1994 – February 25, 1995): 10 games
HIGHEST AVERAGE ATTENDANCE:	Manchester United: 45,856
LOWEST AVERAGE ATTENDANCE:	Wimbledon: 12,360
HIGHEST ATTENDANCE:	Manchester United v Middlesbrough (May 5, 1997): 55,489
LOWEST ATTENDANCE:	Wimbledon v Coventry City (November 11, 1995): 4,578

Individual Records

MOST GOALS:	Alan Shearer (Blackburn Rovers and Newcastle United): 137
MOST HAT-TRICKS:	Alan Shearer (Blackburn Rovers and Newcastle United): 7
MOST GOALS IN ONE GAME:	Andy Cole (Manchester United v Ipswich Town, March 4, 1995): 5
MOST GOALS IN ONE AWAY GAME:	Efan Ekoku (Norwich City, at Everton September 25, 1993): 4
MOST GOALS IN ONE SEASON:	Andy Cole (1993–94), Alan Shearer (1994–95): 34
YOUNGEST PLAYER:	Andy Turner (Tottenham Hotspur): 17 years, 145 days
YOUNGEST SCORER:	Andy Turner (Tottenham Hotspur): 17 years, 166 days

Season-by-season – Premier League average attendances

Team	1992–93	1993–94	1994–95	1995–96	1996–97	1997–98	Av.
ARSENAL	24,403	30,563	35,330	37,568	37,821	39,053	33,956
ASTON VILLA	29,594	29,015	29,756	32,614	36,027	36,136	32,190
BARNSLEY						18,443	18,443
BLACKBURN ROVERS	16,246	17,721	25,272	27,716	24,947	25,253	22,859
BOLTON WANDERERS				18,822		24,352	21,587
CHELSEA	18,787	19,416	21,057	25,486	27,617	33,387	24,289
COVENTRY CITY	14,951	13,352	15,980	18,507	19,608	19,722	17,020
CRYSTAL PALACE	15,748		14,922			21,983	17,551
DERBY COUNTY					17,888	29,105	23,496
EVERTON	20,447	22,876	31,291	35,435	36,188	35,355	30,101
IPSWICH TOWN	18,223	16,382	16,818				17,141
LEEDS UNITED	29,250	34,493	32,925	32,528	32,117	34,641	32,668
LEICESTER CITY			19,532		20,184	20,615	20,110
LIVERPOOL	37,004	38,493	34,176	39,553	39,776	40,628	38,268
MANCHESTER CITY	24,698	26,709	22,725	27,869			25,500
MANCHESTER UTD	35,152	44,244	43,681	41,700	55,081	55,164	45,856
MIDDLESBROUGH	16,724			29,283	29,871		25,293
NEWCASTLE UNITED		33,679	34,690	36,507	36,467	36,672	35,597
NORWICH CITY	16,154	18,164	18,625				17,648
NOTTINGHAM FOR	21,910		23,633	26,916	24,587		24,053
OLDHAM ATHLETIC	12,859	12,563					12,711
QPR	15,015	14,228	14,613	15,683			14,975
SHEFFIELD UNITED	18,801	19,562					19,182
SHEFFIELD WEDS	27,264	27,191	26,572	24,877	25,714	26,697	26,336
SOUTHAMPTON	15,382	14,751	14,685	14,819	15,105	15,159	14,983
SUNDERLAND					20,973		20,973
SWINDON TOWN		15,274					15,274
TOTTENHAM HOTS	27,740	27,160	27,259	30,510	31,067	29,153	28,815
WEST HAM UNITED		20,572	20,118	22,340	23,242	25,075	22,269
WIMBLEDON	8,405	10,474	10,230	13,246	15,141	16,666	12,360

Overall Premier League Records (1992–93 to 1997–98)

Team	P	W	D	L	F	A	Pts
MANCHESTER UNITED	240	146	60	33	446	202	498
BLACKBURN ROVERS	240	115	60	65	371	253	405
LIVERPOOL	240	111	64	65	386	260	397
ARSENAL	240	105	72	63	322	179	387
ASTON VILLA	240	89	63	78	302	263	360
LEEDS UNITED	240	90	72	78	306	280	342
NEWCASTLE UNITED	198	97	48	53	323	209	339
CHELSEA	240	88	69	83	325	304	333
TOTTENHAM HOTSPUR	240	83	68	89	318	328	317
WIMBLEDON	240	82	70	88	298	335	316
SHEFFIELD WEDNESDAY	238	80	75	85	330	341	315
EVERTON	240	74	68	98	288	326	290
COVENTRY CITY	240	68	85	87	265	322	289
SOUTHAMPTON	240	70	64	106	298	356	276
WEST HAM UNITED	198	66	53	79	229	263	251
QUEENS PARK RANGERS	164	59	39	66	224	232	216
NOTTINGHAM FOREST	160	53	50	57	194	218	209
MANCHESTER CITY	164	45	54	65	180	222	189
NORWICH CITY	126	43	39	44	163	180	168
LEICESTER CITY	118	31	36	51	142	175	129
CRYSTAL PALACE	122	30	37	55	119	181	127
MIDDLESBROUGH*	118	32	33	53	140	185	126
IPSWICH TOWN	126	28	38	60	121	206	122
DERBY COUNTY	76	27	20	29	97	107	101
SHEFFIELD UNITED	84	22	28	34	96	113	94
OLDHAM ATHLETIC	84	22	23	39	105	142	89
BOLTON WANDERERS	76	17	5	41	80	132	69
SUNDERLAND	38	10	10	18	35	53	40
BARNSLEY	38	8	9	21	37	71	33
SWINDON TOWN	42	5	15	22	47	100	30

* Three points deducted

Premier League Top Scorers by season

1992–93

	Player	Goals
1	TEDDY SHERINGHAM (Nottingham Forest/Tottenham Hotspur)	22
2	LES FERDINAND (Queens Park Rangers)	20
3	DEAN HOLDSWORTH (Wimbledon)	19
	MICK QUINN (Newcastle Utd/Coventry City)	19
5	ALAN SHEARER (Blackburn Rovers)	16
	DAVID WHITE (Manchester City)	16
7	CHRIS ARMSTRONG (Crystal Palace)	15
	ERIC CANTONA (Leeds Utd/Manchester Utd)	15
	LEE CHAPMAN (Leeds United)	15
10	BRIAN DEANE (Sheffield United)	15
	MARK HUGHES (Norwich City)	15
	MATT LE TISSIER (Southampton)	15
	MARK ROBINS (Manchester United)	15
	IAN WRIGHT (Arsenal)	15

1993–94

1	ANDY COLE (Newcastle United)	34
2	ALAN SHEARER (Blackburn Rovers)	31
3	MATT LE TISSIER (Southampton)	25
	CHRIS SUTTON (Norwich)	25
5	IAN WRIGHT (Arsenal)	23
6	PETER BEARDSLEY (Newcastle United)	21
7	MARK BRIGHT (Sheffield Wednesday)	19
8	ERIC CANTONA (Manchester United)	18
9	ROD WALLACE (Leeds United)	17
	DEAN HOLDSWORTH (Wimbledon)	17

1994–95

1	ALAN SHEARER (Blackburn Rovers)	34
2	ROBBIE FOWLER (Liverpool)	25
3	LES FERDINAND (Queens Park Rangers)	24
4	STAN COLLYMORE (Nottingham Forest)	22
5	ANDY COLE (Newcastle United/Manchester United)	21
6	JURGEN KLINSMANN (Tottenham Hotspur)	20
7	MATT LE TISSIER (Southampton)	19
8	TEDDY SHERINGHAM (Tottenham Hotspur)	18
	IAN WRIGHT (Arsenal)	18
10	ASHLEY WARD (Crewe A/Norwich City)	16

1995–96

1	ALAN SHEARER (Blackburn Rovers)	31
2	ROBBIE FOWLER (Liverpool)	28
3	LES FERDINAND (Newcastle United)	25
4	DWIGHT YORKE (Aston Villa)	17
5	ANDREI KANCHELSKIS (Everton)	16
	TEDDY SHERINGHAM (Tottenham Hotspur)	16
7	CHRIS ARMSTRONG (Tottenham Hotspur)	15
8	IAN WRIGHT (Arsenal)	15

1996–97

1	ALAN SHEARER (Newcastle United)	25
2	IAN WRIGHT (Arsenal)	23
3	ROBBIE FOWLER (Liverpool)	18
	OLE-GUNNAR SOLSKJAER (Manchester United)	18
5	DWIGHT YORKE (Aston Villa)	17
6	LES FERDINAND (Newcastle United)	16
	FABRIZIO RAVANELLI (Middlesbrough)	16
8	DION DUBLIN (Coventry City)	14

1997–98

1	DION DUBLIN (Coventry City)	18
	MICHAEL OWEN (Liverpool)	18
	CHRIS SUTTON (Blackburn Rovers)	18
4	DENNIS BERGKAMP (Arsenal)	16
	KEVIN GALLACHER (Blackburn Rovers)	16
	JIMMY FLOYD HASSELBAINK (Leeds)	16
7	ANDY COLE (Manchester Utd)	15
	JOHN HARTSON (West Ham Utd)	15
	JAN-AGE FJORTOFT (Barnsley)	15
10	GIANLUCA VIALLI (Chelsea)	11

Lethal: Blackburn striker Chris Sutton notched 18 League goals in the 1997–98 season.

Numbers in italics refer to illustrations

Stop press: Last minute transfer details (all other details are correct at time of going to press) – **Arsenal:** *in* – David Grodin (from St Etienne) *out* – Scott Marshall (to Southampton); **Aston Villa:** *in* – Ferraresi, David Unsworth (from West Ham) *out* – Fernando Nelson, Steve Staunton (to Liverpool); **Blackburn Rovers:** *in* – Sebastien Perez (from Bastia); **Charlton Athletic:** *in* – Neil Redfearn (from Barnsley); **Chelsea:** *out* – Danny Granville (to Leeds); **Coventry City:** *in* – Robert Jarni *out* – John Salako (to Fulham), Viorel Moldovan; **Derby County:** *in* – Stefan Schnoor; **Everton:** *in* – John Collins, Olivier Dacourt, Mario Materazzi; **Leeds United:** *in* – Danny Granville (from Chelsea); **Liverpool:** *in* – Vegard Hoggem (from Rosenborg), Steve Staunton (from Aston Villa); **Manchester United:** *in* – Jesper Blomquist (from Parma); **Newcastle United:** Dietmar Hamann, Stephane Guivar'ch, Laurent Charvet, Garry Brady (from Spurs); **Nottingham Forest:** *out* – Kevin Campbell (to Trebgunspon), Ian Moore (to Stockport); **Southampton:** *in* – Scott Marshall (from Arsenal), David Howells (from Tottenham), Mark Hughes (from Chelsea) *out* – Kevin Richardson; **Tottenham Hotspur:** *in* – Paolo Tremezani *out* – Garry Brady (to Newcastle), Paul Mahorn; **West Ham:** *in* – Ian Wright (from Arsenal), Javier Margas, Neil Ruddock (from Liverpool) *out* – David Unsworth (to Aston Villa)